PURPOSE AND A PAYCHECK

FINDING MEANING, MONEY, AND HAPPINESS IN THE SECOND HALF OF LIFE

CHRIS FARRELL

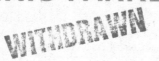

HARPERCOLLINS
LEADERSHIP

AN IMPRINT OF HARPERCOLLINS

Published by HarperCollins Leadership, an imprint of HarperCollins.

Book design by Elyse Strongin, Neuwirth & Associates.

978-0-8144-3962-3 (eBook)

Library of Congress Control Number: 2018960961

978-0-8144-3961-6

Printed in the United States of America
18 19 20 21 22 LSC 10 9 8 7 6 5 4 3 2 1

This book is dedicated to Richard, Billy, Andrew, and Ron for half a century of friendship and the prospect of many more adventures and long conversations.

This book is also dedicated to Rose Veronica Farrell. I can't wait to watch the future unfold through her eyes. The world already is a much better place.

CONTENTS

9
Taking Lifelong Learning Seriously

10
The Personal Finances of Aging—Don't Despair

11
Gains from a Multigenerational Society

12
Reimagining the Common Good

Epilogue
To Have a Go

PURPOSE
AND A
PAYCHECK

The Frontier of Experienced Workers and 50-Plus Entrepreneurs

This is not a moment, it's the movement.
—ALEXANDER HAMILTON (Lin-Manuel Miranda)[1]

The association of old age with inevitable decline runs deep. To carry on with work—or indeed with anything more demanding than afternoon lectures, a movie, and an early dinner—during the traditional retirement years is cute at best and depressing at worst.

Economist John Kenneth Galbraith called these commonplace reactions—surprise laced with condescending admiration or misplaced concern—the "Still Syndrome."

"The Still Syndrome is the design by which the young or the less old daily assail the old. 'Are you still well?' 'Are you still working?' 'I see that you are still taking exercise.' 'Still having a drink?' As a compulsive *literatus* I am subject to my own special assault, 'I see you are still writing.' 'Your writing still seems pretty good to me.' The most dramatic general expression came from a friend I hadn't seen for some years: 'I can hardly believe you're still alive!'"[2]

Galbraith wrote the essay "Notes on Aging" when he was 90 years old. He stayed active and engaged until he died seven years later.

No one would think "decline" on meeting Luanne Mullin, age 71. Mullin has assembled a portfolio of activities in recent years, some paying gigs and others volunteer jobs. "Life is full," she says, laughing.

That's an understatement. Among her jobs with incomes are project manager for a nonprofit organization in Marin County, California, that focuses on older adults and the disabled; her own coaching business and workshops; and acting gigs in the backgrounds of television and movies. (She was one of the people running down San Francisco's Russian Hill as the building behind crumbled during the disaster film *San Andreas*.)

Mullin has a portfolio of volunteer ventures, too. She's a volunteer leader for the mature student organization at the College of Marin, focusing on lifelong learning. She helps produce a local documentary film series. She organizes salons bringing people together to discuss critical topics. "I do feel lucky," she says. "I am in the right place and at the right time to do a lot of really neat things."

I wasn't surprised to learn that Mullin had created a full portfolio combining purpose and a paycheck. That seems to be the story of her life.

We first met in 2013 on the Mission Bay campus of the University of California, San Francisco (UCSF). The area was once dominated by shipyards and industrial businesses. The university and biotech offices now hold sway. Mullin was a mediator and project manager on campus. She was almost done with her job overseeing the construction of an 8,000-square-foot laboratory for university scientists when we got together.

Her career had been an eclectic mix of jobs and occupations. She moved with the grace of the dancer she had been early in her career. She later became head of marketing for a dance company, opened her own theater company in Boston, and ran a recording studio in San Francisco.

As her time at UCSF was coming to an end, she was looking for a new adventure, a different challenge. "OK, what's my next career?" she wondered. "What do I want to do that's fulfilling?"

Like many people working in what is still considered the traditional retirement years, Mullin needs to work for an income and wants to work for engagement. Not one reason or the other. Both purpose and a paycheck. Earning an income helps pay the bills.

"I need a paycheck. I will always need a paycheck," she says. "I'm OK with that. A paycheck puts a roof over my head and shows that I am needed, wanted, and worth paying."

We've talked several times since our first meeting, including at an Aging in America conference held in downtown San Francisco in 2018. She enjoys her work and volunteer activities. They often involve solving problems and designing solutions. Her work keeps her mentally sharp and physically active. Paid work and volunteering are how she stays connected to a wide circle of friends, colleagues, and clients. "Many of us are looking for purpose," she says.

Mullin is still searching for her calling. She believes there is more for her to accomplish, a commitment that will make a bigger difference to her sense of self and to her community. She hasn't found her calling yet. She continues to experiment and test new paths. "I keep thinking I will find one big thing that I am passionate about and give my life to it," she says. "I don't know what it is. Maybe doing all these things will lead me to that one thing."

Mullin has plenty of company in her entrepreneurial quest. Stories like hers are increasingly common with the aging of the population. The demographics of aging ranks as one of the most significant long-term forces shaping the U.S. economy and society, alongside globalization, automation, and climate change.

The numbers are striking. The U.S. Census Bureau forecasts that those individuals 65 years and older will account for more than 21 percent of the U.S. population—about 73 million—in 2030. The comparable figures in 2016 were 15 percent, or some 49 million. Put somewhat differently, roughly 10,000 baby boomers—the generation born between 1946 and 1964—are celebrating their 65th birthday every day until 2030. That year, the surviving members from the leading edge of the boomer generation will turn 85.[3]

Older Americans are also living longer, on average. Thanks to improvements in sanitation, nutrition, education, and medical care, life expectancy for people reaching age 65 now averages 19.4 years. That's up from 13.9 years in 1950. The biggest impact on the nation's aging comes from Americans having fewer children. The U.S. fertility rate has dropped to record lows. Taken all together, the Census Bureau predicts the number of people over 65 years of age will outnumber children under age 18 by 2035 for the first time in U.S. history.[4]

The combination of an aging population and the Still Syndrome fuels ominous economic forecasts. The typical doom-and-gloom story runs along these lines: Too few young workers will have to support too many dependent elderly. Older Americans will be forced to cut back on spending because they haven't saved enough to maintain their lifestyle. The wellsprings of creativity, innovation, and risk-taking—long linked with youth—will dim with rising numbers of elders. The economy is slipping into a permanent state of slow-growth or secular stagnation at best, and possibly worse.

America's best days are behind it.

Hardly! Think Luanne Mullin and millions more like her throughout the country. The aging of America's population represents a historic moment to create a more inclusive society and vibrant economy. Age is nothing but a data point. Chronological aging tells us little about an individual, let alone society. As the poet Samuel Ullman eloquently observes:

> *Nobody grows old merely by a number of years.*
> *We grow old by deserting our ideals.*
> *Years may wrinkle the skin,*
> *But to give up enthusiasm wrinkles the soul.*[5]

Older Americans are showing plenty of zest for life at work and at home. They aren't doddering life away as antiquated stereotypes and tasteless jokes suggest. The swelling numbers of Americans age

50 and older and their experiments in rethinking and reimagining the second half of life will have a profound impact on everyday life in America. "In coming decades, many forces will shape our economy and our society, but in all likelihood no single factor will have as pervasive an effect as the aging of our population," said Ben Bernanke in a speech when he was still chair of the Federal Reserve Board.[6]

For instance, the future trajectory of housing markets, public transportation networks, and urban design will be shaped by growing numbers of mature adults. The global age-friendly city initiative is encouraging many urban communities to better accommodate an aging population. Specifically, well-connected transportation networks of public transit, ride-sharing apps, and on-demand vans can ease trips among modern elders to work, the grocery store, restaurants, yoga studios, and medical appointments. America's postsecondary education system will eventually abandon its near-exclusive emphasis on educating younger generations and become multigenerational institutions welcoming certificate-seeking and degree-desiring students in their 50s, 60s, and older.

Health care services will shift from a primary emphasis on delivering medical care in hospitals and nursing homes. Instead, comprehensive care will be routinely offered at home and in group settings with an emphasis on improving the quality of everyday life. Even expectations about death and dying are changing as the medical profession grapples with how to help people plan and prepare for the end of life. Just as doulas have become commonplace aiding mothers with birth, so-called death-doulas or palliative care doulas increasingly offer elders companionship toward the end of life.

The transformation this book focuses on is entrepreneurship and work for an aging population. Many adults in the second half of life will start their own business or keep working well into the traditional retirement years. An impressive body of scholarly research suggests that, given the opportunity, people in the second half of life can be as creative, innovative, and entrepreneurial as their younger peers, if not more so. Experienced adults are experimenting with different ways to stay attached to the economy, including self-employment, entrepreneurship, full-time jobs, part-time work, flexible employment, and encore careers.

Here's one indication of the embrace of work: According to the Bureau of Labor Statistics, between 1995 and 2016, the share of men ages 65 to 69 in the labor force rose from 28 percent to 38 percent. The comparable figures for women were 18 percent and 30 percent. For men ages 62 to 64, participation rates rose from 44 percent to 57 percent and for women from 31 to 47 percent. Less than full-time employment is popular with some 27 percent of workers 55 and older. The figure rises to 40 percent for workers 65 years and older.

Experienced workers are productive workers. At least that's what the wage data tells us. Wages are one way to measure productivity, and older workers are taking home bigger paychecks than in the past. Inflation-adjusted average monthly earnings of persons age 65 and older were $4,092 in 2015, substantially higher than the comparable figure of $2,276 in 1994, according to the Census Bureau. The pay gains for those in the 55-to-64-year-old age group went from $3,928 in 1994 to $5,557 in 2015.

Here's another critical number with a similar message: The 55-to-64-year-old age cohort accounted for 25.5 percent of new entrepreneurs in 2016, up from 14.8 percent in 1996, according to the Ewing Marion Kauffman Foundation.[7] The Bureau of Labor Statistics reports that the unincorporated and incorporated self-employment rate among workers age 65 and older was the highest of any age group. The 65-plus rate of self-employment was more than triple the unincorporated rate and five times the incorporated rate of the 25-to-34-year-old age group. (An unincorporated business is usually a sole proprietor or partnership; an incorporated business or corporation is separate from the business owner with its own legal rights.) Put it this way: The 50-plus population will start more businesses in the years ahead than any other demographic.

The significance of figures like these lies in the underappreciated promise an aging population holds for boosting economic growth and household incomes. America's aging population is an extraordinary moment to celebrate and an opportunity to seize, especially now.

The economy has failed too many families struggling to make ends meet. Middle-class living standards are under assault. Economic insecurity is on the rise. Income inequality is higher than it has been in decades. Dark undercurrents of economic and financial insecurity have fed and reinforced angry political tensions. Concern about the future is spreading, especially among parents worried about the job and career prospects of their children and grandchildren. Drug abuse in parts of the country is leading to an enormous toll of despair and unemployment. One way that Donald Trump beat the odds and propelled himself into the White House in 2016 was by tapping into disturbing wellsprings of gloom and doubt.

This era of widespread pessimism demands bold actions to boost the incomes of the typical worker and revive optimism about the future. The trials of our time call for "big ideas" and "dreaming big again," declares David Leonhardt, opinion columnist at the *New York Times*. He's right.[8]

Here is a big, grassroots idea that is already making its presence felt: Experienced workers and 50-plus entrepreneurs rethinking and reimagining the second half of life. A new era of broad-based prosperity is within our grasp. Older adults are in the vanguard of inclusiveness by breaking down barriers to staying employed. The fight for purpose and a paycheck is a battle for respect and recognition. The struggle isn't partisan-Democratic or partisan-Republican.

"Perhaps the greatest opportunity of the twenty-first century is to envision and create a society that nurtures longer lives not only for the sake of the older generation, but also for the benefit of all age groups—what I call the Third Demographic Dividend," writes Linda Fried, dean of the Mailman School of Public Health at Columbia

University. "To get there requires a collective grand act of imagination to create a vision for the potential of longer lives."[9]

Fried is spot on.

Older adults are already exercising their imagination as productive workers and motivated volunteers and engaged entrepreneurs. They're battling against age discrimination, taking actions to remove pernicious stereotypes holding down experienced workers. Older Americans represent an enormous market for goods, services, and experiences (and not only for burial insurance and Life Alert). Many of those products and services will be built and designed by older adults with a flair for understanding the 50-plus market. The widely touted innovative benefits of employing a diverse workforce include tapping into the insights of older workers.

How much growth? Oxford Economics (in a briefing paper prepared for the AARP) forecasts that consumer spending by Americans 50 and older will increase by 58 percent to $4.6 trillion by 2032, compared to a 13 percent rise in spending for people ages 25 to 50.[10] (This calculation excludes health care.) Another Oxford Economics report with consulting firm Accenture estimated that increasing the number of experienced workers could boost U.S. gross domestic product by an additional $442 billion by 2020.[11]

Several factors are coming together and reinforcing one another, bringing new ideas and different expectations about the second half of life from society's fringes to the mainstream. Boomers are better educated than previous generations. They're also healthier, with a sixty-five year old today having the the same risk of mortality or serious illness as those in their mid-50s a generation ago.

The realization is growing that retirement—defined as full-time leisure—may be hazardous to your health. Research sponsored by the National Institute on Aging and the Social Security Administration suggests that full-time retirement is associated with a 23 to 29 percent increase in difficulties involving mobility and daily activities, an 8 percent increase in illness, and an 11 percent decline in mental health, notes Columbia University's Fried.[12]

Her Columbia University colleague John Rowe, former chair and chief executive officer at the insurance behemoth Aetna, was emphatic about the results at the conference on aging at Columbia University in 2018. "Retirement is bad for you," says Rowe. "It is bad for your brain. It is bad for your health."[13]

The personal finances of delaying full-time retirement are compelling. A paycheck makes it practical to delay filing for Social Security benefits, which are more generous at age 70 than at age 62. The incentives to work longer have increased with the decline in traditional pensions and the rise of 401(k) plans. There was no added pension benefit to continuing to work past the age of plan retirement with traditional pensions. But employees can continue contributing to a 401(k) and similar defined contribution retirement savings accounts so long as they're on the job. Your portfolio compounds longer, and you need to live off your accumulated savings for fewer years.

The combined effect is compelling. Take this example drawn from the scholarly paper "The Power of Working Longer." Four scholars looked at older workers ten years from retirement. If these workers delay retirement by one month at the end of their careers, they can get the same increase in their retirement income as they could by adding one percentage point to their retirement savings rate over that ten-year period. "Primary earners of ages 62 to 69 can substantially increase their retirement standard of living by working longer," the scholars write. "The longer the work can be sustained, the higher the retirement standard of living."[14]

The prospect of steep health care costs feeds into the desire to delay retirement. The financial services company Fidelity estimates that the average 65-year-old retired couple on Medicare may need approximately $280,000 saved (after taxes) to cover expected health care expenses. (The Fidelity calculation doesn't include the cost of long-term care, such as a stay in a nursing home.)[15]

Work is less physically demanding these days, easing the transition to longer work lives. The historically accurate perspective that "work is an unpleasant necessity and only the prelude to happier times" is less true with the rise of service industries and the spread of information technologies. The decline in the "assembly line" version of work means "working 100 percent until retirement and then suddenly moving to zero percent at an arbitrary age of around 65 is one of the great anachronisms of today's labor market," write World Bank economists Wolfgang Fengler and Johannes Koettl.[16]

The most underappreciated aspect of work may well be that it's a social activity. Colleagues care if you show up. They'll share a coffee or a joke on the job. Work offers the possibility of creativity and purpose, a reason to get up in the morning, an opportunity to tap into skills and knowledge developed over the years. Work helps people stay physically fit and mentally active. Social connections are one of the best contributors to meaningful longevity and, for many older adults, the community in which they spend the most time is the workplace.

Employers are finally looking at experienced workers with greater appreciation. Yes, stereotypes die hard. Too many employers still believe older workers are expensive, slow, and resistant to new technologies and organizational initiatives. There's also no doubt employer attitudes about experienced workers are shifting in a positive direction. Case in point: The fastest growing segment of the civilian labor force from 2006 to 2016 was the 65-plus age group. The age cohort showed an annual average growth rate of 2.3 percent. In sharp contrast, the comparable labor market growth rate for the 25-to-34-year-old age group was 0.2 percent.[17]

A big reason behind the change in employer attitudes is the relatively tight labor market of recent years. Employers constantly complain they can't find the qualified labor they need. I've never found the lament particularly convincing. Seems to me many experienced workers could do the job, given the chance and perhaps with some training. But executives seemed blind to the opportunity experienced workers offered—until now. Management teams are finally learning they can't afford to ignore experience. "The only thing that makes the employer move is a sense that there is a lack of qualified labor," says Ursula Staudinger, professor of sociomedical sciences and psychology at Columbia University. "Then they become very creative and inventive with their employees."

Older Americans are a remarkably diverse group. Some adults 60 and older are well educated and healthy, while similarly credentialed peers have fallen into ill health. Nearly one in ten Americans 65 and older lives in poverty while a majority are financially secure. A lifetime of work handicapped by gender bias or racial stereotyping (or both) diminishes household resources available to fund the retirement years. Some 80 percent of Americans 65 and older own their home. Yet from 2000 to 2018, the only group whose homeownership rate fell among the 65 and older population was African Americans.[18]

Not everyone has had the kinds of jobs that have tapped into their ingenuity and allowed for a degree of individual autonomy. Women are more likely than men to live in poverty in their elder years, largely reflecting a combination of lower lifetime earnings from gender discrimination and taking time off from the job for caregiving of children and aging parents. People who worked in industries or jobs that don't provide employer-sponsored retirement savings plans and health insurance are also vulnerable. Health setbacks can sideline any career. Age discrimination is real, and a job loss around age 60 can force early retirement. The business cycle hasn't been tamed, and more recessions lie in our future. The timing of the next recession is uncertain. But it's a safe bet that the unemployment rate will climb higher at some point, including for experienced workers in the second half of life.

That said, there is no going back. America is past a major inflection point when it comes to experienced workers and mature entrepreneurs creating a more welcoming economy and labor market. Experienced workers are no longer obsolete. They're a valuable asset—productive and creative—with older entrepreneurs in the vanguard.

Picture an S-curve. The S-curve is a famous concept closely tied to the diffusion and impact of technological innovations on the economy. Productivity typically declines when a major new technology is introduced into the economy. Workers and managers struggle to master different techniques and skills. The pioneers are often small companies with few resources except a willingness to experiment. Larger competitors mostly stick with what has worked in the past, while keeping an eye on developments. People and organizations move up the learning curve, helped by additional advances that promote ease of use. The pace of adoption accelerates until a critical mass is achieved. Productivity growth picks up smartly.

A good example is personal computers. The business productivity promise of early personal computers was quickly recognized, but the machines weren't easy to use. The market was dominated by enthusiasts willing to deal with the finicky demands of the new technology. Additional innovations like Microsoft Windows and Apple's Mac opened computers to the average worker and person at home. People moved up the learning curve. Larger companies invested resources in the new technology and reorganized work around advanced information technologies. The rise of the internet in the mid-1990s, additional software developments in the early 2000s, and other advances sped up the process of adoption by companies and individuals.

A similar diffusion-of-innovation pattern occurs in the broader society. The S-curve begins with majority opinion relatively stable and in keeping with the "natural" order of things (e.g., married women shouldn't work outside of the home; homosexuality is wrong and illegal). Alternative visions and expectations emerge. Opinions start changing, engendering a divisive period marked by social struggle and passionate disagreements. Eventually, a major shift in public attitudes accelerates, racing toward a new shared vision of the good life (e.g., married women have careers; gay marriage is legal and embraced by many). Although the S-curve transformation is much messier with social change than with technology, a new consensus does emerge.

The rise of these popular narratives reflects and reinforces broad changes in social norms and individual expectations. They have real effects on the development of new products and services. "When a culture changes, it's often because a small group of people on society's margins find a better way to live, parts of which the mainstream adopts," notes *New York Times* columnist David Brooks.[19] Adds Nobel laureate Robert Shiller: "Narratives are major vectors of rapid change in culture, in zeitgeist, and ultimately in economic behavior."[20]

Retirement has been closely associated with leisure and inevitable decline since the 1950s. The popular image of the elder years was living in segregated adult retirement communities with finances supported by employer pension plans, Social Security, and Medicare. Retirement meant playing golf in the morning and enjoying cocktails in the evening, until the frailties and maladies of old age set in. This vision of the elder years didn't include everyone—far from it. Lower-income elders and many minorities were excluded. Employees of small businesses didn't get company pensions. Elders with long successful careers rarely withdrew from the world of work (although they worked at a reduced schedule).

Nevertheless, persistent stereotypes depicted older people as leisure seeking, increasingly frail, and definitely unimaginative. "Good riddance!" seemed to be the prevailing workplace sentiment when someone retired. They were obsolete. Time to go play shuffleboard. The attitude seemed to be, "Enjoy your retirement as much as possible during your declining elder years. Leave the productive and creative sides of the economy and society to the younger generations."

This "retirement" view of the elder years dominated over the past half century. "In an industrial age, and perhaps in a postindustrial age as well, these assumptions include, *inter alia*, that persons *retreat* gradually from public life, from the world of work, that they make way for younger workers who are presumably fitter and more able to competently perform tasks, whilst they necessarily, because of their state of being 'old,' are more prone to self-absorption, and have a diminished interest in the world around them," writes philosopher Howard Harriott. "It supposes that *creativity and youth are correlates*. . . . It is certainly a fact that the received view of the self in old age is that one is likely to be burdensome, garrulous, miserly, and malicious."[21]

The Grumpy Old Men trope of portraying older people as technological illiterates, borderline senile, and antisocial is fading (thankfully, although I wish much faster). The vision of the elder years is changing toward a model of engagement in the broader community and creativity at work. The unretirement phase of life increasingly includes earning some income. Workers are negotiating phased retirement with their employer; finding part-time work with the same or different employer; shifting to bridge jobs and encore careers with different employers and organizations; tapping into the gig economy; and returning to part-time and flexible employment after a spell of not working.

"It's not about people being older," said Andrew Scott, professor of economics at the London Business School and coauthor of *The 100-Year Life*, during a lecture at Columbia University. "It's about people living younger lives."

The leading edge of the S-curve when it comes to an aging population is entrepreneurship, including self-employment. The core argument in this book is that launching a business is smart and sensible for experienced workers. Entrepreneurship is rapidly becoming a defining activity in the second half of life. This doesn't mean everyone will embrace entrepreneurship. But the men and women with an entrepreneurial drive are in the vanguard of reimagining the good life in the unretirement years. Their grassroots energy is the major reason why the S-curve movement redefining aging is gathering momentum.

Yes, I know that American culture considers entrepreneurship an elite venture only open to youthful talents like the superstars of Silicon Valley, such as Mark Zuckerberg, founder of Facebook, and Evan Spiegel, cofounder of Snap (formerly Snapchat).

Think again. Americans in the second half of life are embracing entrepreneurship in large numbers. Owning a business with or without employees is a source of income that offers opportunities for exercising creativity and engagement. You get to be the boss. Owning your business is a smart way to sidestep sclerotic human resource departments and their ageist algorithms. Why wait around for management to abandon ridiculous stereotypes? Why waste precious time in meetings, only to hear someone make the inevitable ageist insult: Sorry, my memory is failing me. I'm having a senior moment! (Let's retire that catchphrase forever.) Many men and women have harbored dreams of starting their own enterprise. "Entrepreneurship is a reflection of our culture," said Bruce Wolfe, formerly executive director of the BlackRock Retirement Institute, in a talk at Columbia University.

Like Cecilia Wessinger, age 53. She has embarked on her entrepreneurial venture, experimenting with a portfolio of activities that will bring in both money and meaning. Hers is a journey of discovery and creativity.

Wessinger lives in Tulsa. She took a circuitous route before landing in Oklahoma. She was born in Japan to Taiwanese parents and raised in New York City. She lived in Taiwan for three years after college, met her future husband there and followed him back to Dallas, Texas. She had a two-decade career in the travel business wearing numerous hats, including stints in the timeshare business and hotel management. Along the way, she divorced and settled in Tulsa, where her son attends the University of Tulsa.

Wessinger was nearly 50 years old when she parted company from her self-described "soul sucking" hotel job in downtown Tulsa. She jumped into her car and drove more than 10,000 miles to visit the four states she hadn't been to yet. "I was about to turn 50, and I didn't know what I wanted to do with my life. You think a lot about the things that are important," she says. "What is your purpose?"

Answering that question took time for her. We met at Guthrie Green, a park on the edge of downtown Tulsa. The Woody Guthrie Center with its giant mural of the folk music legend with his guitar on an outside wall alongside the park. So are the Philbrook Contemporary Art Museum, art galleries, and restaurants. We had lunch at the Lone Wolf, a Vietnamese-influenced restaurant. Wessinger took me on a walk around downtown Tulsa, introducing me to the city's history, from its stunning art deco architecture to searing memorials to the horrendous race riot of 1921.

Wessinger's journey initially began by dusting off an idea she had had for nearly a decade: Spring Noodles, a healthy Asian noodle bar. She thought she might franchise the restaurant if Spring Noodles was successful. She developed the idea, won a local startup competition, and joined the inaugural class of Kitchen 66, a foundation-backed program designed to help food entrepreneurs launch their ideas in Tulsa.

Wessinger teamed up with local entrepreneur and restauranteur Nancy Bruce, owner of the New York-style deli Lambrusco'z. Bruce gave her some space for her noodle products and mentored her in the restaurant business. Wessinger ran Tulsa's One Million Cups entrepreneurship program sponsored by the Kauffman Foundation. (The Kauffman Foundation is among the nation's leading researchers into entrepreneurship. The foundation is also a practical advocate for creating a larger startup ecology.) Each week, the One Million Cups meeting offers two local entrepreneurs the opportunity to present their startups to an audience of mentors, advisors, and entrepreneurs. She also attended a Kauffman Foundation conference with some 450 people from forty-eight states and nine countries. Nearly half the participants were women and a third were people of color, she recalled. The focus of the conference was how to create a vibrant local entrepreneurial ecosystem.

Eventually, Bruce gave her some timely advice. She recommended Wessinger drop her restaurant dream. "She said, 'You're not like me,'" Wessinger recalled. "She added, 'I'm a cook. But that's not your strength. I like it when you talk to customers.'"

Wessinger said she had to agree with Bruce's assessment. Her work with the One Million Cups and her participation in the entrepreneurial ecosystem conference reinforced to her that what she liked doing was building networks and linking organizations. She is passionate about increasing diversity, inclusion, and belonging in the community. Her favorite word, she told me, is *liminality*, the condition of being on a threshold or at the beginning of a process. "I am a convener," she said.

She has founded or cofounded several initiatives. Civic Ninjas focuses on contracts for nurturing entrepreneurship and civic engagement. Unigus Investments consults on projects and offers workshops to strengthen connections as well as promote an inclusive culture in organizations. Wessinger is an active board member of a local theater group and other nonprofits. She participates in numerous activities with All Souls Unitarian Church, which holds the largest congregation in the Unitarian Universalist Association. When she needs money to help pay bills, she works at Lambrusco'z.

While she is figuring out how to make a living from her portfolio of activities, she is sure of one thing. "I will go back kicking and screaming to Corporate America," said Wessinger. "I never want to work for an organization that judges me solely by how much money I brought them last month."

I've run across that sentiment many times interviewing second-life entrepreneurs.

Many of these businesses started in the second half of life will be small and serve various niches in the local community. Thanks to the rise of digital technologies—internet, mobile, and sharing apps— it often takes little money to open for business. The office is typically the home or maybe a low-rent shared workspace. "Very few businesses require capital these days if you're willing to start small," says Steve King, cofounder of Emergent Research, a consulting firm based in Lafayette, California, focused on the small-business economy.

Experienced entrepreneurs often create an earnings stream from several different money-generating activities. They're emulating the approach of artists, such as writers, dancers, and musicians. Most artists develop several side businesses to make a living while continuing to practice their craft. A modern dancer might teach youngsters at an after-school studio and work as a part-time trainer at a local gym. An author may offer manuscript-editing services and sell books online.

Kevin Costello is an artist living in Sarasota, Florida, who emigrated from England to California in the early 1970s. He taught at the San Francisco Academy of Art, the San Francisco Museum of Modern Art, and was an artist-in-residence for the San Francisco Art Commission. He moved to Sarasota in the early 1980s, where he was on the faculty of the Ringling College of Art and Design and was head of the Education Department for the Ringling Museum. For more than ten years, Costello was the art, dance, and architecture correspondent for the *Sarasota Herald Tribune*.

"There isn't much money available for contemporary art here. This city puts its money into the performing arts. The advanced artists—the big artists—don't live here." Yet Costello has managed to practice his craft. Throughout his varied career, he has created large-scale sculptures out of wood, marble, and granite. He paints and takes conceptual photographs. Costello has written poetry since he was 14. "Poems help me understand what I think," he says. After a moment of reflection, he adds that he feels at his age, now 70, he is more creative than ever. "It took a lifetime to have something to say," he observes.

These days, when not in the studio, Costello lectures on art appreciation and history at many of the area's senior communities and country clubs and for Sarasota's Adult Community Enrichment program, where most of his students are his peers. He enjoys them, noting that the "only art that isn't commoditized is the art of conversation. Conversation is an art."

Costello is an entrepreneur with a portfolio that provides both purpose and a paycheck. "Artists don't retire," he says. "I don't see an end to what I am doing. I enjoy it. Why do something else?"

Some entrepreneurs in the second half of life look to build durable enterprises with employees who will outlast them. They're often serial entrepreneurs who get a kick from starting businesses. Other 50-plus entrepreneurs turn a passion or skill into a lifestyle microenterprise. The embrace of entrepreneurship is increasingly a family affair. The adult children bring hustle to the venture and facility with the latest technologies. The parents usually put up some investment money and plenty of work experience into the enterprise.

Rick Harris, age 62, has gone into business with his son Tim Harris, 27 years old. They have big ambitions for their commercial interior enterprise. "Tim wants to grow the business," says Rick. "He can be a lot more successful than I ever was."

Rick grew up in segregated Texas, living in a segregated town and attending a segregated school until he was 5 years old. His family had to drive to the next town to shop. He left Texas in 1975 at age 20 for opportunities in California. He embraced the diversity of California and "never looked back." He spent years working on factory floors before starting his own small business with a partner in the Bay Area. His business specialized in quickly setting up office interiors for small Silicon Valley startups. There were lots of clients in the Bay Area. New companies were constantly failing and the ones taking their space needed the interior space redesigned and furnished fast. Business fell off sharply during the Great Recession.

Meanwhile, in 2009, Rick's wife was offered a job as head of a private high school in Minneapolis. With their five children launched, the empty-nesters decided to move to Minnesota. His business partner bought him out over a two-year period. Rick tried to start a new full-service commercial interior venture in the Twin Cities, his new hometown. His office is housed at a nondescript but recently renovated one-story office building on the outskirts of Minneapolis. The other tenants represent a variety of service businesses. His office is small and functional with black cabinets and a white desk. It's neat and clean.

He got some business, but the market proved tough for an outsider to break into. The buyers of commercial interiors had known their existing suppliers since grade school. California, he muses, is "like a river," always flowing, always creating new opportunities. In sharp contrast, Minnesota is a land of lakes, moving slowly, defined by long-established relationships.

He looked for a niche. He joined the National Association of

Minority Contractors, and he kept learning about the local market, especially government, large nonprofits like the University of Minnesota, and big private companies. He landed some business installing flooring even though it wasn't his stock-in-trade. He started to think about retirement. "How long do I want to work?" he wondered.

Turns out, many more years. The reason for his change of heart at age 62? Tim, his then-24-year-old son and recent college graduate, asked to join the business, Ideal Commercial Interiors (essentially Rick at the time). "What got me rejuvenated is my son wanting to come into the business," says Rick.

Tim had played college basketball at St. Mary's College of California and Concordia College in Irvine, graduating in 2015 with a degree in communication studies from Concordia College in St. Paul, Minnesota. Tim pursued jobs with advertising and public relations agencies in the Twin Cities after graduation. He had plenty of interviews, but they went nowhere. He decided he wanted to learn how to run a business. "I said: 'Dad, I want to work at the company. I don't want it to be an allowance check. I want to use my skills and talents I've learned in college and help the business grow with the understanding I don't know anything about the business.'"

Tim is excited about joining his father. He laughs that his father still leafs through office interior catalogues when talking to a customer when all the information is online. Yet his father is faster at unearthing the needed information than Tim is on the computer. Tim's title is operations manager. "In short, it means I do everything," says Tim. "It's cool to learn what it takes to build a business," he adds.

They're succeeding. Ideal's revenues have more than tripled since Tim joined the company. Profit margins are improving, too, reflecting a better mix of business. They're hustling for more contracts, developing their network, and hiring.

Experienced workers-turned-entrepreneurs often embrace craft and artisan businesses. Locally made cheese. Craft beer. Farm-to-table restaurants. Handmade shoes, camping packs, and furniture. Upscale barbers and custom cabinet makers. Craft businesses are fun. The enterprise calls for creativity and mastering traditional skills, and then adapting the craft to modern technologies and sensibilities. Consumers are open to buying craft products, especially if the product or service has a strong local presence. "There is a shift in the culture," says Kieran Folliard, the 60-something founder of Food Building in northeast Minneapolis, home to local artisan producers. "There's a movement back toward getting value from craft production."

The typical image of the artisan producer is a bearded, hoodie-wearing millennial and his tattooed, fleece-wearing partner operating out of a warehouse in Brooklyn, a locally sourced restaurant in Chicago, or a small organic farm outside Portland (Maine or Oregon). Yet craft products are just as likely to be created and distributed by someone with graying hair combining a homebrewed passion and hard-earned experience into a small business. Someone in their 60s like Howard Field.

His career had been in sales. In 2010, he was working for a company that markets fuel oil to homeowners around bucolic Lancaster County, Pennsylvania, also known as Amish country. Sales were slow that summer, and his employer let him go. "Thank God," booms Field. "Two hours later, I came home and told my wife I was going into the cheese business."

Sales and marketing may have been Field's career, but at home he loved to cook. His four daughters travel the world for their jobs. Wherever they go, they pick up a local cookbook for him. In February 2010, snowed in for the week, he decided to follow a cheese-making recipe from the newspaper to pass the time. Field enjoyed the process and started imagining himself as an amateur, home-based cheese-maker. "It didn't taste too bad," he says.

His daughters got him a cheese-making book. He was excited about his new career. That is, until he followed a small, handwritten, "goat milk for sale" sign on the side of the road in Lancaster in April. He met Amos Miller, an Amish farmer whose dairy operation had just expanded into cheesemaking. Field knew a good product when he tried Miller's blue cheese. It was one of the best he had ever tasted.

He also learned that Miller "didn't have the slightest idea how to market it," says Field.

He immediately abandoned his amateur cheesemaking ambition. Instead, he tapped into his real skill—marketing. "You have to figure out what you're good at, what you love, what your passion is," he says. "Then do it. If everyone did that, the world would be a better place."

He started Farm Fromage, which sells local cheeses created by the region's Amish, Mennonite, and English small family farmers. The artisan cheeses are sold at several venues, including farmers' markets, farm-to-table restaurants, craft fairs, and online. The business started out with two farms, and it has expanded to fifteen farms. Farm Fromage sells thirty-four different kinds of cheese. "All our cheeses are local, aged raw milk cheeses," he says. "I saw that there was an opportunity to help us get good food and to help the small family farm get more money for their milk and hard work."

Farm Fromage is now a family business. Howard's wife lost her job as a bank teller in 2016, and she joined the enterprise. "The key to starting a business is keep plugging away," says Field. "See what works. See what doesn't work. I know it sounds like common sense. But it's important."

What about retirement? "We have no choice but to work," he replied. (Largely the price of putting four daughters through college. No regrets about that financial decision.) His daughters enjoy their careers and are married with "husbands I like," he says. They now have several grandchildren and love taking care of them when possible.

The work is good, too. "But we love so much what we're doing that we'd do it anyway." Later, he adds that "The bills are paid, and we're having fun. Maybe I'll retire the day after I pass away."

Those sentiments may well be the mantra for many people looking for meaning and money, purpose and a paycheck in the second half of life. The ranks of second-life entrepreneurs will continue to expand rapidly as the choice becomes more mainstream, the personal finance media devotes greater resources to the topic, and the startup ecosystem welcomes the opportunity to work with older entrepreneurs.

Entrepreneurship is in the vanguard of rethinking old age. But the tight labor market is pushing more large employers to try and retain experienced employees. Small-business owners are another (and too often underappreciated) rich source of employment for workers in their unretirement years. While most small businesses don't offer employees benefits, they also don't have human resource departments too often biased against hiring experienced workers. Small-business owners are willing to strike deals to retain good employees, especially by designing part-time hours and flexible schedules. Older workers know the business and customers. They can help train the next generation.

"I think it is true overall and more likely that small businesses develop personal relationships with their employees, and there is more flexibility," says Ruth Finkelstein, executive director of the Brookdale Center on Aging at Hunter College, City University of New York. "People care about each other."

A good example is Metro Optics Eyewear, a four-decade-old chain of retail optometry stores in the Bronx. John Bonizio, owner of the company, was on a panel about multigenerational workforces at Columbia University in 2015. About a third of Metro Optics' employees are 50 years and older. "I do this by design. I want mature, experienced people," said Bonizio. "The older employees train the younger ones. It works the other way, too."

Little Wolf Cabinet Shop is a custom cabinetmaker for commercial and residential customers. The company dates back seven generations starting in a small town in Munich, Germany. The current business opened in New York City on the Upper East Side in 1922. The owner convinced a 70-year-old employee to delay retirement for a year to teach his son the basics of the business. Ristorante Settepani and Settepani Bakery have been operating in Harlem for almost two decades. The company cross-trains its multigenerational staff to allow for flexible schedules.

These examples are drawn from Columbia University's Age Smart Employer program.[22] The awards highlight and recognize age-friendly employers who embrace multiple generations in the workplace. Not all the award winners are small businesses, but it's striking how many smaller companies are represented. "When we think about small business, we think they have limited resources," says Finkelstein, who spearheaded the Age Smart program before moving to the Brookdale Center. "At the same time, they can be idiosyncratic to adjust to motivate and retain workers."

Finkelstein's own story about how she got involved in aging and work is illustrative. Ruth is both a leading scholar and an enthusiastic advocate for practical policies to improve the quality of life of older people. Her enthusiasm for embracing diversity and inclusion, as well as creating opportunities for flourishing, is infectious. Back in 2006, the World Health Organization (WHO) held a meeting in Vancouver, Canada. The WHO wanted to draw greater attention to the prospect that, by 2030, three out of every five people in the world would live in cities. Aging is a global trend, and many urban dwellers will be in the second half of life. The conference marked the beginning of the Global Age-Friendly Cities initiative. The goal is to transform urban environments in ways that make it easier to navigate for older people. (Initiatives that boost the livability of cities for older people are good for younger generations. Several years ago at a conference Allen Glicksman, director of research and evaluation at Philadelphia Corporation for Aging, gave a talk. He said the main lesson he learned over the years about the generations living together was this: "What's good for old people is good for everybody and what's bad for older people is bad for everyone in the community.")

Finkelstein was senior vice president for planning and policy at the New York Academy of Medicine and she directed the Big Apple's Age-Friendly initiative. One of the first things she did was set up community consultations all over the city. The size of the audiences ranged from around twenty to several hundred. The goals emphasized transportation, social inclusion, housing, communication, and civic engagement. Yet at these meetings, the older people kept coming up to her saying they needed work and how could they get a job. "It wasn't on my radar or agenda," says Finkelstein. "It made me interested. This is a big thing."

The instructors at New Century Careers in Pittsburgh, Pennsylvania would agree with her. New Century teaches machining to the younger generations, including the Machinist Training Program, the National Tooling and Machining Association Apprenticeship Program, and the Manufacturing 2000 Machinist Training Plus. The instructors range in age from their 50s to their 80s. The machinist instructors love their craft. They want young people in the program to succeed so they can have a fulfilling career, own a home, and support a family—to live the American Dream.

Among the instructors is Stan Kulczyski, who is 80 years old. Kulczyski is from southside Pittsburgh. The neighborhood he grew up in isn't far from the New Century building. He went into machining after attending a vocational high school in Pittsburgh. He picked up additional skills in night school and on the job. Kulczyski worked at thirteen different machine tool shops during his career. He worked on everything from giant power turbines to nuclear submarines to small plastic products.

When we met at New Century, he showed me several items he had machined. Among them was a thin, clear plastic rectangle about the size of a credit card. The plastic had tiny ridges on it and thirty little holes. Technicians put blood or urine on the plastic card and put it into a centrifuge to run tests.

Kulczyski is busy. A fan of legendary California winemaker Robert Mondavi, he makes red wine from Napa Valley grapes in his garage. (Key to his wine is adding a small amount of blackberry brandy and Spanish red.) He's in a men's club, and they make pierogies (filled dumplings) and haluski (cabbage and noodles) for their church. He works at Costco two days a week, handing out food samples to customers. He's also a caregiver. Married for fifty-seven years, his wife has been ill recently. The income from New Century and Costco helps the household budget. "I want to keep her," he says. "That's life."

Kulczyski retired at age 68 when the company where he worked was bought out in a takeover. For more than the past decade, he has worked part-time as an instructor at New Century, training the next generation of machinists. He regaled me with stories of young people he has helped put on the path toward mastering the craft. "I like the students," he says. "I have a lot to pass on. That's why I am here."

I love it.

Much of the conversation about prospects for finding work later in life ignores how creative people are at coming up with solutions that offer both purpose and money. Kulceski is admirable for his passion and engagement. But he is far from alone in finding meaningful work. Many people I've interviewed over the years who have managed to construct intriguing ways to earn extra income and do new things in their unretirement years. The job may be in an occupation they never considered before retiring. The work is often part-time or seasonal. Housesitting for wealthy families. Waxing skis for racers in Park City, Utah. Repairing used tractors for neighbors in rural South Carolina. Supplementing retirement income by working for publishers creating indexes for books. (All true stories.)

John Kerr's experience stands out. After a career that spanned forty years as fundraiser for public broadcasting's WGBH Radio and Television in Boston, he retired at age 65. "It took the shock of the change to rattle my bones a bit," says John Kerr. "I had way too much energy and experience to sit around."[23]

His exploration for new challenges took him to the high-mountain west. While visiting Bozeman, Montana, he walked unannounced into the Yellowstone National Foundation office, now called Yellowstone Forever. The Foundation raises money to support Yellowstone National Park. He met the organization's president and learned about an internship they had. Kerr applied and for the next season he was the "world's oldest intern," talking to visitors about wolf restoration in Yellowstone's beautiful Lamar Valley. "I earned my stripes," he says.

That internship led him to a seasonal job as a park ranger in Yellowstone National Park between May and September. The money helped his bank account. "Volunteering is fine, but a paid job makes what you do more legitimate," he observes. "So be open to any opportunity that comes along."

He is still at it. Now 80 years old, Kerr loves his shift to seasonal work as a Yellowstone Park ranger. He spends his winters back in New England to be near his family. "It continues to be a great adventure," says Kerr.

Speeding up the S-curve transition calls for more institutional support. Transitions are rarely easy in the second half of life. (Actually, transitions are always hard. Think of going from high school to work or college, getting married, having kids, losing a job, starting with a different employer.) Transitions always seem to take longer than expected, even when the leap into something new has been carefully planned. People need the support of services and institutions—well established on-ramps and off-ramps—to lessen the risks from shifting into an encore career or getting additional education for the next unretirement gig. Institutional innovations would accelerate the transformation toward late-in-life work.

"Without a vision of opportunity, there cannot be a struggle for self-realization," writes the late Nobel laureate and economic historian Robert Fogel. "For opportunity to be realistic, an individual must also have a sense of the mainstream of work and life, a sense of where the opportunities are and how to pursue them."[24]

Expectations are changing. The boomer generation absorbed a simple model of the typical span: School, work, and retire. Boomers went to school in their youth. When they graduated from school, they got a job, and within a short time, they settled into a career. When they reach their early 60s, the expectation was to say goodbye to colleagues for the last time and retire. Leisure was the defining activity during the retirement years.

Even decades ago, this vision often didn't square with reality. Many people didn't live that idealized progression. Life threw them too many curves, some positive and others negative. The story remained powerful and widely shared.

The school–work–retirement silos are coming down, thanks to the powerful combination of an aging population, globalization, and technological innovation. The rewrite of the new life course is still being drafted, but a more complex narrative is being scripted. The baby-boom generation is the lead writer, but other generations will weigh in, too.

The narrative's basic outline is clear. Career shifts will become commonplace, perhaps taking a job at a large business for a time, leaving it to start a business, later joining the staff of a nonprofit organization, shifting to another firm in a few years. Workers will need to pick up additional education and training throughout their careers to ease transitions and create new opportunities. What kind of education and training opportunities should exist for careers that may last for 60 to 70 years in the future? Fascinating to think about, isn't it?

The rewrite puts pressure on policymakers to overhaul the safety net established for a different economy and society. More resources need to be devoted to worker training, retraining, and lifelong learning. Health and pension systems should be redesigned to support a mobile workforce and to encourage experienced workers to stay in the job market, often through part-time jobs and work with flexible schedules and self-employment.

The rewrite will force employers to overhaul employee benefits in ways that encourage longer work lives. Benefits might include paying for late-career training programs to invest in phased-retirement and semiretirement schedules. Elizabeth Isele, founder of the Global Institute for Experienced Entrepreneurship, advocates for a new benefit: lessons in entrepreneurship. Employees could learn what it takes to start a business by having their employers pay for workshops and classes, mentorship programs, membership in incubators and accelerators, and other startup opportunities. The idea is intergenerational, but I suspect quite a few experienced workers looking to transition into their unretirement would take advantage of this benefit. "In truth, every job needs an entrepreneurial mindset. It boosts engagement, which, in turn, boosts productivity," says Isele. "It's a win-win for employers and employees."[25]

A theme of future benefits—public and private—is flexibility. Flexible work arrangements help parents with young children and older adults caring for aging parents. Flexibility is desirable among experienced workers ready to leave full-time employment behind, but not eager to retire.

The rewrite also shifts the focus of public policy discussions when it comes to the economics of an aging population. Too much attention is currently paid to the financial shortfalls in Social Security, Medicare, and household retirement savings. Don't get me wrong. These are critically important topics, and Social Security, Medicare, and household finances need shoring up. But the focus on these topics limits the scope of fundamental questions raised by the aging of society. Policymakers aren't putting enough emphasis on labor market reforms that would boost the participation rate of all workers, including those 50 years and older. The same holds for postsecondary education and training initiatives that would allow workers to add to their skills in their 50s, 60s, 70s, and later. Entrepreneurs and the self-employed who are 50-plus need better support from local incubators, accelerators, and other initiatives designed to boost startups and innovation.

The scale and scope of the rewrite are illustrated by a chart put together by Columbia University's Staudinger, an internationally recognized aging researcher. Her focus is on the workplace "because it is such a crucial setting for human development," she told me in an interview at her book-lined Columbia University office. Part of our discussion focused on a slide she had presented several years ago during a talk at a Columbia University Age Boom Academy—an annual gathering of scholars studying aging and journalists that cover aging. She highlighted seven key ideas for employers and society to embrace:[26]

- Flexibility in payout of retirement funds
- Cumulating overtime to make room for family, training, or life beyond work
- Education becomes lifelong learning
- Support for transitions in and out of the labor force (for example, parental leave, eldercare leave, sabbaticals)
- Easier access to activating volunteer activities
- Leisure: Striking a balance between activity and rest
- No life course flexibility without health. Health promotion needs more attention.

These are all worthwhile aspirations. The theme that ties these ideas together is the desire to improve the quality of everyday life over the long haul—the life course. We can't do that without cultivating and devoting resources to better the experience of work. Let's focus on boosting the odds of healthy aging and purposeful aging—including on the job. Everyone should have the opportunity to pursue purpose and a paycheck, the ability to exercise creativity and engagement throughout a long-lived life.

This conversation about aging shifts the focus of attention away from savings, Social Security systems, leisure, and decline and toward ideas to improve the quality of work, boost education and skills, and promote entrepreneurship and an entrepreneurial mind-set throughout a lifetime, including the last third of life.

"All Utopias that have hitherto been constructed are intolerably dull," shrewdly observed philosopher Bertrand Russell. "Social reformers, like inventors of Utopias, are apt to forget this very obvious fact of human nature. They aim rather at securing more leisure, and more opportunity for enjoying it, than with making work itself more satisfactory, more consonant with impulse, and a better outlet for creativeness and the desire to employ one's faculties."[27] (Russell himself lived for 97 years. He was remarkably engaged and active throughout his long life until pneumonia felled him in 1970.)

∎

The impact of experienced workers and 50-plus entrepreneurs is bigger than positive prospects for aging individuals. The hope of their pioneering struggles to redefine aging lies in the tantalizing vision that their efforts will improve prospects for younger generations (who will get older).

Policymakers, business leaders, public intellectuals, and others with a voice in the community routinely praise work and the work ethic. The reality is that work and workers have been given relatively short shrift in recent decades. Wealth creators, private equity buccaneers, Wall Street financiers, and senior management have received the lion's share of attention—and much of the economy's wealth. Instead of the work ethic, it seems maximizing shareholder value holds primacy. The contributions of employees are too often an afterthought. Worker jobs and livelihoods are increasingly insecure and financially fragile.

The rise of shareholder value maximization—the "world's dumbest idea," notes behavioral financier James Montier—is telling. The modern twist is often dated to a 1970s article by conservative economist Milton Friedman. "There is one and only one social responsibility of business—to use its resources and engage in activities designed to increase its profits," he argued.[28]

Finance economists led by Harvard Business School professor Michael Jensen believed professional managers of large publicly traded companies weren't acting like owners of the business. The critics scorned corporate executives as empire builders more interested in their office perks than aggressively investing in the business like the ruthless capitalists from another era (such as nineteenth-century robber barons). Jensen and his fellow travelers didn't like it when chief executive officers talked about the company's need to consider the interests of shareholders, employees, customers, and community.

The "solution"? Turn executives into capitalist owners by turning the bulk of their compensation into stock options. The options would pay off big if the company's stock price improved. Corporate America and compensation consultants ran with the idea. Chief executive pay skyrocketed, thanks to option-laden pay packages. Most CEOs figured they could earn more sacrificing long-term gains for short-term results. Business leaders had a financial incentive to scrimp on investments. The pursuit of shareholder value maximization helped fuel the rise in income inequality and labor's falling share of gross domestic product.

The ideology of shareholder capitalism has made the country worse off. "Shareholders are but one very narrow group of our broader economic landscape," writes Montier. "Yet by allowing companies to focus on them alone, we have potentially unleashed a number of ills upon ourselves. A broader perspective is called for. Customers, employees, and taxpayers should all be considered. Raising one group to the exclusion of the others is likely a path to disaster. Anyone for stakeholder capitalism?"[29]

Sign me up.

The search for purpose and a paycheck in the second half of life is a force for focusing on improving the quality and rewards of work, from the janitor to the lawyer. People spend much of their lives measured in hours, physical presence, and mental activity at work. Little wonder the desire for both purpose and a paycheck on the job is powerful. "Work is the experience of life," says Nobel laureate Edmund Phelps while we talked in his spacious book-lined office at Columbia University. "To participate in the economy is essential to being part of society's central project—working together to do stuff."

The late Studs Terkel beautifully brought that search alive in his 1972 masterpiece, *Working*. Terkel recorded the hardships, humiliations, and disappointments ordinary workers suffered from their daily labors. Except for a few luminaries, his interviews were with people in occupations like receptionist, miner, farmer, railroad worker, car salesman, and hotel switch operator. He chronicled their dignity and pride in a job well done, and the sense of community and connection that came from their work.

"It is about a search, too, for daily meaning as well as daily bread, for recognition as well as cash, for astonishment rather than torpor," wrote Terkel. "To be remembered was the wish, spoken and unspoken, of the heroes and heroines of the book." As Nora Watson told Terkel during her interview, "I think most of us are looking for a calling, not a job."[30]

Nearly a half century later, older adults are also looking for a "calling, not a job." A job that nourishes the spirit as well as pays the bills. Work is one of the principal ways people get to feel both needed and wanted by their community. Forging connections that keep people engaged in the economy in the second half of life rather than labeling them unproductive and uncreative is a recipe in the twenty-first century for fueling creativity, encouraging innovation, and boosting economic growth.

"Two hundred years ago, business and political leaders learned the importance of investing in physical capital," writes Michael Mandel, chief economic strategist at the Progressive Policy Institute. "One hundred years ago, they learned the importance of investing in human capital. Today, business and political leaders are learning a new lesson: the importance of investing in connections."[31] Those valuable connections include the insights, experience, and willingness to take risks on people in the second half of life.

Perhaps we're simply relearning an old lesson about multigenerational connections (and adapting it for our technological age). The American economy went through enormous changes from the early days of the Revolution through the Civil War. A new society was being built and the contributions of the elders were seen as critical.

"Our predecessors would have been surprised to learn that the elderly as a group would be described one day as roleless and unproductive persons who inevitably and willingly disengage from active life," writes historian W. Andrew Achenbaum in *Old Age in the New Land*. "In sharp contrast, Americans between the Revolutionary and Civil [W]ars believed that their infant republic depended upon the commitment and ability of men and women of all ages to work together in creating a new society."[32]

Social convention held that work also helped the older Americans enjoy a healthier, longer life (anticipating current scientific and social science research). Work kept them engaged. "In fact, Americans considered it foolish for the elderly to quit their jobs merely on account of age: medical and popular writers noted that deterioration in later years less often resulted from natural decay than from disuse," notes Achenbaum. "The prevailing notion that the old were seasoned veterans of productivity, whose advice and participation enhanced prospects for successfully accomplishing many tasks, justified ascribing to aged persons a variety of important societal tasks to perform."[33]

Perhaps we're having a back-to-the-future moment. Thankfully, older Americans have access to earned-benefit programs unavailable to early Americans, such as Social Security, Medicare, Medicaid, and retirement savings plans. Early American elders had no choice but to labor away, unless or until their health failed them.

Nevertheless, the observations drawn from the young Republic's first century resonate. Experienced workers and older entrepreneurs in the twenty-first century are "seasoned veterans of productivity" who have a "variety of important societal tasks to perform." They're redefining aging for a high-tech global economy.

The Mt. Washington Hotel in New Hampshire is a majestic white building with a Spanish-style red tile roof alongside the White Mountain National Forest. The railroad-era hotel was built in the early 1900s. Toward the end of World War II, delegates from forty-four Allied nations gathered there to design the international economic architecture for when the war was over. Among the achievements of the 1944 Bretton Woods agreement (named after the town near the hotel) were the International Monetary Fund and the World Bank.

One of the speakers at a human resources conference held at the hotel in 2015 was Anna Eleanor Roosevelt. She is the granddaughter of Eleanor and Franklin Roosevelt, the former First Lady and President of the United States. She gave her talk in the Grand Ballroom, a fitting scene considering it was where the delegates met. Anna Roosevelt had a long career in the private sector and, in her encore career, she was head of Goodwill in Maine, New Hampshire, and Vermont.

Her remarks focused on the dignity of work. She got a good laugh from the audience when she said she didn't learn her economics from her grandfather President Roosevelt but from a children's book—Babar the elephant. In Babar's fictional town of Centerville "everyone had a job and every job was important," she said. "To have a thriving economy every person who wants to work can work. We each have to do our part, but we all reap the benefits. Its' not just about the job. It's about the community."

What makes for a life of significance, a life that matters? What good have we done and what more can we do in the time remaining to us? What gives meaning to life? What is my calling? Questions like these often begin in religious settings and late-night dorm room conversations. They're haunting and timeless and crop up at unexpected moments. Perhaps the questions are sparked by book club reading or staring at the vista of a national park like Yosemite. Satisfying answers are elusive, of course. The search for purpose can take different directions, sometimes depending on our stage of life and at other times reflecting the dominant concerns of the era.

We spend much of our days at work. Little wonder that the desire to get more from the workplace than a paycheck is strong. "We want work that is challenging and engaging, that enables us to exercise some discretion and control over what we do, and that provides us opportunities to learn and to grow," writes Barry Schwartz, professor of psychology at Swarthmore College. "We want to work with colleagues we respect and with supervisors who respect us. Most of all we want work that is meaningful—that makes a difference to other people and this ennobles us in at least some small way."[34]

Although Schwartz isn't addressing experienced workers in particular, his exhortation underlines why reimagining the second half of life is a deeply moral and practical enterprise. Experienced workers and entrepreneurs are grappling with timeless questions at the workplace. The issues are shared among the generations. Still, the search for purpose does seem somewhat more pressing with age. Most of us don't know when we'll die. We do know that life gets shorter with each tick-tock of the clock.

There is much more to life than work. Family. Friends. Spirituality. Holding a grandchild. Taking a walk around the neighborhood with friends or enjoying a drink with strangers after running a 5K.

The goal is about choice. If experienced Americans still want to work, they should be included and valued. They still have much to contribute to the workplace, the economy's dynamism, and the wider community. Many experienced workers are ready for new adventures. They're willing to experiment. They're curious and they want to keep earning a paycheck.

A note on language. Words matter. Words reinforce stereotypes or combat them. Words reflect and affect the way we think about work and spending, love and friendship, gender and ethnicity. Many people studying, researching, and talking about aging are deeply dissatisfied with many common terms.

Some catchphrases are insulting and easy to avoid, like "geezer," "over-the-hill," and "silver tsunami." Many people increasingly refuse to use less incendiary terms that have fallen out-of-favor, such as senior citizens. "Senior" seems to imply that anyone over age 60 is in retreat from society. "Boomers" seems to carry too much baggage for comfort most of the time.

"Old" is usually on the list of words to avoid. Too bad. "Old" is simple and chronological. I don't find it offensive. I agree with Laura Carstensen, the distinguished head of the Stanford Center on Longevity. She campaigned to get people to embrace the word "old." But, as she wrote in a *Washington Post* column, she failed. No one seemed to like the word. Carstensen gave up. Instead, she proposed following the lead of a fashion technologist who refers to her older customers as "perennials."[35]

I can't get behind being called a plant or a flower. It also takes too much time to explain what the word means in everyday conversation.

I don't have an easy and satisfying solution. My approach is to vary a handful of terms. Among them: *Experienced workers* (my preferred term), as as *older adults, second half of life, older workers* and *aging entrepreneurs*. I like "unretirement" to signal people continuing to work into the traditional retirement years. I'll try to be specific when I can, say, identifying people 65 years and over or between ages 64 and 74.

As for myself, I turned 65 in 2018. I'm *still* working. I *still* plan on sticking with journalism and writing (assuming I can continue publishing with *PBS Next Avenue,* the *Star Tribune,* and other outlets); *still* show up on public radio and exchange ideas with colleagues (so long as Minnesota Public Radio/American Public Media will have me); *still* love spending time with family and friends; *still* enjoy exploring new restaurants and experimenting with recipes; *still* like hiking and book club meetings; and I'm *still* trying to learn how to play a musical instrument for the first time, a guitar (a truly pathetic exercise so far).

2

The Myth of Creative Decline

The great thing about the work, and particularly work later in your life, is that you can still maintain the sense of possibility that at the end of the day you'll know something that you didn't know at the beginning of the day. And I just find that an extraordinary gift.

—MILTON GLASER[1]

The crowd in the lobby at the Museum of Modern Art was reminiscent of Grand Central Station during rush hour. I was there to see the exhibition, "Henri Matisse: The Cut-Outs."

Matisse was born in 1869 in northern France. Initially trained as a lawyer, he turned to art in his early twenties and, during his rich and varied career, he became one of the giants of modern art. This sketch of Matisse is familiar to the average museum-goer.

Less well known is that, in 1941, Matisse barely survived colon surgery. He was a semi-invalid until his death at age 84 in 1954. Yet in those years he created a new art form—the cut-outs. They're magnificent, visually stunning, constructed out of white paper, gouache, and scissors. He mostly made the cut-outs from his wheelchair and bed, which makes the large size of many of them even more impressive.

"My terrible operation has completely rejuvenated and made a philosopher of me," he wrote in 1942 to the French painter and lifelong friend Albert Marquet. "I had so completely prepared for my exit from life that it seems to me that I am in a second life."[2]

Many artists enjoy the heights of creativity in their second life, such as painter Paul Cézanne and sculptor Auguste Rodin. Matisse was 82 years old when he created his famous Blue Nudes series of cut-outs.

"Matisse's final decade was arguably more prodigious than any period of his magnificent career, which endured for more than sixty years and produced countless masterpieces from the time of his revolutionary Fauvist painting *The Woman with the Hat* (1905) and *The Joy of Life* (1905–06)," writes Alastair Sooke in *Matisse: A Second Life*. "In an astonishing burst of creativity, he produced hundreds of new works in his seemingly effortless late style that came to be known as his 'paper cut-outs.'"[3]

I like Matisse's expression a "second life." He used the phrase to tell his son, friends, and fellow artists how glad he was to be alive despite an awareness that time remained short for him (although it turned out he had thirteen years of productive work ahead). Clearly, second life presages second act, encore career, next chapter, third age, unretirement, and other phrases currently used to describe people reimagining their jobs and careers in their 50s, 60s, and older.

When I visited the Matisse exhibition, my engaging companion was Bruce Nussbaum, former assistant managing editor at *Businessweek* magazine. Bruce is a master of reinvention. He was head of the magazine's editorial page for much of the time we worked together at the magazine's headquarters in New York. When a new editor-in-chief eliminated the editorial page, Bruce quickly pivoted to create a new position covering the hot field of industrial design. He leveraged that gig into a decade-long position as professor of innovation and design at the Parsons School of Design at The New School in New York City. He wrote *Creative Intelligence: Harnessing the Power to Create, Connect, and Inspire* when he was 65 years old. And now, at age 71, he is mentor-in-residence at New York City's NEW INC, the art-and-technology incubator in the United States.

Bruce and his wife are passionate birdwatchers (passionate and birdwatching may be one word). While at MOMA, he described how veteran birdwatchers develop the ability to quickly name birds despite not seeing all identifying marks. Birders get a vibe or a reading from a brief sighting. "You see only a fragment, and you know what it is," says Bruce.

That birdwatching skill is useful for identifying creativity later in life, he added. The broader society doesn't appreciate how many artists and elders in all kinds of endeavors did some of their most imaginative work in their later years. But once you start looking, you get a vibe and begin identifying patterns about the accomplishments of older people exercising their creativity.

Laura Ingalls Wilder, for one. When our family lived in Bremerhaven, Germany, in the early 1960s, my younger sister and I eagerly shared her "Little House" series of books. We had no idea Wilder didn't start writing in earnest until she was 57. Her first manuscript, a memoir, was rejected by editors. She reworked it into a fictional story about nineteenth-century life on the Great Plains aimed at young readers. *Little House in the Big Woods* was published when Wilder was 65 years old.[4]

How about *A River Runs Through It* by Norman Maclean? My friends and I read his story about family and love and reckonings through the lens of fly fishing in Montana. We spent many evenings talking through the themes of the tale that begins with the memorable line, "In our family, there was no clear line between religion and fly-fishing." Maclean wrote *A River Runs Through It* at age 74, three years after retiring from teaching at the University of Chicago in 1973. Marilynne Robinson published her Pulitzer-winning novel *Gilead* when she was 61 years old. Among my favorite observers of current affairs is basketball legend Kareem Abdul-Jabbar. Now in his 70s, he enjoys a remarkable second career as movie producer, author, documentarian, and columnist.

Many musicians improve at their art with the passage of the years, testing boundaries and trying new compositions. Madonna, age 60, has enjoyed a music and entertainment career defined by multiple reincarnations. She released her ambitious album *Rebel Heart* in 2015 and she is working on another album to be issued in 2019. Still, Madonna seems a favorite target of critics telling her to "act her age." Her reaction? A topless photo shoot for *Interview* magazine and another in suspenders for *Vogue*. "I don't think artists think about their age when they create," she said to Jon Pareles, the music critic.[5] The late Leonard Cohen came out with his last studio album at age 82, the bleak yet powerful *You Want It Darker*.

Like Madonna, musician and multimedia pioneer David Bowie reinvented himself many times over the span of his 69 years. Yet some of his most innovative work came in the last five years of his life, long after a 2004 heart attack led fans and critics to expect a quiet retirement. The HBO documentary *David Bowie: The Last Five Years* celebrates these inventive years marked by collaborations with jazz composer Maria Schneider and saxophonist Donny McCaslin.

The same story holds with visual artists. Lubaina Himid was awarded the Turner Prize, the United Kingdom's most important contemporary art prize, at age 63 in 2017. (She could win because of a rule change eliminating the previous 50-or-younger age restriction.)

How about Faith Ringgold, the brilliant multimedia artist? Born in 1931, her posters and paintings from the 1960s powerfully captured the tensions enveloping race relations in America. In the early 1980s she began her signature series of painted "story quilts." (Her first was "Who's Afraid of Aunt Jemima?".) She is best known for her painted "story quilts." Her quilts showcase large painted scenes and narrative text panels. She has written a memoir, authored and illustrated numerous children's books, and designed a game for mobile devices. The game Quiltuduko was inspired by Sudoku."[6]

Architects also show progress in their work and imaginations with age. During a tour with friends of Frank Lloyd Wright's Taliesin estate in rural Wisconsin, our silver-haired docent was thrilled to report that the famed architect did a third of his work after age 70. Wright designed some of his most famous buildings during this inspired period, including the Guggenheim Museum in New York City and Falling-water, the home constructed over a waterfall in the Pennsylvania countryside.

See the pattern? Older artists like these and many more would agree with Keith Richards, the 70-something guitarist and songwriter for the Rolling Stones. "You don't stop growing until they shovel the dirt in," he memorably growled in an interview with *The Guardian*.[7]

These artists are exceptionally talented. They're famous for their cre-ative drive. They managed to imagine something new and different with their art throughout their long careers. What does their flourishing in their 60s, 70s, and 80s tell us about the average American worker and entrepreneur in the second half of life?

Everything.

The pernicious stereotype is that people in the second half of life aren't creative. Older workers are set in their ways, reluctant to learn new skills, unwilling to embrace new technologies and new ways of doing business—or so we're told. You've probably heard dismissive sentiments like that at work or at a neighborhood gathering, haven't you? Sayings like, "You can't teach an old dog new tricks," or "I'm having a senior moment."

"People who would never make a racist or sexist joke will make an ageist joke without thinking about it," says David Neumark, economist and director of the Center for Economics and Public Policy at the University of California, Irvine.[8] "The social acceptability of that is remarkable."

Adds David DeLong, president of Smart Workforce Strategies, a consulting firm based in Concord, Massachusetts, "The older job seeker is the last group where it's culturally acceptable to be biased against. Not legally acceptable. But it's a widespread position."[9]

The negative stereotype is wrong on so many levels. The scholarly evidence is convincing that creativity and inventiveness don't fade with the accumulation of birthdays. Like Matisse, the creative impulse often improves with time and experience, not just in the arts but in the skilled trades, sciences, engineering, the professions, and other occupations and industries. (It's fitting that 'create' and 'creativity' come from the Latin words *creatus* and *creare,* which mean "to grow.")

Meet Iris Shiraishi. She's in her early 60s. Shiraishi is in her most creative period yet. I met Shiraishi at a day-long conference held at the University of Minnesota Landscape Arboretum. Arts organizations from around the state were promoting their efforts to encourage engagement among older adults. Advocates and scholars—some local, some national—talked on topics such as brain-health research and advice on building an arts program for older adults.

Shiraishi was in a large room with attendees. She was demonstrating *taiko* drumming—Japanese ensemble drumming. The instruments were five-gallon white buckets she had picked up at a big box hardware store. She supplied the drumsticks. Shiraishi teaches *taiko* to a group of mostly older adults for a local music academy. She also teaches *taiko* to elders with dementia and their caregivers. The demonstration at the conference was designed to show participants how *taiko* could physically and mentally engage older individuals. The attendees enthusiastically hit their "drums" in rhythm and with power. The reverberations were loud and intense.

I met with Shiraishi several times to learn about her art and portfolio of activities. A self-described band geek, she grew up in Hawaii where her parents still live (and perform concerts at senior centers with a group of 80-something peers). She got her undergraduate degree in classical music and composition at the University of Hawaii. She got an advanced degree in the same field at the University of Iowa. She later attended the University of Minnesota for her doctorate in music therapy. The degree led to her first career helping children and families in the foster-care system rebuild trust and connections through music.

She loved her job, but over time she began to feel something was missing. Shiraishi still hadn't found her creative outlet. Living in the Twin Cities, she saw an ad for *taiko* lessons. The drumming has deep roots in Japanese history, but the modern art form was born after World War II. *Taiko* combines music, movement, and even martial arts. She started taking classes at age 42. *Taiko* became her passion.

"I finally felt compelled to start writing music again," she says. "Once I started doing that drumming, I realized this is my medium."

Eventually, Shiraishi started a new career, going from *taiko* student to *taiko* teacher. For fourteen years, she was the artistic director of the *taiko* ensemble at Minneapolis-based Mu Performing Arts, one of the largest Asian-American arts organizations in the country. She's a dynamo in concert, small in stature, fluid in her motions, a natural with large Japanese drums.

In her early 60s, she embarked on her next chapter. She left her steady job and paycheck at Mu in 2014 to form her own *taiko* group— Ensemble Ma. She makes her living from a portfolio of *taiko* activities, from performing to teaching.

Shiraishi is experimenting with her *taiko* music, taking risks with her compositions and breaking traditional rules. She's making creative leaps. "It has been what has kept me alive and growing," she says.

She's enjoying her second life (or maybe third). "I feel if I'm not going to do this now, then when am I going to do it?" she says. "As you get older you really start asking the 'why' and start prioritizing. I am rethinking and refocusing the next phase of my life."

Tom Rusu is also in his early 60s. He's another creative artist, though you might not immediately think of him that way. He does oil paintings, sculpture, and other art in his spare time. But his main creative outlet is machining. He creates prototypes and fabricates parts with lathes, milling machines, and other shop tools. Rusu has worked in machine shops from California to Oregon to Pennsylvania. "Machining isn't a skill," says Rusu. "It's an art form. I sculpt metal into something new."

He graduated from high school in Pittsburgh in 1973. His father gave him a one-way train ticket to California where his uncle worked as a machinist. He didn't plan on going into the machining occupation, but after he was laid off from his hardware store job, he gave it a whirl. Rusu says he "just took to it." He's moved around to different machine shops, always looking to add to his skills, find new problems to solve, and gain greater insight into his craft. "I would stay until I couldn't learn more," he says. "Then I'd go to another shop."

He's learning again. When I talked to Rusu, he was three months into a new job. He's an instructor at Carnegie Mellon University— one of the nation's premier technology and engineering schools— teaching engineers and graduate students the basics of machining. He works with them on their projects, too.

He got the job despite not having a "B.A. or anything else," he says, laughing. "They said, 'We're looking for experience.' And I'm having a blast doing this."

Rusu enjoys the students. He's picking up new skills, including 3D printing. He intends to continue to practice his art for many more years. "I don't plan on retiring," he says. "I like what I do."

Entrepreneurship is creative. Entrepreneurs are rightly celebrated for their innovations. If you travel, you might stay at an Airbnb rental (founded in 2008), get around with Lyft or Uber (2012), and make restaurant reservations online at Open Table (1998). Most entrepreneurial enterprises are far smaller than these now-megacompanies. Many startups fail, too. That said, it takes creativity to bring a business idea to life.

Just ask Ken McCraley, the 50-something owner of KMS Air Duct Cleaning. While hosting a radio interview for Minnesota Public Radio on minority entrepreneurship, I asked McCraley why start a business rather than work for someone?

"I always wanted to own my own business. I didn't know what that looked like," he replied. "I didn't see myself working nine to five. I didn't see myself working in a factory. So, for me, it was just having the opportunity to say, 'That's my artwork,' create a business. For me, it was being able to create something that was my own."[10]

Jean Cannon is in her 70s, and she is an entrepreneur. She is trying to transform the region surrounding the city and county of Sarasota on Florida's southwest coast, which has one of the state's oldest populations. The median age is 50-plus. Sarasota's white sand beaches and rich cultural life have long attracted retirees.

Cannon's mission is to help turn the area into a hotbed of entrepreneurial activities—the kind of place younger and older generations alike will gravitate toward to turn their ideas into commercial enterprises. She started an online business to fulfill her vision. Her ambition is for the business to grow and continue for the long haul.

"We need to jump-start entrepreneurship in our community," says Cannon. "Our mentality is that the pie is only so big. We have to realize that we have to make the pie a little bit bigger."

Cannon is a former high-tech employee who retired from IBM in 2013. By that time, she and her husband had lived for years in Sarasota, since IBM didn't care where she lived so long as she was conveniently near a major airport. She took advantage of an IBM option to work half-time for a year in 2012 before retiring.

That said, the word *retirement* is misleading. She's putting in long hours building a virtual entrepreneurial ecosystem for her community. Her website is designed to make it easy for entrepreneurs, investors, and others in the region to connect, find resources, share information, and learn the nuts and bolts of starting a business from scratch. Cannon's ambition is to eventually attract partners and outside investors to grow the enterprise.

Like many people switching from working at a large business to starting a company, Cannon has had to learn to carry out many tasks on her own. For instance, at IBM she had a worldwide network of knowledgeable colleagues to tap into. No longer. When I met her at her Sarasota townhouse near the beach, she was struggling with WordPress, a software program popular with bloggers. She's already taught herself to become familiar with Facebook, MailChimp, and other programs critical to modern entrepreneurs. "It's not difficult, but it's a lot when you're wearing four to five hats," she says, laughing.

We had a wonderful conversation about what business model would work for her fledgling enterprise. She loves using the web tool Canvanizer to help her brainstorm various options, ranging from subscription series to mentor and referral fees to some combination of several revenue streams. "What are customers willing to pay for?" she asked.

As if that weren't enough, she has also embraced politics. Specifically, she has become active in the Democratic Party. For example, she is vice chair of Florida's District 10 Democratic Women's Club and this covers five counties. She is working with various civic clubs and organizations to get out the vote and set up events to bring in volunteers. She is working with other local organizations to identify and mentor qualified candidates to run for office now, as well as to prepare for the 2020 election cycle. "After the last election, I had decided that if I don't go bold and act now I'd better go home," she says. "And I am not ready to go home.

When I asked her about retirement, she replied, "I think 80 is about the time to think about it. Maybe." Sounds about right.

Cannon's experience fights against so many ageist stereotypes. She is in her encore career. She is teaching herself new skills, including mastering several unfamiliar high-tech programs. She is exercising her creative imagination to try and implement a vision for her community, building an entrepreneurial incubator. Thing is, she isn't an exception. She has plenty of company, experienced workers undertaking similar grassroots efforts in communities around the country.

Self-employment is entrepreneurial. You're running a business. You need to find customers, price your product or service, maintain the books, set money aside for taxes, and deliver the goods. The self-employed show up in most occupations. For example, according to the Bureau of Labor Statistics, common self-employed occupations include craft artists, fine artists, hairdressers, hairstylists, cosmetologists, massage therapists, musicians, photographers, and tailors.[11]

A study by economists Joseph Quinn of Boston College, Kevin Cahill of Analysis Group, and Michael Giandrea of the Bureau of Labor Statistics demonstrates the growth of self-employment among experienced workers. The scholars found that 41 percent of men ages 51 to 61 were self-employed in 2010, a huge increase from the 20 percent self-employed in 1992. Among women, the comparable figures were 10 percent in 1992 and more than 22 percent in 2010.[12] Not everyone joins the ranks of the self-employed by choice. Going into business for yourself often is the best (and maybe only) option when getting hired through human resources isn't succeeding.

Joe Anania is in his late 50s, and he chose to redefine his second life. He's a maestro at repairing motorcycles, especially vintage Japanese bikes. He's self-employed.

Anania grew up racing and repairing motorcycles in Pittsburgh. When he had a family, he became an airline mechanic for the steady paycheck. He eventually settled in the Twin Cities area. He worked twenty-one years as a mechanic for Northwest Airlines (now Delta). He loved the job and the camaraderie with coworkers. He continued to ride motorcycles with friends on the weekends, often with his dog Daisy sitting on the gas tank. When Daisy passed away, he taught his new dog Ginger to ride with him.

Northwest Airlines mechanics went on strike in 2005. When the strike ended, Anania decided he didn't want to go back to the airline. A proud man, he was disgusted watching his colleagues gradually cross the picket line. He retired and started his own business, repairing and restoring vintage motorcycles. Now, he plans on sticking with the venture for the long haul. "It's nice being your own boss," he says. "I can always back off and take less work."

Anania fixes older motorcycles that regular repair shops can't handle well. If he can't get the parts he needs, he makes them. He's even machined some of his specialized tools. When I visited his shop in a St. Paul suburb, he was working on some twenty-five to thirty vintage motorcycles, many of them Hondas and Kawasakis. The place looked like a jumble of tools and motorcycles at first glance. The more time I spent in the shop, the more I realized how neat, clean, and well organized was the work space. It reminded me of an artist's studio. Everything was in its place.

He took me to the basement of his home and showed me a beautifully restored classic British motorcycle from the 1920s. The motorcycle was mostly black, with a small leather saddlebag in back and a big brass light in front. Anania is an artist.[13]

Anania's experience reminded me of the writings of Matthew Crawford. He owns a motorcycle repair shop in Richmond, Virginia. He's also an essayist and author. Like Anania, Crawford finds working on older motorcycles deeply satisfying and intellectually challenging. "I have found the satisfactions of the work to be very much bound up with the intellectual challenges it presents," he writes in an essay on the value of working with your hands. "Put differently, mechanical work has required me to cultivate different intellectual habits."[14]

Creativity doesn't diminish with the march of time. The desire to learn continues to burn bright. Novelty keeps the "little gray cells" working, to paraphrase Agatha Christie's famed detective Hercule Poirot. Better yet, as more and more people in the second half of life fire up their imaginations and devise creative pursuits, others join in. The community of second-life creative individuals will expand, feeding on itself, growing in scale, scope, and impact. "No longer is it the rare person writing poetry, but lots of people doing creative things," says Claude Fischer, sociologist at the University of California, Berkeley. "You start to see an increase, but an accelerating increase."[15]

The study of creativity is an industry. The commanding heights of gov-ernment, business, education, and nonprofit organizations are eager to promote creative thinking. The emphasis on creativity is partly driven by the sense that encouraging people to discover their inner artist is good for their overall sense of well-being. Exercising creative abilities nurtures people's mental and emotional health. Philanthropists and foundations spend considerable sums supporting creative programs in local communities, from elementary schools to assisted living centers. The satisfaction we get from tapping into our creative impulses is why so many of us have hobbies, passions, and pursuits. "Creativity is an adaptive human quality," says Rex Jung, assistant professor of neurosurgery at the University of New Mexico. "It's a quality of the human brain."[16]

The bigger factor behind the creativity push is the belief that nourishing America's widely admired entrepreneurial spirit—the "animal spirits of capitalism" in economist John Maynard Keynes' memorable phrase—is increasingly critical to the health of our living standards in a highly competitive global economy. The challenge is how best to keep unleashing the designer, the innovator, the high-tech visionary, and the problem solver among employees and entrepreneurs. Imagination and innovation are vital for developing new technologies, new services, and new ways of doing business. Creativity, imagination, and innovation are considered core competencies in industry after industry. Creativity and economic dynamism are almost synonymous these days. "Creativity drives capitalism," says Bruce Nussbaum. "Creativity is the source of economic value."[17]

Leaders eager to spur networks of creativity and innovation on the job should fling open doors of opportunity to experienced workers. Welcome them into high-tech endeavors, social enterprises, brainstorming sessions, cosharing work spaces, and factory teams. Solicit their insights. Challenge them. See what solutions they have to offer. Experienced workers with the freedom to exercise their creativity are engaged workers.

Scholars and business consultants disagree about the precise definition of creativity in general. There is agreement that creativity involves devising a product, service, or insight that is novel, useful or valuable (not necessarily monetarily), and relevant. My reading of the literature also emphasizes that scholars appreciate the role social ties and social connections play in generating creative insights.

Creativity has long been treated as something of a mysterious act, an almost supernatural moment of insight enjoyed by a rarified few, typically young. Wolfgang Amadeus Mozart. Lord Byron.

Albert Einstein. When he was 22 years old, Facebook founder Mark Zuckerberg infamously captured the association of creative brilliance with precocious youth by telling an audience at Stanford University, "Young people are just smarter."[18]

An apt metaphor for uniquely creative individuals is *The Thinker* by French sculptor Auguste Rodin. The bronze sculpture is of a nude man sitting alone with his chin in his hand. He's deep in thought, devising the next breakthrough. *The Thinker* model is associated with what's often referred to as Big-C creativity—the artist or scientist who produces something appreciated over decades and centuries.

Scholars are moving away from *The Thinker* model. The research has broadened to include an appreciation of the creativity of factory workers who figure out how to cut assembly costs without compromising quality and the neighbor who develops a delicious homemade barbeque sauce in her kitchen. For example, scholars James Kaufman of California State University at San Bernardino and Ronald Beghetto of the University of Oregon have proposed an intriguing Four-C model of creative activity. The first is the traditional Big-C kind, the product of genius. There is also Little-c creativity, activities most of us can participate in, such as taking leftover Chinese and Italian food and making a tasty dish by merging the two cuisines. Mini-c creativity highlights focused efforts at getting students to come up with innovative or novel ideas. Pro-c creativity represents advances in professional level expertise.

Creativity is part of the human condition.[19] "There is no doubt that scientists, artists, and inventors, for example, bring forth innovations," writes Robert Weisberg, director of the Brain, Behavior, and Cognition Cluster at Temple University. "It is just that those innovations are based on ordinary thought processes that we all carry out."[20]

Herbert Simon stressed the shared traits for innovative problem solving. Simon himself was a renaissance man who advanced many disciplines during his life, 1916 to 2001. His multidisciplinary pursuits included landmark contributions to economics, political science, administrative theory, psychology, organizational theory, computer science, artificial intelligence, the philosophy of science, and more— much more. Simon was a genius.

His outlook on creativity was democratic and pragmatic. People with knowledge, interests, and perseverance come up with novel solutions. "Fortunately, it is not necessary to surround creativity with mystery and obfuscation. No sparks of genius need be postulated to account for human invention, discovery, creation," he observed. "The same processes that people use to think and to solve problems can explain the thinking and problem solving that is called creative. My basic claim is that creativity is 'thinking writ large.'"[21]

Since everyone shares an ability to think, it's logical to assume that everyone can be creative and innovative, although to different degrees. Simon also recognized that creativity is social. People work in organizations and networks. They collaborate with colleagues. Creativity thrives from feedback, even if unwelcome. Creativity blossoms through connections with teams, groups, and the wider society.

The social connection that feeds into creativity is a major reason why isolating any one group as unproductive is wrong on the economics as well as the ethics. Inclusion is economically smart and morally right. "We all know intuitively that connections between people fuel creativity, innovation, and economic growth," writes economist Michael Mandel.[22]

John Seely Brown is a high-tech maven and educator. He is best known as director (1990–2000) of the legendary high-tech think tank PARC (Palo Alto Research Center, previously known as Xerox PARC). In a talk, Brown proposed an alternative formulation of the famed expression from seventeenth-century French philosopher René Descartes "I think, therefore I am." Instead, said Brown, "'We participate, therefore we are': we come into being through participation with others, and our own understanding is socially constructed."[23]

The same holds for thinking about creativity. Instead of saying, "I'm creative, therefore I am," it's "We're creative, therefore we are."

These observations help explain why aging brains can flourish on the job. Adults tap into decades of experience and knowledge gained at work. The everyday expression "connect the dots" is a useful metaphor for thinking about creativity with age. Thanks to their experience, older adults are good at drawing connections from various memories and shards of knowledge. *Connecting the dots* is also called wisdom.

"This wisdom includes good judgment in difficult situations, understanding of the way in which the events of life go together to form a consistent context, the ability to place events into perspective, a grasp of the fact that life is full of uncertainty and imponderability and that all planning must take this into account, and similar knowledge and skills," writes Arthur Cropley, a prolific scholar of creativity and professor emeritus at the University of Hamburg, in *Creative Performance in Older Adults*.[24]

Older adults are often willing to experiment and take a risk. Maybe they're more aware of the "why" for getting up in the morning. They're motivated to solve problems and come up with creative solutions. Like Shiraishi.

What's sometimes taken as intractability among experienced workers often reflects hard-won self-knowledge. They've learned over time where they excel and what skills they'd like to develop rather than waste efforts on endeavors that don't intrigue them. The fact that older workers may be less willing to embrace management's latest organizational scheme or exhortation to "do more with less" doesn't mean they don't want to engage.

"Particularly important is the fact that differences in intellectual performance at different ages may be due more to differences in interests, motivation, self-image and the like than in ability," writes Cropley. "With increasing age adults possess more clearly developed personal goals, better articulated ideas about what constitutes worthwhile subject matter, and a stronger desire to apply the results of their intellectual efforts."[25]

Julie Skye, at age 64, is using her veteran money management skills to build her own firm with a social and environmental conscience. "I tell clients that by 60 years old you should be doing what you love," she says. "You should be able to work for yourself and cover your expenses and not drive down your savings."

She is living her talk. Skye works out of a small, narrow office with multiple computer screens alongside one wall at the cosharing workspace 36 Degrees North in Tulsa, Oklahoma. The renovated Universal Ford Building built in 1917 was originally a Model T dealership. The members are mostly entrepreneurs, startup companies, social enterprises, and community organizations. Glancing around the mostly open floor space, the age range seems to be from recent college graduates to veteran workers. Skye moved into the building in late 2017. "This place is the wave of the future," she says. "Every person here is positive about the future. They think today is better than yesterday."

Count her among the optimists. Back in 1983, she found herself divorced with two children. She quickly earned her undergraduate degree at the University of Tulsa (she had accumulated credits elsewhere) and got her MBA at the school. Skye entered the financial services industry in 1986. She worked at a number of firms over her long career, including investment advisory, wealth management, bank trust departments, and her own registered investment advisory firm.

Skye has a strong commitment to social change. Her concerns eventually led her to embrace ESG investing standards. ESG stands for environmental, social, and governance. The goal is to invest money in companies with high ESG standards. The appeal of investing in companies with a sustainable track record is growing, with studies and experience suggesting there is little financial difference between investing to make money and investing to make money and express values. Her sustainability ethos pushed her to help with the Unitarian Universalist Association's movement to divest itself of fossil fuel investments. She belongs to the All Souls Unitarian Church in Tulsa.

However, her environmentalism didn't go over well with her last wealth management firm. Time to set up her own shop—Skye

Advisors LLC—and manage money for clients the way she believed was best for them and society. Assets are invested through Colorado-based First Affirmative Financial Network, which specializes in sustainable and ESG investments. Advances in software technology have driven down the cost of setting up and operating a personal finance firm to several thousand dollars a year. Clients stuck with her, and she is managing about $33 million, charging low fees. Skye expects to earn about $150,000 to $160,000 a year and has plans to hire an office manager.

Work isn't everything, of course. Skye is an avid gardener; cycles with a group of women, the Tulsa Tough Divas; and she's active in the Unitarian Church. She also has a "terrific boyfriend." Her children are launched in their careers. Skye is having a blast.

A better image than *The Thinker* for aging and creativity is improv. Improv encourages open-minded communication and collaboration in a group. The improv method gets people to welcome ideas and build on them. Improv is fun and engaging. The "basis of creativity is the ability to make non-obvious connections between seemingly unrelated things," writes Barry Kudrowitz, director of product design at the University of Minnesota in his dissertation with the suggestive title, *HaHa and Aha!*.[26] Sounds like improv, doesn't it?

Brave New Workshop is an improv theater in downtown Minneapolis. Founded in 1958, among its better-known graduates are comedians Louie Anderson, Al Franken, and Lizz Winstead. Brave New Workshop runs numerous classes for schools, companies, organizations, and other groups. I participated in its 55-plus improv class taught by Jim Robinson, theater veteran and recently retired university professor in psychology.

The class was held at a building owned by Brave New Workshop in downtown Minneapolis. The fourth-floor room is long and narrow. A large window takes up most of the wall at the far end. The concrete floor is mottled. The walls are painted different colors, mostly dark—blue and black with touches of red. Plastic black chairs are scattered along one wall. This is a working theater room. Nothing fancy.

About a dozen students were in the class the times I visited. Each time, we went through several exercises and improv games. We did exercises like "Clams are Great." One person stands in the middle of a circle and lists all the reasons clams are great. They taste good with pasta. Clams look great wearing suspenders. Clams are great because they have good self-esteem. Everyone surrounding the person yells "YES!" after each statement, encouraging them to keep coming up with different reasons for praising clams. Eventually, the circle senses inspiration is fading. Someone tags the person out, takes their place in the middle of the circle, and starts listing clam-loving sentences.

The exercises were fun. The takeaway lesson from improv lay in the expression "yes, and. . .". Most of us at work and at home respond in conversation with "yes, but. . .". Improv encourages openness to new ideas and opportunities with the mantra, "yes, and. . .". The "yes, and. . ." phrasing encourages experimentation.

The catchphrase builds on what another person has said or done. Positive collaboration makes extemporaneous scenes more plausible and (hopefully) amusing. Here's an example drawn from instructor Robinson: The scene starts with one person pensively munching on Fritos. She says she hasn't been the same since her mom died. Another person contradicts her by saying, "Mother isn't dead; she's just working late at the mall." The scene flounders with the "yes, but" response. Where do you go from that, asks Robinson?

However, new improv possibilities are opened if the person responds instead with, "Yes, a tragedy to see another of our brethren cut down by the family's fatal Frito allergy."

After one class, Robinson confirmed my observation that the 55-plus students are willing to experiment. "They don't have any inhibitions," he laughs. "They have nothing to lose now. So they take risks I don't think the younger improvisors do."[27]

A very different scene unfolds in the sunlit common room at the adult daycare facility at Ecumen Parmly LifePointes in Chisago City in rural Minnesota. The message is the same.

Professional folksinger Charlie Maguire, age 66 at the time, and fifteen older adults are sitting around a table, some in wheelchairs, writing a song.[28]

> *Pour me another cup of coffee*
> *Make it as strong as it can be*
> *Because I have a lot of things on my mind*
> *So pour one for you and one for me. . . .*

Maguire strums his guitar and blows on his harmonica. He stops to talk about the weather, trips he's taken in an RV, and the joys of reel-to-reel tapes. Everyone laughs at the mention of reel-to-reel-tapes. No explanation needed. When he talks about the news, he always refers to something he read in the newspaper. Maguire is a longtime musician who started singing for money back in 1974. He's probably best known for long stints on the national public radio show, *A Prairie Home Companion* (now named *Live from Here*). He enjoys his time at Ecumen.

"You want to give back," says Maguire. "I have a gift. You want to share it. You can bring so much happiness and joy into a senior's life. You always get more out of it than you put into it."

The mix of song and conversation inspires the elders to contribute lyrics captured on a large flip chart. The last stanza comes together:

> *Keep that coffee pot handy*
> *And the milk and sugar for the crew*
> *So we can talk together*
> *And we can listen, too.*

Imaginations unleashed were also apparent thousands of miles from rural Chisago City at the Burbank Senior Artist Colony in Burbank, California. The residents are deeply involved in creating their own art. "Erase the idea in any way, shape, or form that people's brains stop learning with age," says Tim Carpenter.

The Colony is the brainchild of Tim Carpenter. He worked in senior health care early in his career. He became disillusioned with the medical approach to aging, treating the process of getting older as a disease. He was horrified watching residents at senior centers gluing popsicle sticks together during arts and crafts period. Where was the creativity? The challenge? The engagement? "Getting older is actually a good thing," says Carpenter. "What I saw was pathetic."[29]

There had to be a better way, he thought. In the late 1990s, he founded the nonprofit EngAGE. He tried out his ideas on arts engagement at a building refurbished by a developer. Carpenter was brought in to create a curriculum for the residents. The building didn't have an arts studio, but it did have a shuffleboard court outside. The first painting class was held on the shuffleboard court, and paint was deliberately splashed around. "We spilled plenty of paint all over the shuffleboard court as a message," he laughs.

Carpenter took his ideas to the next level when he joined forces with developer John Huskey, chief executive of Meta Housing. In 2005, in Burbank, they opened the first of their "art colonies," an affordable, 200-person elders complex designed to encourage residents to participate in the arts. Professionals teach classes in theater, painting, screenplay writing, short-story telling, and other crafts. The classes are taught on a college semester system with the expectation that the low-income elders will learn a craft and produce art. Residents work on projects and present their results. "Expect a lot from people," says Carpenter. "Create a space for people to take risks, stretch and use their creativity."

By 2018, Carpenter had developed seven art colonies, affordable housing complexes built around the arts with theaters, multimedia rooms, and art studios. Working with a variety of developers, Carpenter has also created three intergenerational buildings and thirty-nine other facilities. All his facilities in Oregon, California, and Minnesota offer residents multiple art classes and creative opportunities. A number of other buildings are in the works. "The elephant in the room with aging is isolation and loneliness. We see the arts as a way to combat it," he says. "Art creates a reason for people to come together in a social way that has a purpose to it."

What about the persistent belief that elders can't be creative? "Everything we have seen firsthand, as well as the research, [says] it's the opposite," says Carpenter. "We have all kinds of people saying that it's life changing."

Among the instructors at the Burbank facility is Food4Thot. The South Central Los Angeles resident teaches creative expression, spoken word, poetry, and rap at charter schools in the area. He offers a similar curriculum at the Burbank Senior Artist Colony. His students range in age from 75 to 95. They call themselves OWLs, for "Oshea's Wise Ladies." "It's a beautiful time. They are at the top of their artistry," he says. "They don't care what society thinks. They express from a place of true authentic experience. It blows me away."

Expectations matter. Older workers often don't get enough opportunity to exercise their creativity and insights. If employers believe older individuals aren't creative, productive, and innovative, they don't get the chance to refute such falsehoods, which is why so many turn to entrepreneurship and self-employment. Negative cues about gender and race exert a long-term influence on education outcomes and career performance for the worse. The same goes with age bias. And, of course, age bias can compound with other prejudices, such as race and gender.

Change expectations and you change outcomes. That's the message of Daniel Kish. He had his eyes removed because of cancer when he was a toddler. Despite being completely blind, he walked to school on his own. As a young adult, he hikes and travels to foreign cities. Kish is best known for riding a bike.

Think about that. What he learned when he was young was to make a clicking sound that lets him understand his surroundings, which is why he is known as "batman." In a public radio documentary about him by *This American Life*,[30] Kish had this to say about expectations:

"I definitely think that most blind people could move with fluidity and confidence if that were the expectation," he said. "If our culture recognized the capacity of blind people to see, then more blind people would learn to see. It's actually pretty simple and straightforward."

Similarly, the more society recognizes the capacity of older workers to be creative, the more experienced workers will be creative.

Neuroscientist Oliver Sachs at age 79 looked forward to his 80th birthday. Sachs was a remarkable scholar, author and, by all accounts, a mesmerizing raconteur. He hoped he had a few more years to be "granted the liberty to continue to love and work, the two most important things, Freud insisted, in life," he wrote in a *New York Times* opinion column. He more than got his wish. Oliver Sachs died at age 82.[31]

His neuroscientist colleagues are moving away from characterizing aging as an inevitable process of physical and mental decay. The technical term describing the brain's ability to develop and adapt is *neuroplastic*. New neurons are born as well as die.

Scientists have long known that cognitive processing speed declines with age. Various tests have been performed to document that people's ability to process new information is quicker when young and slows with the passage of time.

But scientists also know that other mental functions improve with age. Semantic memory, for example. Semantic memory captures things that are common knowledge, such as the names of colors, the capitals of countries and other basic facts acquired over a lifetime. Language and speech can improve with time. The lessons of experience accumulate. On various tests, older adults perform well on vocabulary and crossword puzzles, so-called crystallized intelligence. The reason is that when using crystallized intelligence, older adults tap into their pre-existing knowledge base, things they have learned at school and on the job. The evidence is strong that crystallized intelligence is maintained or strengthens throughout a lifetime. "The bottom line is that older people do things differently, but they don't do it worse," says Johannes Koettl, economist at the World Bank. "They have different advantages vis a vis young people."[32]

The insight that older adults can learn new skills is the new normal with aging. Take a fascinating study by Joshua Hartshorne and Laura Germine of the Boston College Department of Psychology and the Laboratory for Brain and Cognitive Health Technology at McLean Hospital, respectively. The scholars created two websites featuring cognitive tests that can be completed in a few minutes, and gathered data on nearly 50,000 people who participated. They found that the standard perception that the young are best at fluid intelligence (the ability to think quickly and recall information) and older people do better with crystallized intelligence isn't wrong. But the distinction is too blunt and simple, they say.[33]

Their findings suggest brain functions peak at different ages with some abilities starting to decline around high school graduation and others not until people reach their 70s (basically the life span). Specifically, young people process new information fast, with peak ages around 19; short-term memory improves until about age 25; and vocabulary peaks in the late 60s and early 70s. "On the practical side, not only is there no age at which humans are performing at peak on all cognitive tasks, there may not be an age at which humans perform at peak on *most* cognitive tasks," write Hartshorne and Germine. (Personally, I find their results reassuring.)

Other studies find older adults are emotionally mature compared to their juniors. Emotional maturity is a valuable resource in an organization. Experience is probably why older workers often show less stress and stay calm during a workplace upheaval or crisis. Intriguingly, age may offer another advantage. Mature adults are more aware that time runs out. Older adults try to cut through the turmoil of the moment and remember what really matters. That doesn't mean they always succeed, but they are more aware that it doesn't pay to get caught up with short-term static.

Lifespan psychologist and aging researcher Ursula Staudinger, during a talk at Columbia University's Age Boom Academy, summed up the research this way: "We can really improve ourselves."Older workers have the intangible skills that make organizations operate (relatively) smoothly, the kind of knowledge not captured by organizational handbooks. Managements rely on intangible knowhow to meet deadlines and accomplish tasks. The intangibles are vital to an organization's culture, the rules and norms that motivate and guide people on the job. Intangible knowledge is a major factor behind worker productivity.

Scholars are figuring out what common sense tells us: Younger and older employees complement one another. The combination of younger employees with their energy and older employees with their expertise improves organizational productivity, creativity, and innovation. "They reduce turnover, they create stability, and they create high-performing units in levels we've never seen in youth alone," says Patricia Milligan, senior partner and global leader for Mercer's Multinational Client Group. "We need to be talking about the role of the older worker to drive growth and innovation through those multi-generations."[34]

Case in point: the 2010 Cogito Study. The European study compared the performance of 101 young adults (ages 20 to 31) to 103 older adults (ages 65 to 80). They were measured working on twelve different tasks over 100 days, including tests of cognitive abilities and working memory. The scholars assumed that younger workers would perform at a consistently higher level than the older workers.[35]

Wrong. The older workers performed their jobs with less day-to-day variability than younger peers. They learned more, remembered more, and took less time to learn than the younger workers. The team of scholars behind the study at the Germany-based Max Planck Institute for Human Development suspects older workers did better at work by tapping into experience to solve problems.

Another scholarly paper looked at whether decision-making abilities declined with age. Gary Charness, economist at the University of California, Santa Barbara, and Marie-Claire Villeval, research professor in economics at the National Center for Scientific Research in France, compared the performance of "seniors" (50 years and older) to "juniors" (30 years and younger). The scholars conducted three experiments in the field and in the laboratory. Each session consisted of a team working on a task. The experiments were designed so that competition was key to any payoff; cooperation among team members was important to accomplishing the task; and a simple investment decision was thrown into the mix to uncover worker willingness to take on or avoid risk.[36]

Competition, cooperation, and risk-taking are valuable traits in any organization. What the scholars found, contrary to "negative stereotypes" is that the "seniors" did well. They weren't risk averse; they reacted to incentives and the competitiveness of the environment as strongly as their younger peers; there was no significant difference in performance across the generations; and older workers were more cooperative than the junior workers.

They concluded: "Overall, the implication is that it may well be inadvisable to exclude seniors from the labor force; instead defining additional short-term incentives near the end of a worker's career to retain and to motivate older workers may provide great benefits to society."

Inclusiveness pays.

Steve Kempf would agree. He's the chief executive officer of Brooklyn-based manufacturer Lee Spring, a 100-year-old company. Lee Spring was founded on Union Street in Carroll Gardens, Brooklyn by immigrant Robert Lee Johannsen. You can trace the history of manufacturing and gentrification in New York City by the various locations for its Brooklyn factory and global headquarters.

Lee Spring has been at its current location for a decade in the old Brooklyn Army Terminal, a massive four-million-square-foot complex designed by famed architect Cass Gilbert. Lee Spring has several factory facilities in the United States, as well as manufacturing and distribution facilities in Europe, Asia, and Latin America.

The headquarters and factory floor are on the third floor of the terminal. A glass divider splits the floor. On one side of the glass partition is the office with the typical open floor plan composed of cubicles, file cabinets, and conference rooms. Management, marketing, customer relations, and other functions are run out of the office.

On the other side is the factory. The walls are lined with coils of stainless-steel wire of different grades, some thin and others thick. The smaller springs are made at the manufacturing machines closest to the office. The farther away you get from the office, the thicker the springs. A small machine tool shop on one side is for small-batch orders, say, less than 100. When I visited the factory, the machinist was making custom springs for a Pilates studio. With the exception of the machine tool shop, much of the spring-making process is automated.

Springs are fascinating, once you start thinking about them (which I hadn't before touring the factory). Springs are in so many products, like toasters, mattresses, watches, automobiles, garage doors, water valves, and pacemakers. Lee Spring designs and manufactures more than 25,000 types of springs. Specialty springs were packaged for Boston Scientific, the medical-device behemoth, and Watts Water Technologies, maker of flow control products, during my visit.

Lee Spring received a 2018 Age Smart Employer Award from Columbia University. Among its ninety or so employees in Brooklyn, about half are over 50. "It's just smart," says Kempf. "We're getting experienced workers."

The day we met, Kempf had just hired a guy who had worked at another factory for twenty-five years. He had been recently laid off. "Why wouldn't I hire him?" asks Kempf during our interview, held in a conference room at Lee Spring. "One of the advantages of hiring someone who is more experienced, usually they are looking for a place to stay. They are tired of jumping around. Training is a big cost of any employment; whether programmed or on-the-job training, we put a lot into it," he adds.

Kempf is willing to tailor jobs to the desires of the company's older workers. The typical request is to reduce the number of hours, usually starting with going to four days a week and, over time, as little as a day. Kempf muses that that there are two kinds of older workers at the factory. There are those who "look forward to retiring and those that want to keep working." The latter, he quickly adds, "are the best. They want to keep working. They are doing it by choice. They want to stick around. They have experience. That's the best of the best of the best."

Think about that.

The Economics of Optimism

Aging is not "lost youth" but a new stage of opportunity
and strength.

—BETTY FRIEDAN[1]

Deirdre McCloskey is an economic historian, author of a magisterial three-volume treatise on the origins of modern capitalist growth and an enthusiastic storyteller.

I had interviewed McCloskey over the years for columns on economics, but I met her for the first time at the 2016 Nobel Conference at Gustavus Adolphus College in St. Peter, Minnesota. The conference participants were asked to focus on the "search for economic balance." (I'm not sure McCloskey addressed balance. Disruption or upheaval might be better descriptions.) She gave a lively talk on the most important question in economics: How did the average person become ten times, thirty times, or one hundred times richer (depending on the measure) starting around 1800 to the present? How did we get so rich, she asked?

Moving energetically around the stage before an audience of more than a thousand people, many of them students, she ran through common explanations, such as exploitation, capital accumulation, institutional innovation, and education. Each of these factors had a role, yet she found them wanting in overarching explanatory power.

What is her theory? She believes it all comes down to one phrase: To have a go. From 1800 to the present, the idea and the ideal of human equality spread. Equality of social standing. Liberty to open a business. Equal justice before the law. "The key is that the mass of people feel entitled, feel empowered to open a hair salon, or start a computer business in a garage or invent the Chicago Board of Trade," she said during her talk. "Masses of people feel free 'to have a go.'"

The catchphrase "to have a go" has stuck with me. Isn't that what everyone wants? Certainly, growing numbers of older adults with energy and health are looking to "have a go." If older Americans are encouraged to work longer, welcomed in the workplace, treated with respect, and given the opportunity to use their skills and abilities on the job, they will become a powerful force for rejuvenating organizations and the economy.

"The shrinkage of younger cohorts means that the nation will need to turn to older workers if the economy is to remain globally competitive," writes historian W. Andrew Achenbaum.[2] *Bloomberg Businessweek* economic journalist Peter Coy is even more emphatic: "By working longer—and more productively—boomers will help the U.S. economy thrive even as their personal odometers keep clicking forward."[3]

Thrive is the right word, a welcome turn of events.

The American economy's underlying rate of growth decelerated since the early 2000s. The slowdown is particularly noticeable following the global credit crunch and Great Recession of 2008 and 2009. The economy grew at an average annual rate of about 3 percent from the 1950s to 2007, after adjusting for swings in the business cycle on the upside and the downside. Growth has averaged about 2 percent since 2007.

The current consensus forecast is for growth to average 2 percent or less over the next decade—at least a percentage point below historic levels. While that's only a forecast, it reflects a distinct lack of optimism about the economy's prospects among professional prognosticators. To be sure, GDP (gross domestic product) growth has been in the 3 percent range in 2018. The extra economic boost seems to stem from the massive corporate tax cuts signed into law in late 2017. The impact is likely to fade with time.

What accounts for weaker underlying growth? Politicians, policy-oriented think tanks, and much of the public understandably pay most attention to fiscal and monetary policy. A common refrain is that taxes are too high or that inflation-hawks on the Federal Reserve Board are holding back the economy. Regulations come in for some blame. So does widespread industry consolidation. The dramatic widening in income inequality since the late 1970s is a culprit. Each of these factors has its merits and flaws as an explanation.

However, most economists focus on two main concepts when trying to understand growth prospects: labor force growth and productivity growth (or output per worker hour). The basic (simplified) formula is economic growth equals the sum of labor force growth and productivity growth. The demographic side of the growth equation is more important for the theme of this book. (I'll touch briefly on productivity in the next chapter.)

The aging of the population is the single biggest factor behind the conventional gloomy growth predictions. Labor force growth is expected to decline and stay low, thanks to the combination of lower fertility rates (fewer children) and longer life expectancy (more retirees). Fewer working-age adults will support too many dependent elderly, a toxic combination for growth. (We could add more immigrants to boost births and offset retirements, but that's unlikely in the current political climate.)

"The aging of the U.S. population is at the heart of why most economists who focus on demographics tend to maintain a lower economic growth rate for the next twenty-plus years than we have had for the last twenty-plus years," writes David Harris, chief investment officer for Rockefeller & Co., an independent investment and wealth management firm.[4]

The best-known formula reflecting and reinforcing demographic gloom is the "old-age dependency ratio." The ratio compares the number of people between 15 and 64 (workers) with people over age 64 (retired, not working). The ratio paints the familiar picture of an increasing number of nonworking older folks. By 2040, there will be 2.7 workers for each retiree, down from 4.8 in 2010 (and 9.09 in 1940). We won't have enough young workers to support the aging population. The trend looks ominous, doesn't it?[5]

The old-age dependency ratio is deeply flawed. The ratio assumes people 65 years and older don't work. The assumption may have been reasonable at one time, but in recent decades the distinct trend is toward retiring later. For instance, nearly a quarter of this age group is still part of the labor force.

"We observe the world how it is today and make these very simple projections and turn them into a terrible scenario," says Johannes Koettl, senior economist at the World Bank's Social Protection and Labor Global Practice. "This approach fails to take into account that the world is changing. There are good things about aging. You can come up with a different picture."[6]

Koettl proposes getting rid of the concept of putting a limit on working age. He believes it's an artificial constraint on productive aging "whether it be 65, 75, or 105." Some people retire early, say, in their late 50s or early 60s, for health reasons or to care for aging parents. Other older adults may stay gainfully employed well into their 80s and 90s.

Koettl prefers a different ratio: The "adult dependency ratio." This ratio compares the number of inactive people (not working and not looking for work) with active people (working or looking for work) in the adult population, ages 15 and older. His adult dependency projections include the past trend toward rising labor force participation rates of women and older people. He additionally assumes the effective retirement age is extended by ten years between 2030 and 2060.

The adult dependency ratio for the United States remains relatively constant until it eventually starts improving in the early 2030s. The bottom line: The ratio says older adults aren't a deadweight on the economy.[7]

Working longer is a practical option for many people. Contrary to images of frail older adults with failing memories (the target of tasteless jokes), most older adults are reasonably healthy, particularly for people from age 50 to the late 70s. Most Americans at those ages aren't crippled by disabilities.

Of course, we move slower with the passage of time. The body and mind take longer to recover from a late night at work or a long evening out. My knees protest every time I get out of a chair or a car. I'm careful not to strain my back. More seriously, the physical toll from some jobs is severe, such as maintenance and the assembly line. Repetitive and boring jobs wear people out mentally and physically. There are worrisome trends with obesity and diabetes. The opioid epidemic is destroying lives.

Nevertheless, the real question for many people is are there things that can be done to stave off cognitive decline? Tom Rando, neuroscientist at Stanford University, believes the research sends a clear message. "Summing up a lot of data, the kinds of things people should do are physical activity and social engagement and learning new things," he says. "All common-sense stuff—grandmother's wisdom."[8]

Staying attached to work is one of those commonsense activities. For instance, the federal government's *Older Americans With a Disability: 2008–2012* defines disability as having one or more "difficulties" related to hearing, vision, cognition, ambulatory ability, self-care, and independent living. Almost 74 percent of those 65 to 74 had no disability by these measures. Another 14 percent had one. Even the 75-to-84 age group fared well with 55 percent without disability and almost 19 percent with only one.

There does come a time when most people deal with physical and cognitive limitations. The onset is typically much later than popular culture assumes. For instance, the big shift comes at 85-plus. Among that group, only 28 percent had no disabilities while 42 percent had three or more. That's more than six times the percentage for adults ages 65 to 74. (When I've given talks on aging, I've found it intriguing how many seem to believe people go from robust 60 to frail 90 in a mere year or two!).[9]

A 65-year-old today has about the same risk of mortality or serious illness as a mid-50-something a generation ago. "The percentage of the population over age 65 who are at serious risk of mortality or life-threatening illness will grow by only about 16 percent between now and 2035, which means that there will be a huge cohort of healthy individuals in that age group who want and need to work," writes Peter Cappelli, professor of management at the Wharton School, in the *Harvard Business Review*.[10]

Organizations benefit from the participation of experienced workers. They're productive employees. That's the conclusion of a series of studies by economist Axel Börsch-Supan and colleagues at the Munich Center for the Economics of Aging. These studies in the aggregate systematically debunk the notion that workers are less efficient and creative with age. The opposite may well be the case.

Börsch-Supan and colleague Matthias Weiss looked at worker productivity data generated at a Mercedes-Benz truck assembly plant in Germany. The scholars concluded that productivity progresses all the way up to retirement. They measured productivity as the absence of errors during production. Experienced workers made more small errors, but major errors are more frequent among their younger peers.

"Even in a work environment requiring substantial physical strength," they write, any decline in physical ability "is compensated by characteristics that appear to increase with age and are hard to measure directly, such as experience and the ability to operate well in a team when tense situations occur, typically when things go wrong and there is little time to fix them."[11]

Börsch-Supan led a similar study with white-collar, cubicle-based workers at a major German insurance company. The conclusion was the same. "Experience accumulates," Börsch-Supan told me at an economics conference in Washington, DC.

Results like these don't surprise Laura Carstensen, director of the Stanford Center on Longevity. She summed up the scholarly research into aging, productivity, and work this way: "There is no evidence older workers aren't as good at their jobs."

Her insight offers an optimistic assessment of the economy's prospects for an aging population. More people working well into the traditional retirement years is good for growth. PwC, the giant consulting firm, created its Golden Age Index to quantify how member countries in the Organisation for Economic Co-operation and Development are harnessing the power of older workers. (The OECD comprises thirty-five member countries.) Iceland has the highest rate of employment of workers 55 to 64 years old at 84 percent. New Zealand was second at 78 percent and Sweden third at 76 percent. According to PwC, if the United States increased its employment levels of older adults to New Zealand's, the American economy would expand by over $815 billion. To Sweden's level, the increase in U.S. gross domestic product would be $519 billion.[12]

The global consulting firm Accenture, in collaboration with Oxford Economics, arrived at a similar calculation. Increasing the number of older people in the workforce and making productivity-enhancing investments in their skills could boost U.S. gross domestic product by $442 billion and lift employment levels by 5 million by 2020.[13]

President Trump was ridiculed by many economic commentators early in his administration when he said the economy could expand at a sustainable 3-percent or 3-percent-plus rate. He was right about the possibility. Critics were mistaken to dismiss the possibility of higher rates of growth.

Trump was wrong on how to get there, however. Tax cuts and large fiscal deficits won't do the trick, at least not over the long haul. Increased labor force participation rates among adults of all ages, including people in the second half of life, will get us closer to those growth rates (before taking any productivity improvements into account).

The economic benefit of working longer has several striking implications. Government policies and organizational benefits should be restructured to keep experienced workers attached to the labor market longer, say, with well-established phased retirement or semi-retirement programs. More and better matchmaking services are called for to steer experienced workers to organizations needing their skill and experience. Resources need to be brought to bear on combatting and razing age discrimination.

"I would suggest that the ability to spot, mobilize and deploy older workers is the next biggest source of competitive advantage in the U.S. companies," writes Tyler Cowen, professor of economics at George Mason University. "The sober reality is that many companies should retool their methods to fit better with the experience and sound judgment found so often in older workers."[14]

Organizations could well find that their ranks include more innovators like John Goodenough, the battery pioneer. He turned 96 years old in 2018. Goodenough could have been basking in memories of his remarkable achievements with batteries. After all, four decades ago, he was co-inventor of the lithium ion battery used to charge smart phones, tablets, and other mobile devices. As the professor of engineering at the University of Texas, Austin told *The Wall Street Journal*: "My mission is to try and see if I can transform the battery world before I die. When I'm no longer able to drive and I'm forced to go into a nursing home, then I suppose I'll be retiring."[15]

In the meantime, the *Journal* notes that he has recently published research with three coauthors on the prototype of a new kind of battery—liquid free, cobalt free, and longer lived than the lithium ion battery. If his team of scientists solve the puzzle they're working on, the battery "would be so cheap, lightweight and safe that it would revolutionize electric cars and kill off petroleum-fueled vehicles," according to the *New York Times*.

"I'm old enough to know you can't close your mind to new ideas," Goodenough told the *Times*. "You have to test out every possibility if you want something new."[16]

There isn't a standard definition of phased retirement or semi-retirement. Any arrangement that offers older workers flexible, part-time, or reduced hours should be considered phased retirement or semiretirement. Many of these deals are negotiated between an employee and his or her boss. There are formal programs, although they aren't common—yet. "If employers would accelerate the drive for flexible work arrangements everyone would be better off," says Richard Johnson, labor market expert at the Urban Institute. "Flexibility is important."[17]

Flexibility matters to Mark Keefe. He retired from Atlantic Health System, headquartered in Morristown, New Jersey, in 2014 at age 66. He was a human resources manager for the company's Overlook Medical Center in nearby Summit. When he retired, Keefe stayed busy by going through a long list of jobs around the house. His wife still worked, so he took on household chores and cooked evening meals. "It was really a time to relax," he says.

The twist is that in March of 2017, Keefe began putting on a suit and tie and returning to work every Wednesday at his former employer. His job is counseling employees nearing retirement about their benefit package as they exit the company. The soon-to-be-retired always have plenty of questions, and Keefe enjoys offering them information and guidance, including insights gleaned from his own experience. "They feel good. They don't have a lot of information about retirement," he says. "Since I've been through it, I can help them with questions on Social Security and Medicare. I can at least give them some guidance, some information."

He adds that the work helps keep him sharp and, although the income isn't much, the added income helps. "I look at it this way: I have a six-day weekend," he says. "I love it."[18]

Keefe is a member of the company's Alumni Club (previously called the 1,000 Hour Club). The company established the formal program in 2006. Alumni Club members can return to the company to work part-time—no more than 1,000 hours a year. About 300 Atlantic Health retirees are on the company's payroll in various capacities through the program. "They're engaged employees. They're productive," says Lesley Meyer, Atlantic Health manager, corporate human resources. "They're a stable talent pool."

Pat Waller is passionate about her work and colleagues. She was an intensive-care nurse for thirty-nine years at Atlantic Health. "I loved the work," she says.

Waller retired at age 66 in 2005. She joined the Alumni Club in 2007 after receiving a phone call from her former manager. The hospital she had worked at had applied to qualify as a federal center of excellence in knee and hip surgery. Her boss wondered if she would help gather data. Waller has since worked on several projects. "It's enjoyable to use my expertise and knowledge," she says.

Her portfolio of activities includes time with her six grandchildren and traveling with her husband. She mostly works from home, sometimes three to four days a week and other times one to two days a week, depending on the project. "I always said when I was at work I learned something every day," she says. "Since I've come back, I feel the same way."[19]

Of course, not every employee has the option of joining an organization's alumni club. Most arrangements are negotiated on a case-by-case basis. However, matchmaking services are springing up in many metropolitan areas. A common denominator is bringing together a soon-to-be-retiree who wants an encore career with an organization that needs their skill. For example, Experience Matters in Phoenix is a nonprofit organization that works with retiring private-sector workers and professionals looking for their encore with community-based nonprofits. RetirementJobs.com is an online job board that offers "jobs lists" and guidance sources for workers 50 and older. RetirementJobs.com also has its Certified Age-Friendly Employer program identifying organizations it deems the "best places" to work for employees age 50 and older. Other matchmakers include Empowered Age, Operation A.B.L.E., Reboot Careers, Retired Brains, and ReServe.

Harnessing the potential of older workers means crushing age discrimination. Age discrimination is widespread, well-documented, and deeply entrenched in the American workplace. A U.S. Government Accountability Office report from 2012, *Unemployed Older Workers*, reports that focus-group participants "believed employer reluctance to hire older workers was their primary reemployment challenge, and several cited job interview experiences that convinced them age discrimination was limiting their ability to find a new job."[20]

A 2018 AARP survey of workers age 45 and older had three in five experienced workers witnessing or facing age discrimination. Of those surveyed who reported ageism at work, 91 percent believed it was very or somewhat common. Women are more likely than men to deal with age discrimination. The survey notes that more than three-quarters of African-American respondents, 60 percent of Latinos, and 59 percent of whites had seen or experienced age discrimination.[21]

Formal age discrimination claims filed with the U.S. Equal Employment Opportunity Commission (EEOC) peaked at 24,582 in 2008 during the Great Recession. Yet in 2016, filings remained at an elevated 20,857, and 18,376 in 2017.[22] These claims are the tip of the proverbial iceberg. Most older workers don't bother to formally protest age discrimination, figuring it isn't worth the time or expense to litigate. But sit down and have several drinks with aging colleagues and neighbors, and it won't be long before people are swapping stories about age prejudice on the job or on the job hunt.

Age discrimination is illegal, and it has been for the past half century. The U.S. Equal Employment Opportunity Commission enforces the Act, yet in a historic overview, the agency reached this dismal conclusion:

"Despite decades of research finding that age does not predict ability or performance, employers often fall back on precisely the ageist stereotypes the ADEA was enacted to prohibit," notes the

EEOC review, *The State of Age Discrimination and Older Workers in the U.S. 50 Years After the Age Discrimination in Employment Act (ADEA).* "After 50 years of a federal law whose purpose is to promote the employment of older workers based on ability, age discrimination remains too common and too accepted."[23]

Age discrimination tears at people.

Workers 55 years and older also have higher rates of long-term unemployment than their younger peers. Government statisticians define long-term unemployment as six months or more. At a presentation at Columbia University in the summer of 2018, Carl Van Horn, director of the John J. Heldrich Center for Workforce Development at Rutgers University, put up a slide on the long-term unemployed. In December 2017, among workers out of work, the long-term unemployment rate for those 55-plus was 30.6 percent. That compares to 20.8 percent among the 16-to-54-year-old group. Benefits quickly run out for workers unable to land a job. "The long-term unemployed don't get much help from the government," he added.

Patricia, in her mid-60s, ranks among the long-term unemployed. "Who Am I? I ask myself that question every day," she wrote to me. "I've reached and reached, have been interviewed, talked about, called all kinds of names, been told over and over and over again, 'how overqualified' I am, that it makes me cry and cry often."

When I talked to Patricia—she asked that I not use her last name—the basic outline of her story is sadly familiar. She had been a paralegal on and off for some twenty years in the New York City area. She also worked as an insurance claims rep on Long Island. Her last full-time job was legal secretary in New York, driving two hours from her home into the city. She lost that job in 2008 during the Great Recession. New York State sent her to school in 2009 to earn two certificates, one as a certified biller/coder and the other in medical business administration.

In 2010, she moved to a Florida town about an hour drive from Tampa to lower living costs. (It didn't work.) She went through all her retirement savings. Patricia filed for Social Security at age 62 to pay the bills. Two years later when we spoke, she was still looking for a full-time job. The most common rejection is that she's too qualified for the position. "How many times do you need to be told they don't want you anymore," she said. "It's an awful way to live."

Yes, it is an awful way to live.

The federal Age Discrimination in Employment Act (ADEA) was passed in 1967 as part of a flurry of government initiatives during the Kennedy and Johnson administrations to boost civil rights and improve the quality of life for older adults. The law became effective in 1968. (Other legislation around the time included liberalizing Social Security and the passage of Medicare, Medicaid, and the Older Americans Act.)

The original ADEA protected workers between ages 40 and 65 from discrimination in hiring, firing, and other conditions of employment. Congress strengthened the ADEA in subsequent years and eliminated the upper age limit. The law covers firms with twenty or more workers.

By any measure, there has been progress with the ADEA. When Secretary of Labor W. Willard Wirtz testified before a Senate subcommittee in 1967, he noted that applicants over 55 years of age were barred from half of all job openings in the private sector. Workers over 65 weren't welcome, period, he added. As U.S. Senator Ralph Yarborough, a Democrat from Texas and ADEA supporter, put it, "There is simply a widespread irrational belief that once men and women are past a certain age they are no longer capable of performing even some of the most routine jobs."[24]

These days, experienced workers on the payroll are less vulnerable on average to being the sole target of layoffs during a restructuring. That said, more needs to be done. For one thing, the federal courts have made age bias claims difficult to prove. The Supreme Court and many lower courts increasingly defer to employers when it comes to what the ADEA calls "reasonable factors other than age" for handling older workers without legal penalty. For example, employers can justify laying off their most expensive workers who happen to have seniority and are mostly older as a reasonable business decision.

The landmark moment that highlighted judicial skepticism toward age discrimination is the Supreme Court ruling, Gross v. FBL Financial Services. The Supreme Court justices decided in 2009 that claimants must prove age discrimination was the primary factor behind a bias claim. For plaintiffs to prove that age was the main factor in their discrimination claim is an extremely difficult if not impossible standard to meet.

An example of the high legal hurdle is the June 26, 2015 decision by the Supreme Court to let stand a lower court ruling in Villarreal v. R. J. Reynolds Tobacco Co. Here's a (very) brief synopsis:

Richard Villarreal applied online for a territory sales manager job at the tobacco company in 2007 when he was 49 years old. No response. Several years later he learned about internal guidelines stating the ideal candidate would be "two to three years out of college." Job reviewers were told to "stay away from" applicants whose résumés showed that they had been "in sales for eight to ten years."

Villarreal sued under the ADEA. The courts dismissed his claim on the grounds the ADEA employment discrimination claim he brought only protected existing employees, not job applicants. The courts also agreed with Reynolds that Villarreal hadn't "diligently" pursued the reasons he got no response to his application. Seriously?

"The high court's decision will make it harder for some people later in their work lives to prove they were victims of bias," writes Peter Gosselin, when he was an investigative reporter at ProPublica, the nonprofit journalist organization.[25] Laurie McCann, senior attorney at AARP Foundation, echoed Gosselin's insight in testimony before the EEOC. "There are reports that private attorneys, and the workers who walk into their offices seeking representation, have been discouraged from bringing ADEA cases," she said.[26]

Outrageous, isn't it? Older Americans want to work, and some combination of ageism and algorithms denies them that opportunity. That's what happened to this 60-something correspondent who emailed me:

"I was laid off in mid-January 2017. . . . I need and want to work. I am healthy and available now. . . . BTW, a lot of jobs that I qualify for require me to fill out an application that requires me giving the year I graduated from college. . . . As soon as a candidate gives the year they graduated from college, the HR reviewer trashes their application because age discrimination is practiced daily. It is a real shame."

Experienced workers have even found that online job portals can be discriminatory. In 2017, Illinois Attorney General Lisa Madigan warned six major job search portals that potential age discrimination lurked in their menu options. Madigan began an investigation into the online job portals after a 70-year-old man told her office that he couldn't use a résumé-building tool on Monster's app because its drop-down menu required choosing your year of college graduation or first job and the dates stopped at 1980. (That would effectively rule out people over 52.) Other sites used dates ranging from 1950 to 1970 as cutoffs to apply for available positions.

"Today's workforce includes many people working in their 70s and 80s," Madigan said. "Barring older people from commonly used job search sites because of their age is discriminatory and negatively impacts our economy."[27]

The portals made adjustments. New examples keep popping up and big data algorithms will likely be designed in ways that block older workers from the job pool. That said, the evidence strongly suggests that online job boards are mostly a waste of time at any age. Older workers typically find jobs by tapping into their most valuable asset—their network of friends, family acquaintances, former colleagues, and others at three-to-six degrees of separation. Experienced workers must reach out to people in their formal and informal networks. (The same is true for younger workers.) Technology makes it easier to track down connections and research potential employers, including online networking sites such as LinkedIn and Facebook.

Sad to say, there are employers and human resource professionals who can't see past calendar age. The problem is particularly ingrained in the technology business. IBM, Intel, Google, Hewlett Packard, and other high-tech firms have been accused of systemic age discrimination in culling their ranks and in their hiring and promotion practices.

Still, there are reasonable grounds for optimism now and into the future. Some successes on the enforcement front are worth celebrating. For instance, the EEOC acted aggressively in the Texas Roadhouse discrimination case it brought in 2011. Texas Roadhouse is a national chain of steakhouses based in Kentucky. Federal officials say the company had "a history of labeling workers over 40 such things as 'Old 'n Chubby' and rejecting them for jobs where customers see them," writes Peter Gosselin. Texas Roadhouse eventually settled with the EEOC—without any admission of guilt—by agreeing, among other things, to pay $12 million and to change its hiring and recruiting practices.[28]

At some point, reform legislation might gather enough votes to pass. The AARP proposed legislation—Protecting Older Workers Against Discrimination Act—is a good starting place. The legislation would ensure the same standards are used for all employment discrimination victims, including age, race, gender, and sexual orientation. In an interview in 2018 with the acting chair of the EEOC, Victoria A. Lipnic, she didn't endorse any legislation. But she was emphatic about what needed to be done. "The public policy question is, Do we want that to be the case? Congress has to decide," she says. "It's up to Congress to change the situation."

And for all of us to put pressure on Congress.

The demographics of an aging workforce will push policymakers to embrace breaking down barriers to employment in the second half of life—perhaps slowly, but inexorably.

"Most significantly, population aging means that public policy must be increasingly concerned with the employment of older individuals, because continued employment implies lower dependency ratios, greater income, more tax revenues, and decreased public expenditures on health insurance, retirement benefits, and income support (depending on the age of the individual and their economic circumstances)," writes Neumark in *The Age Discrimination In Employment Act and The Challenge of Population Aging.*[29]

Age discrimination is exerting less influence on the job and in the economy in the aggregate, largely thanks to the tight labor market of recent years. This judgment isn't to minimize the pain of those discriminated against. But employers are rethinking their attitudes. The proof is in the rising labor force participation rates among older workers and greater attention being paid by organizations to phased and partial retirement programs. Employers are learning that their experienced workers are valuable to the organization's mission and purpose. Management is absorbing real workplace lessons about the worth of their experienced workers, and they're not about to forget. The insights are driving changes in attitudes and expectations, and for the better.

Of course, many older adults aren't waiting for the inevitable. They've decided the better solution is to go into business for themselves, perhaps with family, friends, and colleagues. They're also tapping into their networks and finding owners and managers at smaller businesses that want a good worker, period. No point in wasting valuable time waiting for the future to arrive.

This is a good point to get rid of a common and understandable fear: that experienced workers are denying younger adults the opportunity to get a good job by staying employed longer. They aren't. The job market is not a zero-sum game. More jobs for one group doesn't mean fewer jobs for another group. Economists call the zero-sum view on jobs the "lump of labor fallacy."

The belief is understandable because it can be true at the level of the firm or organization. For instance, a job held by an older colleague doesn't open up to a younger peer until she retires. But at the level of the economy, the number of jobs can increase. Think of the rise in women's labor force participation rate and the increase in immigrant labor over the past half century. Research shows that the greater employment of older people accompanies reduced unemployment, increased employment, and a higher wage for younger workers.

Scholars find the pattern consistent for both men and women and for different levels of education. Higher rates of employment of older people won't reduce the wages and hours of younger workers.

"There isn't a fixed number of jobs," says Carstensen. "You grow the pie."

4

What about the Robots? Not.

Whether it's the best of times or the worst of times,
it's the only time we've got.

—ART BUCHWALD[1]

What about productivity growth? Productivity, or output per worker hour, is the basic building block of higher living standards. The rate of productivity growth has been disappointing for more than a decade, averaging about 1.2 percent annually from 2007 to 2017. That rate of growth is lower than the 2.8 percent average annual rate from the previous decade.

The factors behind the productivity slowdown are hotly contested, but most of the discussion focuses on the economic impact of recent technological innovations.

One popular explanation for anemic growth is that the current generation of digital-based innovations aren't the kind of economy-wide transformations that generated strong job growth in earlier eras. Many of the technologies seem to boost the productivity of leisure rather than business. Facebook, Twitter, Snap, and similar products allow for easily staying in touch with family, friends, colleagues, and the wider community. You can create your own videos and post them online for friends to see. You can try your hand at podcasting your restaurant and travel adventures. These products are fun, too.

Still, businesses tap into these technologies to bolster their marketing messages and brand identification. Organizations take deep dives into their data to devise effective sales strategies. Efficiencies have been gained from investing in automation, such as robots on the assembly line and in warehouses. Companies have built high-tech platforms for internal sharing of information to encourage innovation. Nevertheless, in the aggregate, the job-generating impact of these high-tech investments pale in comparison to, say, the rise of the internal combustion engine and the spread of electricity in the late nineteenth and early twentieth centuries—at least so far.

A competing explanation counsels patience. History suggests it takes time for new technologies to live up to their potential. There is nothing new or unusual about the current experience.

A classic example comes from a famous essay by Henry Adams, the social philosopher and scion of the prominent American family. He visited the Great Exposition in Paris in 1900, a remarkable world's fair celebrating technological innovations, art, and architecture at the beginning of the twentieth century. In the essay "The Dynamo and the Virgin," he marveled at the Gallery of Machines with its massive engines, transformers, and electric dynamos. He felt he was looking at a new economy.[2] But it took many more years before the new economy took hold. In 1900, when he stared at the dynamos, electric lighting was installed in about 3 percent of U.S. homes. Electric motors were in fewer than 5 percent of factory mechanical drives. It wasn't until the 1920s that these measures of electrification reached 50 percent.[3]

This historically informed perspective holds that artificial intelligence, robots, algorithms, automation, 3D manufacturing, and other advances will drive productivity growth higher—eventually. The moment of higher productivity growth is simply taking longer than most prognosticators expected. The timing of the next productivity boom is uncertain, but it's coming. (I'm in the optimistic camp. The combination of higher rates of labor force participation by experienced workers, more aging entrepreneurs, and strong technology-led productivity growth is an enticing recipe for robust growth and low unemployment.)

The future could be nearing. The high-tech infrastructure is gaining critical mass. Artificial intelligence and machine learning are making rapid strides. The global race to build autonomous driving vehicles is accelerating investments in sophisticated software and hardware. High-tech juggernaut Amazon is pushing several major industries to boost their technology investments, including grocers, retailers, and delivery businesses.

I find the debates over the likelihood of a productivity rebound fascinating. But the big issue for the current and future aging work-force is this: Will the rise of robots, artificial intelligence, automation, and algorithms lead to massive job destruction? Why bother calling for breaking down age bias, instituting phased retirement, and other concrete steps for creating work opportunities for experienced adults and entrepreneurs if advanced technologies will lay waste to the job market?

The belief in a jobless future is strong. Job gloom is a cottage industry. Global consultant PwC predicts about a third of jobs in the United States (as well as in Germany and Britain) will be eliminated by automation by the early 2030s.[4] An Oxford University study concludes that some 47 percent of jobs in the United States are at "high risk" of being eliminated by automation over the next 20 years.[5] Among the jobs most vulnerable to being replaced by automation are in transportation, logistics, and office and administrative support. Vivek Wadhwa, the veteran high-tech entrepreneur and faculty member at Carnegie Mellon University in Silicon Valley, has argued that "some 80 to 90 percent of jobs will be eliminated in the next ten to fifteen years."[6]

These are frightening numbers. There have been periodic eruptions of anxiety about a tech-led job apocalypse. A classic is the 1957 romantic comedy *Desk Set* starring Katherine Hepburn and Spencer Tracy, which captures the 1950s fears that mainframe computers would replace humans on the job. The economy and job market have swelled over the past sixty years, however.

Another high-tech episode of gloom came about during the so-called jobless recovery in the early 1990s. A good example is futurist Jeremy Rifkin's 1995 *The End of Work*. In the introduction, Rifkin argues, "We are entering a new phase in world history—one in which fewer and fewer workers will be needed to produce the goods and services for the global population."[7] Yet by the end of the decade, the U.S. unemployment rate had dropped to an average of 4 percent.

Just because technology has ended up creating more jobs than it destroyed in the past doesn't mean the future can't be different. The worry about a jobless future seems particularly acute with the rise of robots and artificial intelligence. The scenarios of intelligent and powerful machines replacing labor seem more persuasive with the latest technologies. Science fiction writers certainly have imagined economic Armageddon, including Skynet in the *Terminator* series and in the *Matrix* movies.

The odds are high that America doesn't confront a dystopian job market. "The fears of runaway AI systems either conquering humans or making them irrelevant aren't even remotely well grounded," writes MIT computer scientist Rodney Brooks. "Misled by suitcase words, people are making category errors in fungibility of capabilities. These errors are comparable to seeing more efficient internal combustion engines appearing and jumping to the conclusion that warp drives are just around the corner."[8]

What I find frustrating is speculations about a high-tech, jobless future make it easy to avoid tackling nitty-gritty economic challenges confronting an aging society. Instead of spinning tales of a jobless future, let's spend time working on implementing universal retirement and universal health care and universal family leave policies. These three reforms alone would support increased job mobility and entrepreneurial risk-taking over a lifetime, well into the traditional retirement years. Equally pressing is designing policies that boost the incomes of low-wage workers, including experienced workers.

I wouldn't fear the march of the robots. For one thing, if the robot-led productivity gains are as great as some tech futurists predict, the economic wealth created by the new technologies will be staggering. The added wealth will inspire entrepreneurs to devise new products, new services, and new markets. (Never underestimate the ability of entrepreneurs to come up with new ways to make money.) Meeting these needs and wants will create jobs, many we can't even imagine now. (In the early 2000s, a quarter of American workers were in jobs that weren't listed in the Census Bureau's occupation codes in 1967.)

For another, the American economy has created many more jobs than technological innovation has eliminated. "Such innovation allows workers and firms to produce more, so wages go up and prices go down, which increases spending, which in turn creates more jobs in new occupations, though more so in existing occupations (from cashiers to nurses and doctors)," write Robert Atkinson and John Wu in their look at 165 years of U.S. economic history, 1850 to 2015. "There is simply no reason to believe that this dynamic will change in the future for the simple reason that consumer wants are far from satisfied."[9]

Of course, jobs will be eliminated. Walk into a movie theater and you're just as likely to buy your ticket from a machine as from a human. ATMs have replaced human tellers at banks. Supermarkets are investing in self-service checkout stations. There is always destruction when jobs are automated out of existence. Maybe the jobs lost weren't particularly challenging or glamorous, but they often provided a first job to teenagers or decent work for people without sterling résumés. Conversations between customer and clerk add to the overall quality of life, and machines can't replace human contact.

Technology also creates jobs. Here's an intriguing example: Consultants at McKinsey's Paris office in 2011 found that the internet had destroyed 500,000 jobs in France in the previous fifteen years. The consultants also discovered that the internet had created 1.2 million other jobs at the same time. In other words, the internet led to a net addition of 700,000 jobs or 2.4 jobs created for every job destroyed.[10]

Similarly, economists at Dartmouth College estimate that new oil and gas extraction technologies (fracking) between 2005 and 2012 increased employment by 640,000.[11] Michael Mandel of the Progressive Policy Institute calculates that jobs related to mobile apps in the United States totaled 1.7 million as of December 2016. Put somewhat differently, app economy jobs nearly quadrupled over the previous five years—a 30 percent annual growth rate.[12]

Results like these aren't surprising. Boston University economist James Bessen, in a series of studies, examined the historic relationship between automation and jobs in the textile, steel, and automotive industries. During the Industrial Revolution, the introduction of automation transformed the weaving industry. The labor input into per yard of cloth plunged by 98 percent. In other words, productivity soared. Cloth became much cheaper to make. The demand for clothing expanded with lower prices. Weaver tasks changed in many instances, but jobs for weavers quadrupled between 1830 and 1900.[13]

Bessen examined the impact of computers to see if the same dynamic held in modern times. Employment in occupations that used computers grew significantly faster. Computer use on average is associated with about a 1.7 times increase in employment annually, he found.[14] Anthropologist Benjamin Shestakofsky spent some two years studying a company that uses the internet and mobile technologies to connect buyers and sellers of local services, such as wedding photographers and plumbers. He assumed his research would show machines replacing humans. Instead, the company kept hiring more humans to monitor, manage, and interpret the data. Shestakofsky concludes that "high-tech tools can be more powerful when they're interwoven with high-quality, low-cost human labor that is flexible and scalable."[15]

The job benefits of the digital economy aren't limited to a highly computer literate global elite. Many less-rarified jobs are redefined and redesigned. For instance, nursing can be physically demanding. Management at medical complexes are eager to keep experienced nurses on payrolls. Hospitals are installing formal flexible hour and part-time programs to prolong the careers of their nurses. They're also investing in automation, such as mechanical systems that shift patients from gurney to bed.

"It's not that nurses' aides are being replaced by health-care robots; rather, what nurses' aides do is being redefined," writes Barry Eichengreen, economic historian at the University of California, Berkeley. "And what they do will continue to be redefined as those robots' capabilities evolve from getting patients out of bed to giving physical therapy sessions and providing emotional succor to the depressed and disabled."[16]

Job losses are visible, but the gains are there, too. The net benefit is real.

The debate over truck drivers is illuminating. The American Trucking Association reports that more than 70 percent of goods consumed in the United States move by truck. Truckers also have help-wanted signs out. You might have noticed all the hiring signs on rigs driving on the highway. The industry is grappling with worker shortages to meet rising demand.

To find long-haul truckers, companies are turning to older workers. About a fifth of long-haul drivers are 55 to 64 years old.[17] Many of these drivers are in their second and third careers, says Rob Reich, senior vice president of maintenance and driver recruiting for Schneider, the giant transportation company headquartered in Green Bay, Wisconsin. Reich emphasizes that automation is easing the physical demands of the job. Key is the trucking industry's transition away from manual transmission to automatic transmission. "That's one reason it's a good second or third career," he says.

I caught up with 61-year-old Robert Stanton when he was driving a rig between Peoria and Bloomington, Illinois. He drives a rig and also trains newcomers into the business. Before taking up trucking, he was a park ranger, mostly in law enforcement and firefighting. At age 43, after years of chasing "drug-fueled kids through the woods," he decided it was time for a change and joined the long-haul trucking workforce. His wife is a tax accountant, and they have three children. He's brought each of his kids on the road with him so they could see the life. "Trucking is not a job," he says. "It's a lifestyle. You make money driving, but it's a lifestyle."

A defining part of the lifestyle is long days away from home. Long-haul truckers spend a minimum of twelve days on the road and two days at home. Stanton typically is out for four weeks and returns home for a week. The number-one reason people drop out of the industry is the time away from home. That's one reason husband-and-wife teams are favored by the trucking companies, he notes. They're considered more stable employees and, since they shift back and forth on the driving, the truck is moving all the time. Trucking is increasingly a second career. "Some people are doing it in their 70s," says Stanton.

When I've mentioned the trend of experienced workers joining the trucking business among friends and colleagues, the response is usually negative. Sure, that's a nice example, they'll say, but why bother learning to drive a truck? The jobs will be eliminated by driverless trucks. My response? When? Two years from now? Ten years? Twenty?

The opportunity for older workers to drive trucks exists now and sometime into the fog-shrouded, uncertain future. Assuming you like being on the road, it's a reasonable encore career option to consider. (It's not for me. I don't like driving.) No one knows the timing or even how the trucking job market will evolve with the spread of self-driving vehicles. Few jobs are permanent in any industry. Driving trucks can be a good occupation for people without much formal education. Truckers usually have high school diplomas and professional truck-driving-school certificates. In the meantime, why not embrace trucking, if that's what you want to do in the second half of life?

The real worry isn't the robots. It's that the jobs created in the future will pay too little to ensure household economic security and a high quality of life. What is worth worrying about is low wages. The Bureau of Labor Statistics expects most job growth to come from service-providing sectors between 2016 and 2026. Job projections are dominated by health care and social assistance work, such as home health aides (47 percent), personal care aides (39 percent), physical therapist assistants (31 percent), and massage therapists (26 percent). These sectors of the economy also offer the kind of work people might do in their second and third careers.[18]

Problem is, these jobs typically come with low wages and poor-to-no benefits. "If we don't do anything, wages will stagnate," says Paul Osterman, professor of human resources and management at MIT.

What kind of bold action might best hike worker paychecks? Relying on market forces isn't enough. Markets are amazing institutions for transmitting information, creating incentives to innovate, and for allocating resources. But markets have faltered at sharing prosperity in recent decades. "We don't think there is a path forward without a political solution," says David Hammer, executive director of the ICA Group, a consulting firm that helps grow worker cooperatives, employee stock ownership plans, and other social purpose ventures.

The movement for hiking the federal minimum wage to $15 an hour has spurred a number of states and urban areas to establish a timeline to raise the local minimum wage over several years. E-commerce giant Amazon put pressure on other low-wage businesses to embrace $15 an hour with its decision in 2018 to raise its minimum wage to that level.

An expanded Earned Income Tax Credit, or EITC, would also raise incomes. The anti-poverty program rewards work and it has low administrative costs. The focus of the current program is to help low-income families with children. The amount of the credit varies by marital status and the number of dependent children. The EITC essentially ignores adult childless workers, even though many are living paycheck to paycheck. The program could be made more generous and expanded to include single low-income adults. An alternative to the EITC is tax credits targeted at employers to encourage them to hire low-wage workers. None of these wage-boosting policy ideas are specifically designed to encourage older workers to stay employed. But they would improve household income of lower-income workers, old and young alike.

■

A good example of the challenge is the direct-care workforce. They are on the frontline of caregiving. Home-care workers (also known as personal aides) allow disabled older adults to age in place. They provide light housekeeping services, companionship, and some personal care, such as bathing, dressing, and medication reminders. Depending on the state, some can perform, with training, modest clinical tasks under the supervision of a health professional.

The current supply of some two million paid home-care workers falls short of demand for their services. Government statisticians calculate that with the aging of the population, the home-care industry will need an additional million workers by 2024—an increase of 26 percent from 2014.

The caregiving workforce is an older workforce, with more than half 45 years and older. Home-care workers are also the Rodney Dangerfields of health care: They get no respect.

"Home care has a long history of being undervalued—a glorified babysitter. For decades, it has been seen as companionship and not as a complex profession with a wide range of skills," says Robert Espinoza, vice president of policy at PHI, a nonprofit that looks to improve eldercare and disability services.

Home-care workers occupy the lowest rung of America's vast health care system. The home-care workforce is 90 percent female and 56 percent minority. The median hourly wage rate was only $10.66 in 2016. That's about two-thirds the hourly earnings of veterinary technicians, notes Howard Gleckman, senior fellow at the Urban Institute. "In other words, we pay people $5-an-hour more to care for our cats than to care for our mothers," Gleckman acidly writes.[19]

Benefits are paltry. Only a third of home-care workers are employed full-time and, as with most businesses, part-timers don't qualify for benefits. Some 40 percent of home-care workers rely on public health care coverage (mostly Medicaid). The industry has high rates of on-the-job injuries. The risk of sexual harassment and assault is also high.[20]

Little wonder annual turnover rates at home-care agencies hover around 60 percent. Research by Lisa Gurgone and her colleague Hayley Gleason at the Massachusetts-based Home Aide Care Council has this telling statistic: Home-care agencies in Massachusetts hire eighteen people every three months, on average. They lose fifteen workers over the same period.[21] That's crazy.

In light of high turnover rates, many more workers than the projected one million will need to be hired and trained to meet the demand. Home-care agencies will probably run through some 13 million workers by 2024, assuming the 60 percent turnover rate persists, estimates David Hammer of the ICA Group. The bottom line: The industry needs higher wages to attract and retain workers.

There are efforts underway to upgrade conditions and transform caregiving into a more rewarding job, including for people in their second and third acts. Among the more intriguing experiments are home-care cooperatives. These are worker-owned and worker-controlled. Co-ops provide their members with greater training opportunities, steadier hours, and better benefits. The books are open to members. Any year-end profit is distributed as a dividend to members. The emphasis on mutual commitment and support may be particularly attractive to older caregivers.

"I think the cooperative is the only model for home care," says Kippi Waters, the 62-year old founder of the twenty-three-member Peninsula Homecare Co-op in Port Townsend, Washington. The cooperative was started in 2016. At the beginning of 2017, it raised its hourly wage to $15 an hour, up from $13. The members learn about the business and share information at monthly meetings. "We're trying to change the perception that home care isn't a good job," says Waters. "Caregiving has a bad rep in our culture. It should have the best rep."

Vibeke Danborg, 60 years old, is a convert. Born and raised in Denmark, she came to the United States in her 20s. She was a long-time caregiver in the Seattle area, mostly finding clients through word of mouth. When her husband got a job in Boston several years ago, she joined a private agency to get caregiving work. They moved to Port Townsend, where they plan to retire eventually, and bought a home. She joined Peninsula and plans on working until she is age 67. "I love what I do," she says. "I love it."

She prefers the cooperative business model to the traditional home-care agency. "The difference between an agency and membership is big. The whole thing about being a member of a co-op versus being hired by an agency where you work for the boss," she says. "Members have input into the day-to-day running of the co-op. I am a team player. I have a voice. It's very fulfilling."

Grace Rosen, age 66, echoes her sentiments. Rosen moved in 2016 to Port Townsend from Portland, Maine, where she had her own therapy business. She heard Waters speak about helping people stay in their homes. She decided to give it a go. She became a home-care worker in January 2016. Rosen has several customers, including a 96-year-old former member of the Coast Guard and an 88-year-old former elementary school teacher. "The job has been one of the more challenging things I have done in my life," she says. "To change careers at age 65 seems bizarre. But I love it."

Rosen bought a place in Port Townsend. Her income is Social Security and caregiving. She loves the Pacific Northwest, and she likes the cooperative model. "People are passionate about caregiving. We want people to have quality of life. How can I use my skills that make a difference in people's lives," she says. "It's like an extended family." Danborg and Rosen benefitted from a joint program funded with $200,000 by the AARP Foundation and managed by Washington, DC-based Capital Impact Partner. The AARP money covered the cost, which is several hundred dollars, for them to become state-certified home-care aides in Washington. The goal behind the grant money is to create quality jobs for women 50 years and over. Part of the experiment is to see if the co-op model might offer older workers a second career option in caregiving and, with the passage of time, the chance to stay employed at the co-op when the physical demands of caregiving become too much. "We got the funds to test the model for older workers. Many caregivers have to work until 70," says Candice Baldwin, director of Aging in Community at Capital Impact. "Maybe the older caregiver can transition to training and bookkeeping. It's another career track and gives them the ability not to have to leave the field."[22]

The reality of home-care reform is daunting, however. There are only some ten home-care co-ops currently in operation, with another handful in the formation stage. Co-ops have a long way to go before filling in the gap between the demand for caregiving services and the supply of home-care workers. There is no way to broadly improve the working conditions of the home-care profession without Medicaid reform. Medicaid is the federal and state long-term-care public health insurance plan, and it pays for some two-thirds of long-term care in the United States. Medicaid reimbursement rates for home-care workers are low and inflexible. That's why co-ops concentrate on private clients paying for services through household savings, private insurance, family resources, or some combination of the three.

When I met with Nobel laureate Edmund Phelps at Columbia University, he repeatedly emphasized the positive economic and social returns from engaging in quality work for everyone and not just a talented few. Quality work was a moral and economic imperative for everyone, he said, including caregivers. He nodded when I quickly added older workers to the long list.

Here's what he once wrote that addresses the economic challenge worth thinking about: "A good economy promotes lives of vitality," Phelps wrote. "An economy cannot be good that does not produce the stimulation, challenge, engagement, mastery, discovery and intellectual development that constitute the good life."[23]

His sentiments aren't simply aspirations. No, there are good reasons to believe that, with effort, caregiving could become part of the emerging artisan economy in the United States and a force behind the creation of a new middle class. At least, that's what Harvard University economist Lawrence Katz believes is possible. Artisans bring their individual flair to the job, whether it's the carpenter designing custom kitchen cabinets or a waitress establishing her own catering business. Just as the cooperative movement demonstrates, the job of home-care aides doesn't have to be a minimum wage, low-skill job.

"But it could be done in a way that brings dignity to the patient and their family—that's a skill that requires some education, but a lot of experience would be much more valuable if we reimburse that in a way that took into account the skill of an artisanal dementia coach or home health aide" said Katz in an interview with PBS. "That's the kind of middle class job that's going to be extremely valuable going forward as opposed to a 'McJob' where a person just does a routine."[24]

Isn't designing work along those lines worth trying, not only for experienced caregivers but for every adult looking for meaning and money?

The Returns to Work

Works and days were offered us, and we took works.

—RALPH WALDO EMERSON[1]

When I moved to New York City after graduate school in the early 1980s, I went through a phase living off Nathan's Famous frankfurter. A cheap and tasty meal. When I picked up *Nathan's Famous: The First 100 Years*, written by William Handwerker, the founder's grandson (with Jayne Pearl), I gave it a nostalgic read. The centerpiece of the book is the story of founders Nathan Handwerker and his wife, Ida. An aspect of their lives illuminates a central theme about aging in America.[2]

The rise of Nathan's Famous from one restaurant in Coney Island into a national and, for a time, international chain is a classic bootstrap immigrant tale. The young Polish immigrant Nathan Handwerker arrived at Ellis Island in 1912 with no money. He didn't speak English, but he had relatives in Brooklyn's Jewish community and a work ethic. Four years after coming to the United States, he opened his nickel frankfurter stand. (In the book, readers learn not to call them "hot dogs.") He and his wife, Ida, worked side by side for nearly sixty years as the stand grew into a fast food empire.

When Nathan and Ida's son Murray took over the expanding business, he eventually pushed his parents into retirement in 1971. The move was well-intentioned, writes author William Handwerker, Murray's son. Murray wanted his parents to enjoy a life outside of work, to spend their remaining days in leisure in Florida. They were well off financially. They didn't need to work anymore. Instead, Nathan and Ida were miserable in their retirement. "They clearly felt left out, marginalized, and no longer needed," writes their grandson.

No matter how old we are chronologically, everyone needs good reasons to get out of bed in the morning. Vice President Joseph Biden eloquently captured the idea in his Yale commencement address to graduates in 2015:

"The truth is, though, that neither I, nor anyone else, can tell you what will make you happy, help you find success. You each have different comfort levels. Everyone has different goals and aspirations. But one thing I've observed, one thing I know, an expression my dad would use often, is real. He used to say, it's a lucky man or woman gets up in the morning—and I mean this sincerely. It was one of his expressions. It's a lucky man or woman gets up in the morning, puts both feet on the floor, knows what they're about to do, and thinks it still matters."[3]

He's right.

For some mature adults, it may be grandchildren, hobbies, and the proverbial bucket list. Others find it rewarding to continue tapping into their skills and knowledge at work, being useful by drawing on their accumulated experience. Earning an income is good, too.

Ana Negrini is 64 years old. She is a specialist in accounts payable at Urban Health Plan, a federally qualified community health center founded in the Bronx by Dr. Richard Izquierdo, a pediatrician and family practitioner. Izquierdo opened the San Juan Health Center in 1967, and in 1974 expanded its scope of practice to provide services to the predominately Latino residents of Hunts Point, Mott Haven, and the Morrisania neighborhood in the Bronx. Urban Health Plan and its approximately nine hundred employees have health centers throughout the Bronx, the Corona neighborhood in Queens, and central Harlem.

Urban Health Plan operates 27 health practice sites with its main health center located on Southern Boulevard Street in the Bronx. It's a short walk from the Simpson Street Station. The streets are crowded and lively. Leaving the subway, I'm greeted by a human billboard dressed up as the Statue of Liberty soliciting workers for an employment agency. Stores and restaurants are doing a brisk business. It's hard to believe that this neighborhood was deeply troubled in the 1970s with vacant lots, abandoned buildings, and high crime. Obviously, no more.

Urban Health Plan's main health center operates on several floors offering a variety of medical and health-related services, serving a large number of Medicaid recipients. It also offers its patients health promotion and prevention programs, a large commercial kitchen for teaching people healthy cooking habits, and the Center for Healthy Aging. The youngest employee is 22 and the oldest is 79. Urban Health Plan makes a point of hiring people from the community in their 50s, 60s, and 70s.

"We value people for their skill sets. Age is just a number," says Paloma Izquierdo-Hernandez, chief executive officer at Urban Health Plan and the founder's daughter. "I also think there is something to be said about taking the experience and using it in the organization."

Negrini was born in the Bronx, went to school in the Bronx, and lives in the Bronx. Her résumé includes years in the billing department for a durable medical equipment company in the Bronx; accounts payable at a food company in Hunt's Point, the large food distribution facility based in the South Bronx; and, early in her career, at a bank. She always worked, until she found herself unemployed for about eighteen months in her late 50s. She hated being unemployed.

Her sister encouraged her to talk to Urban Health Plan's Izquierdo-

Hernandez when they were at a funeral together. Izquierdo-Hernandez and Negrini were in fifth grade together. Negrini hesitated, but she finally approached Izquierdo-Hernandez. Here's how she remembers the conversation:

IZQUIERDO-HERNANDEZ: What do you do?
NEGRINI: Accounts payable and billings.
IZQUIERDO-HERNANDEZ: Which do you prefer?
NEGRINI: Accounts payable.
IZQUIERDO-HERNANDEZ: I'll get back to you.

Negrini tears up as she tells the story. She repeatedly dries her eyes with a carefully folded tissue. Two weeks following her conversation with Izquierdo-Hernandez, she got a call from the assistant vice president of finance at Urban Health Plan. A position was available, though it would only last two to six weeks. She took the temporary job. Six weeks passed, and the assistant vice president of finance calls her into her office.

"I figure this is it," says Negrini. "She asks me: Have you liked the work?"

Negrini said she did. To her surprise, she was offered a full-time job in accounts payable at age 60. Her job is located in a historic complex in Hunt's Point, the Bank Note building. It was finished in 1909 and the American Bank Note Company used it to print paper currency (including foreign currencies), war bonds, stock certificates, and coins. The four-building complex houses many businesses.[4]

"I enjoy working. I really do. I enjoy getting up in the morning and doing something," she says. "I still feel I am young at heart. Retire? To do what? Why retire when you still have so much to do and give?"

Later in our conversation, she emphasizes how much she likes her colleagues. "You aren't going to work. It's like going to a family meeting. If I don't show up, I get texts—are you OK?"

Among the most annoying assumptions with the trend toward working longer is the belief that older adults either "need to work" (bad) or "want to work" (good). The reality for most people is it's both—need and want. They are two sides of the same second-life coin. Most older Americans have little in retirement savings outside Social Security and their home. (About 80 percent of Americans over 65 own a home.) For households nearing retirement with 401(k)/IRAs, the median savings was $135,000.[5] The U.S. Government Accountability Office found that 52 percent of households ages 64 through 74 had no retirement savings.[6]

The current retirement savings system is designed to encourage working longer. Defined contribution retirement savings plans like 401(k)s and 403(b)s allow participants to add to their tax-sheltered savings as long as they're employed. Social Security benefits are more than 75 percent higher for those who file at age 70 (the latest you can file) compared to receiving benefits at age 62 (the earliest).

The financial impact from continuing to earn an income is genuine. A well-known personal finance metric is retirees can safely withdraw 4 percent from their retirement savings every year. (Like all finance rules of thumb, the baseline number is adjusted for individual circumstances. It's nothing but a starting place for additional calculations.) Let's say an older worker or self-employed person earns $10,000 in their unretirement. That sum is the equivalent of withdrawing 4 percent from a $250,000 retirement savings plan. Earn $20,000? That equals a 4 percent withdrawal from a $500,000 portfolio.

Mention work and most people automatically think income. Nothing wrong with that association, of course. But the workplace is much more. The workplace is a community. The job can provide people with an identity, status, and respect. A career or job can offer purpose, as well as mental and physical stimulation. The returns from work include pay but are also independent of the paycheck.

"Through work, we seek to justify our own existence, to develop a feeling of participation in a design which is grander than our personal lives," write Sar Levitan and Clifford Johnson in their 1982 *Second Thoughts on Work*. "Through work, we join a community of individuals with common experiences, skills or goals. Through work, we derive feelings of competence and achievement, making contributions which enable us to believe in our own worth."[7]

An intriguing illustration of the psychological and community effects of work is the story of Marienthal. The Austrian town was dominated by its textile factory, which essentially employed most of the population starting in the nineteenth century. The factory closed in 1929 and, with its sole employer bankrupt, unemployment skyrocketed. The unemployed factory workers continued to get an income from the Austrian government so long as they didn't find another job. The unemployed had the time to pursue full-time leisure, perhaps writing, painting, reading books, and learning new hobbies. Except they didn't.

Sociologists studied the town following the mill shutdown. What they learned was that unemployment set the town residents adrift. They felt untethered, and not in a good way. People stopped getting together for dances. Fewer people checked books out of the public library. The town's park fell into disrepair. Families broke down and neighbors quarreled. "Previously healthy individuals, losing the structures that once shaped their lives, progressively experience various forms of physical and mental breakdown," writes Jonathan Gershuny and Kimberly Fisher, sociologists at Oxford University.[8]

The workplace is a community. Depending on your occupation, doing your job involves engaging with cubicle mates, factory workers, suppliers, and customers. Gossip is the lifeblood of organizations. People care if you don't show up for work. You like some of your coworkers and dislike others.

The desire for more than a paycheck from the job is longstanding. The yearning for community and respect is a major theme in the 1950 book *The New Society: The Anatomy of Industrial Order* by Peter Drucker, the late philosopher of management. Drucker was trying to understand how large mass-production industrial enterprises (think General Motors and U.S. Steel) were transforming society. Among his strongest findings was the desire among workers to be part of something bigger than themselves.[9]

"In survey after survey, the major demands of industrial workers appear as demands for good and close group relationships with their fellow workers, for good relations with their supervisors, for advancement, and above all, for recognition as human beings, for social and prestige satisfactions, for status and function," he writes. "Wages, while undoubtedly important, rank well down the list."

The same desire among experienced workers holds some seventy years later. Several years ago, I gave a talk at the community center at the Verrado development on the outskirts of Phoenix. At some point during the discussion, one "retiree" relayed his perspective (drawn from memory).

Chris, here's the thing. You retire. You have a drink on your patio at 4:30 in the afternoon. It's the best drink ever. You're not worried about getting fired or having to fire someone. You don't have to go to a meeting, work late on a report, or deal with an irate customer. Just relax.

Time passes. Now, you have a drink on your patio at 3:30 in the afternoon. The drink still tastes good. But you're disconcerted. No one cares that you're having a drink at 3:30.

More time goes by. Now you have a drink at 1:30 in the afternoon. No one cares. You realize it's time to go back to work.

We all had a good laugh. But his experience is widely shared. "Retirement" these days is more accurately described as a "sabbatical." Older adults want a break from the demands of a job. They retire. But they return to the workforce within a year or two, often by finding part-time employment and flexible jobs. About 40 percent of Americans age 65 and older who are currently employed were retired at some time in the past, according to a research report by economist Nicole Maestas and colleagues for the RAND Corporation.[10]

Recent research emphasizes the health benefits of social connections. We meet people in all kinds of settings, such as religious services and while volunteering at a neighborhood gathering. But for many people, these settings are squeezed into very busy schedules. We have many demands on our time. For many workers, the job is the community in which they spend the most hours. Loneliness is a threat to the quality of life with the passage of time. A lack of social relationships and community interactions heightens the risk of an early death, much like smoking, obesity, and inactivity. (Numerous studies also document that strong social networks are a force for delaying cognitive impairment and even battling the onset of dementia among older adults.)

"The work environment places demands on people. You have to socially interact. You're forced to be there. People are forced to engage," says Michael Hurd, director of the RAND Center for the Study of Aging. As economists Axel Börsch-Supan and Morten Schuth write in "Early Retirement, Mental Health, and Social Networks: "Even disliked colleagues and a bad boss, we argue, are better than social isolation because they provide cognitive challenges that keep the mind active and healthy."[11]

Certainly, work keeps Monte Clausen sharp. He was just shy of his 76th birthday when I interviewed him. He graduated from the University of Arizona law school in Tucson in 1969, back when "By the Time I Get to Phoenix" by Glen Campbell was album of the year and *Oliver!* won best picture at the Academy Awards. Clausen was a civil litigator in private practice in Tucson until 1989 when, around age 50, he was asked to join the United States Attorney's office in Tucson. He has been working out of the criminal division since 2003 on immigration cases.

"I get asked daily, 'Aren't you supposed to be retired?'" Clausen says, laughing. "My stock answer is, 'So long as they want me, I'll keep coming.'"

Clausen talks with affection about the people in his local legal community—judges, court personnel, and fellow U.S. attorneys. He's mentored some of the young lawyers he works with and, he emphasizes, he gleans new knowledge from them. "You would be surprised with the legal talent we have here," he says. "We have high ethical standards."

The job definitely keeps him engaged. "I learn new stuff every day," says Clausen. "It's different all the time. I love my job."

Work can help stave off cognitive decline with age. That's one conclusion from research by a group of scholars studying large databases from Europe, the United Kingdom, and the United States. They're uncovering positive effects of later retirement on body and mind. Among those studies is "Mental Retirement" by economists Susann Rohwedder of the RAND Corporation and Robert Willis of the University of Michigan. Looking at data from the United States, England, and eleven European countries, they concluded that retirement had a significant negative impact on the cognitive ability of people in their early 60s. They speculate that retirement can lead to a less stimulating daily environment. There's wisdom in the expression "use it or lose it."[12]

The research is suggestive and intuitive. But it's also inherently difficult. Just as retirement can influence health, so can health influence retirement. It isn't easy to disentangle whether the data reflects people with better cognition staying employed or whether work protects against cognitive decline. Nevertheless, the research certainly suggests that there are positive mental returns to working longer.

Says Catherine Sullivan, professor of occupational science and occupational therapy at St. Catherine University in St. Paul, Minnesota: "When the mind is stimulated by the need to problem solve it builds cognitive reserve in the brain which is believed to protect against premature cognitive declines associated with aging."[13]

The cognitive benefits seem strongest among people in jobs that require education and judgment, such as lawyers, consultants, and teachers. Blue-collar workers such as machinists, iron workers, carpenters, and electricians also have skills that demand learning and judgment. They can often transfer their knowledge to less physically demanding jobs when they feel the need. Monotonous routine and the lack of novelty are enemies of good cognitive health.

The work-longer movement is most apparent among college-educated cubicle workers, C-suite executives, and professionals. The well-educated tend to have better health overall. They're not as physically drained from the job as their less-educated peers. Their skills often transfer to another career or occupation that may be less demanding or simply more engaging in their unretirement years.

The labor force participation rate for men in the 65-to-69 age group with four years of college or more was 50.25 percent in 2016, up from 41.2 percent in 1995, according to the Urban Institute, the Washington, DC-based think tank. For women, the comparable numbers are 37.5 percent and 28.3 percent, respectively.[14]

But the embrace of longer work lives goes beyond the college-educated. For the 65-to-69 age cohort with only a high school diploma, the labor force participation rate for men was 31.2 percent in 2016. That's an increase from 26.7 percent in 1995. For high-school-only women graduates, the numbers are 24.7 percent in 2016, up from 17.9 percent in 1995.[15]

"It's still the case that better educated people are more willing to work past age 62," says Richard Johnson, labor economist at the Urban Institute. "Still, in the last twenty years we've seen for those with no more than a high school education a big increase working past age 62 and past age 65. It isn't just the best educated people who are extending their work lives. Everyone is."

A decline in the "unpleasantness" of work is helping the shift to later retirement. Between 1971 and 2006, for instance, the share of jobs with high physical demands declined from 57 percent to 46 percent, according to the Urban Institute. The vast improvement in working conditions over the past 150-plus years is one of the most powerful takeaways (and too often ignored) from economic historian Robert Gordon's magisterial *The Rise and Fall of American Growth: The U.S. Standard of Living Since the Civil War.*[16]

Gordon defined "disagreeable work" this way: Being outside and exposed to the elements, heavy lifting or digging, and monotonous repetitive motions on the assembly line. These jobs are mostly in farming, blue collar, and domestic service jobs. Gordon compared those workers to the rest of the workforce, and he calculated that the share of unpleasant occupations since 1870 declined from 87.2 percent to 21.6 percent in 2009.

Gordon sliced the data in different ways in his book. Still, his conclusion was that the various classifications underestimate the improvements in working conditions.

"One only need contrast the 1870 farmer pushing a plough behind a horse or mule, exposed to heat, rain, and insects, with the 2009 farmer riding in the air-conditioned cab of his giant John Deere tractor that finds its way across the field by GPS and uses a computer to optimally drop and space the seeds as the farmer reads farm reports and learns about crop prices on a fixed screen or portable tablet."[17]

People with physically demanding jobs can also take their skills and find something less arduous. They reinvent themselves. They have skill. They have knowledge. They have experience. They just need to find a paying job that doesn't take too great a toll on their bodies.

That's what Steve Guadalupe of Miami, Florida did. He knows the medical building he works in well. He's in his late 60s. He started out in the Air Force working with computers in personnel. Guadalupe left the Air Force in 1983, tapping into his computer background to get jobs at centralized bank data centers in the Miami area. When that work dried up in the late 1980s, he shifted into construction. Among the projects he worked on in the 1990s was a six-story medical building on the grounds of the Baptist Hospital complex in Miami. He stayed on as a member of its maintenance crew.

Guadalupe was a jack-of-all-maintenance-trades. He changed ceiling lights, fixed plumbing, and maintained the electrical and air-conditioning systems. "We did it all," he says. "Unless it was a big job. Then we would hire a contractor."

The work was hard on his body. "Climbing up and down ladders, my legs would be sore when I got home," he says. "As I got older, I decided I wouldn't be able to keep doing that."

When the concierge retired from the information desk around the turn of the century, Guadalupe got the job directing people when they come in for a procedure or visit. His desk is in the lobby. "People will come in. I know where to tell them to go," he says.

A great-grandfather, grandfather, and father of four, Guadalupe needs an income. He likes his concierge job. He has health insurance, a 401(k), and usually a bonus.

"If I stayed in maintenance, I would be making more money. But I wouldn't still be working," he says. "This job I can do until I'm 80. It isn't physical work. It's information."

Guadalupe's job offers daily variety dealing with different customers and their questions. Turns out, variety helps stave off cognitive decline. Variety means learning new skills and taking on new tasks. The health benefits from variety largely stem from breaking with routine and relieving monotony. That's the main conclusion from a 2017 research paper by eight scholars, including Ursula Staudinger of Columbia University.[18]

The scholars studied middle-aged production workers across a seventeen-year time span in one manufacturing company. Through a variety of cognitive tests, along with MRIs on some workers, the scholars found "novelty" on the job—learning new skills and tasks— was associated with improved mental processing speed and working memory. "It's a no-brainer. We spend a lot of time in the work environment. Cumulatively, what does it do to us?" asks Staudinger in a talk at Columbia University. "Use it or lose it isn't enough. It's 'challenge' it or lose it. It doesn't have to be a lot, it just has to be a little bit different. You have to adapt."

The creativity of blue collar workers is underestimated. When I graduated from college, I became a merchant seaman for the next four years, typically working six to seven months on a ship followed by several months on shore. My first job was wiper in the engine room on the container ship *SS San Francisco*. (Actually, that was my second ship; the first was a freighter that hit another ship in New York harbor as we left the Brooklyn piers. A very short trip to the Hoboken repair docks!) The *San Francisco* was an old ship from World War II that had been lengthened and retrofitted into a container ship.

The boilers were still from the early 1940s, durable but somewhat finicky. The able-bodied seamen on deck worked at keeping the rust at bay. Officers had their own quarters. Seamen shared rooms. Everything in the rooms was bolted down.

Wiper is an apt job description. My tasks included cleaning the engine room and the seamen's shared bathroom. The voyage was a round trip run between European ports and the Middle East. For seven months, we went from Rotterdam to Bremerhaven to Genoa to Algeciras (Spain), to Piraeus (Greece) to Dubai, to Dammam (Saudi Arabia), and back again.

During my time at sea, I got to steam through the Suez Canal, the Panama Canal, Guam, the Philippines, Japan, and the coasts of the United States. The job of merchant seaman is marked by long days of work with spells of boredom punctuated by memorable moments of adventure.

A big lesson for me was how skilled even supposedly "unskilled" labor is at their job. Most of the seamen were competent and some brilliant at solving problems in the engine room. A skill several tried to teach me that I never mastered was to think like steam flowing through the miles of pipes in the engine room. The mental trick is an effective way to figure where the trouble lies if you can play that game. I couldn't. One vicious storm, I'll never forget assisting the first engineer and a skilled engine room seaman machine a shaft at the lathe, a critical repair needed to keep the ship safe. Artistry at sea.

I tucked away from my experience at sea how imaginative several seamen were at building a diverse portfolio of income-generating activities. Long before white-collar workers were routinely advised to think of their careers as a mosaic or a portfolio, these seamen had figured out how to make a living in different environments. A seaman might own a small house or a double-wide trailer, perhaps in a rural area. The household owned a small business run by the spouse. The seaman came home timed to hunting season. He'd fill the freezer with game for when he was gone. The family members got their retirement plan and health insurance through the seafaring job. He'd work side gigs on land, say, driving a truck or working at a construction site, sometimes off the books. These workers had built variety and novelty and income into their portfolio of jobs.

Technological advances will help an aging population to stay active. Robotic technologies could even overcome disabilities that prevent many older Americans from working. Autonomous driving vehicles should improve the mobility of older people. Some advances are less than high-tech. Anti-fatigue mats ease the strain of standing for longer periods. "Universal design" takes into account aging in the office with utilitarian and aesthetically pleasing door handles, lighting, and work surface heights.

The experience of John Smith is illuminating. He was in his late 50s when we met. Born with cerebral palsy, Smith worked full time at the Institute for Community Integration on the campus of the University of Minnesota, Twin Cities. The organization's mission is bringing people with all kinds of disabilities into the community.

He has worked there part-time ever since a life-changing accident a decade ago. He fell and badly injured his spinal cord. Smith lost his ability to walk, so now he uses a power wheelchair for mobility. "I was lucky," he says. "I work for an employer who has been committed to keeping me around."

Smith owns a condo near campus. He employs a personal caregiving assistant who comes to his place to help out. Certain basic activities take a long time. For instance, his morning routine takes about two to three hours. His work schedule is flexible, but he usually arrives around noon and stays until 7:00 or so in the evening.

"I need to work as long as I can. I have my money and my savings, but my expenses are going to keep going up." He also works because he's "driven by my rather naïve passion to make a difference in the world, and I am pleased to have a way I think I can do it."

His power wheelchair facilitates his ability to work. Smith uses a trackball rather than a mouse to navigate his computer. The computer has software features that take into consideration his difficulties with the keyboard. Smith's power wheelchair lets him raise his seat almost to eye-level when speaking with someone who is standing up. He can tilt it back to relieve pressure during the long day. Some simpler gadgets are also useful, such as the handle that holds the key he uses to unlock his office door and the rope around the doorknob so he can close the door when leaving at night. "I have no doubt that technology is going to keep getting better and will allow me to increase my productivity for many years to come," Smith says.

The job should feed the spirit as well as the bank account. Another word for spirit is *purpose*, simply defined as why we get up in the morning. Purpose is also a vision of opportunity. Purpose, then, not only gets us up in the morning but keeps us striving through the days and years.

Michael Shoemaker, 69 years old, understands purpose. I met him sitting at a wooden picnic table in front of his RV on an early October evening at the Red River State Recreation Area in East Grand Forks, Minnesota. Shoemaker enjoys jokes. "I woke up to a realization this morning," he deadpans. "The only way I will have a smoking hot body is when I'm cremated." He cracks up.[19]

Shoemaker is a work-camper, part of a growing number of modern-day nomads who live in their RVs and travel from campground to campground for seasonal jobs like working the retail counter in national parks, filling orders for Amazon.com, and taking tickets at NASCAR races. Most work-campers are in the second half of life, many well into the traditional retirement years. Shoemaker was one of some 550 work-campers hired to help stack and store the sugar-beet harvest in October for American Sugar Crystal in the Red River Valley along the border of North Dakota and Minnesota.

Shoemaker retired in 2010 from his gratifying job as a machine operator making armor for the Abrams tank at Idaho National Laboratory in Idaho Falls. His brother and sister-in-law had lived the work-camper lifestyle for about ten years, so he decided to give it a try. He travels in his RV with two Shih Tzu dogs, Kobie and Katie. Among his jobs, mostly at retail counters, Shoemaker has worked at Yellowstone National Park, Grand Teton National Park, Mount Rushmore National Memorial, and the joint spring training camp for the Kansas City Royals and Texas Rangers in Surprise, Arizona. Among the people he met during his travels are Rollie Fingers, the famous pitcher with the wild mustache; Bert Campaneris, the great shortstop; and Meadowlark Lemon, the legendary "Clown Prince" of basketball for the Harlem Globetrotters.

Shoemaker's previous job was at Crazy Horse Memorial in South Dakota. He had never worked the sugar-beet harvest and, since it was only some 600 miles from Crazy Horse, he thought he'd give it a try. How was it going? His job was operating a beet piler—large, elongated, yellow machines reminiscent of a praying mantis—since he's comfortable with machinery. "I can still shovel and work with the best of them," he says. "I am enjoying the heck out of this."

Shoemaker gets a pension from Idaho National Laboratory and Social Security. His RV is almost paid off. He also collects coins. The seasonal work supplements his income. The real lure for him is the lifestyle that keeps him engaged and active. He's intrigued by a job opportunity at a fishing camp in Montana for his next gig after the harvest.

"I watched my dad retire, sit in a chair, and die a miserable death," he reflects. "I won't do that. You have to have a purpose."

The Rise of 50-Plus Entrepreneurship

Walk on air against your better judgment.

—SEAMUS HEANEY[1]

The late Herbert Gutman was a well-known professor of history at the Graduate Center of the City University of New York. A footnote in his book *Work, Culture & Society*, published in 1973, tells a story drawn from a 1972 newspaper article in Rochester, New York. Santo Badagliacca, a master tailor, emigrated from Sicily to Rochester in 1956 with his wife and 5-year-old daughter. He was 40 years old when he came to the United States. The next twelve years he worked for the National Clothing Company, Timely Clothes, and Bond Clothes. He quit working in clothing factories in 1968 to open a custom tailoring shop.

Gutman seemed amazed that Badagliacca would go off on his own. Only three or four people visited his home shop weekly for alterations. In the previous four years, not one single order came in for a custom-made suit. Badagliacca was OK with that, explaining why he had left the factory: "Each day, it's just collars, collars, collars.

I didn't work forty years as a tailor just to do that," he said. Gutman remarked that Badagliacca "seemed to belong to another era."[2]

Not any longer. The suit business is still tough, but Badagliacca would have plenty of fellow entrepreneurial artisans. Craft beer and artisan spirits are growth businesses. The same goes for chef-owned, farm-to-table restaurants. Outdoor gear makers and handcrafted backpacks. Blacksmiths and weavers, small batch soap makers, and shoe cobblers. Artisan businesses like these are often started by people 50 years and older.

The leading edge of the S-curve with an aging workforce is entrepreneurship (including self-employment). Entrepreneurship is creative. Entrepreneurship brings in an income. Entrepreneurship involves purpose. Entrepreneurs are redefining the possibilities in the second half of life. Just ask Richard Williams.[3]

He left behind a tenured job as a university professor in the second half of life to start a Neapolitan pizza restaurant. The journey hasn't been easy, but Williams is glad he has found a new calling in his second act.

"Can you be exhilarated and exhausted at the same time?" he asks, jokingly.

Here's the backstory: Williams was a 51-year-old recreational therapy professor at East Carolina University in Greenville, North Carolina, when we first spoke near the end of 2016. (We stayed in touch for more than a year for a PBS Next Avenue story.) He'd been a professor for some twenty-five years. He had job security. He loved his field of study and his students. Single and frugal, his finances were in excellent shape: a university pension, health insurance, and ample savings.

Yet Williams felt increasingly unsettled and unsatisfied. "The longer I am a professor, the more wooden I have become," he told me. "Do I want to challenge myself? In five to ten years, I might be too tired."

Many people in the second half of life are restless, even those with jobs and careers that have long offered social and professional returns.

They once knew the answer to the critical question, "Why get up in the morning?" But over time, their enthusiasm has flagged. They know they have more to give. The haunting refrain, as the legendary jurist Oliver Wendell Holmes Sr. eloquently said, is that they'll "die with their music still in them."

To Williams, the "music" sounded like owning a restaurant. He always found it rewarding to come up with recipes and cook for friends. A small eatery offered the prospect of taking his creative energy to a wider group of people. "Cooking and serving good food is an artistic experience for me," he says.

Just one problem: He didn't know the restaurant business or have a business background. But professors are great at research. Several years ago, Williams started studying the local market, searching for a gap or opportunity in the restaurant scene.

He leaned toward pizza and learned that most pizza joints in the area were in strip malls. What his growing university town lacked, he decided, was a downtown, sit-down pizza restaurant targeted at adults, especially young professionals on a date. His new mission: create a "small, swanky Napolitano pizza cafe."

Williams knew he had more research to do. Instead of teaching during the summer of 2016, he flew to Florence and took a three-week pizza-making course at Bivero Pizza Academy. While there, he also worked at the popular Pizzeria ZeroZero.

Like many visitors to Florence, he went to the Duomo, the magnificent Renaissance cathedral dominating the skyline. He climbed the stairs to the top of the famous cupola and, halfway up, paused for breath. Then he saw graffiti on the wall saying: "Give more than you get and be blessed." He took that as a sign and committed to take the leap into the unknown and become a restauranteur.

"Now is the time," he recalled saying to himself on the Duomo stairway. (He has since preserved the saying as a tattoo.)

Of course, a long time usually passes between deciding to take a leap into a new career and turning that next chapter into reality.

Reinvention is a tricky business. Poet T. S. Eliot captured the challenge of embarking on an encore:[4]

> *Between the idea*
> *And the reality*
> *Between the motion*
> *And the act*
> *Falls the shadow*

Williams retired from East Carolina University in 2017. He knew he had something of a personal-finance safety net, being vested in the state retirement plan and, as a retired professor, having the ability to stay on the school's insurance plan.

We stayed in touch periodically by phone and email during 2017 and 2018. Sometimes, his enthusiasm was apparent, such as when he sent me a picture of him working with an architect on the kitchen design.

The pressure was intense at other times, like this email from mid-February 2017:

"I have been extremely stressed, and I get caught in moments of terror and regret. A couple of weeks ago, I pulled over on the way to work to throw up in a bank's parking lot," he wrote. "Now that I've resigned, I feel like Cortez and Chuck Yeager. Cortez burned his boats; there was no choice but to fight. Yeager described breaking the sound barrier as a chaotic moment where he thought the plane might break apart, then he broke through, and all became smooth.
I'm almost there."

He found a location for the restaurant in an old Coca-Cola bottling building. The area had been downtrodden, but the Uptown Greenville and the Dickinson Avenue Arts District is undergoing an urban renaissance. Of course, rehabbing the space took much longer than expected.

"Slow, slow, slow, and then slow," is how he describes the remodeling project.

The planned August 2017 debut got pushed back several times, but Luna Pizza Cafe opened on January 2, 2018. The small Neapolitan restaurant offers locally sourced, artisanal pizzas baked in an 800-degree brick oven along with wine, craft beers, and cocktails. Williams's menu highlights Luna's organic tomato sauce and fresh mozzarella, with fresh toppings and local ingredients. "We've been thrilled with the response we've had," says Williams, now 53.

Williams has taken several steps to boost his odds that Luna will be a successful enterprise. He hired an experienced general manager and sent him to the Bivero Pizza Academy for training. The general manager handles the nuts and bolts of the business, such as the nearly forty employees (almost all part-time); Williams focuses on the food and menu.

Luna's finances are also designed for staying power. Williams figured early on that he needed around $300,000 to launch. His original plan was to put in $100,000 from personal savings and borrow $200,000 from a bank. He has since revised the plan. With sufficient savings from his frugal living, he decided to go all-in and own the restaurant outright, partly to avoid interest payments and partly to exercise greater control.

The final tab at opening was a fraction over $300,000. He has nearly $22,000 remaining dedicated to the restaurant. "This way, we keep our monthly nut to a minimum and give Luna the best chance to succeed," he says.

Customer traffic is good. Williams will start drawing a salary soon and hopes to offer employees benefits once the restaurant is on solid footing.

"All I think about is the restaurant," Williams says. "I am at work seventy to eighty hours a week. I'm in at 11:00 in the morning, and I'll be there at 11:00 at night. It's fun."

■

Entrepreneurship at 50-plus is a practical encore career. To be sure, like many people writing about an aging population, I've treated entrepreneurship as Plan D: What to do when Plan A (a part-time, salaried job), Plan B (a flexible schedule with pay), and Plan C (new career, full-time job) don't pan out. Entrepreneurship seemed too risky for most older adults.

Wrong. Really wrong.

The attractions of entrepreneurship are many in the second half of life. Older workers steer clear of human resource departments and their age bias barriers to hiring. Age discrimination is less of an issue (it doesn't disappear), since you're building a business off your experience, knowledge, and contacts. Most people start a business that reflects their passions and skills. The range of businesses is remarkably diverse.

"You see people of all ages trying all kinds of things," says David Deeds, Schultze professor of entrepreneurship at the University of St. Thomas. "Entrepreneurship can be a lifestyle. Do something you love. Make some money at it."[5]

Entrepreneurs include everyone from the solopreneur setting up a lifestyle business to serial entrepreneurs establishing a venture backed by angel investors. Older Americans are particularly suited to join the startup culture, whether they are pushed into it (involuntary retirement, age discrimination) or pulled into entrepreneurship (acting on a dream, wanting to be the boss). There are many paths and triggers to entrepreneurship. Whatever the reason, older workers tend to share several advantages. They're experienced, with networks of contacts developed over the years. Financing for most startups is typically a bootstrap operation and, on average, older households have more money to tap. Self-employment—a category of entrepreneurship—may be a good fit with their stage of life. It's a savvy way to phase into retirement, especially if the business allows for embracing a part-time, flexible work schedule. Self-employed older workers tend to reduce their hours more than their wage-and-salary peers.

You're never too old to innovate and create.

Don't get me wrong. Starting a business is hard work with plenty of stressful nights. You need to learn bookkeeping and understand taxes. You might want to register as a limited liability company, or LLC. You'll need to pick up online marketing skills. You'll have to learn how to price your product or service.

The good news is an ecology of knowledge, advice, and support for would-be entrepreneurs is developing and expanding. The entrepreneurial ecosystem hikes the odds of success. The startup culture is spreading far beyond the well-known high-tech hubs, such as Silicon Valley, Boston, and Austin.

How about St. Petersburg, Florida?

St. Petersburg was famous as a mecca for retirees following World War II. The city's many retirees were famous for spending hours on the green benches lining its sidewalks. The late-night comedian Johnny Carson called St. Petersburg "God's waiting room." (People still flinch telling that quip in St. Petersburg.) The green benches are long gone, although it seems somehow fitting that Green Bench Brewing opened for business downtown in 2013. About one-third of St. Pete's population is 55 years and older. The city has become a creative capital with artists, art galleries, restaurants, and museums.

St. Petersburg also has an emerging entrepreneurial ecology. For example, the Greenhouse offers experts and resources to help new entrepreneurs transform their idea into an enterprise and to encourage existing small business owners to grow. The Greenhouse is housed in the oldest surviving school building in St. Pete's. (The two-story building is constructed of yellow brick but the large front doors are green.)

Not far from the Greenhouse is the Innovation Lab at the Poynter Institute (a leading media think tank). The Innovation Lab is one of the larger coworking spaces in the Tampa Bay region. Among its tenants is REUNIONCare, founded by Monica Stynchula. The company uses information technologies to integrate health care professionals with far-flung family members. Local Eckerd College is active in supporting the entrepreneurial community both on and off campus.

Entrepreneur ecology stories like St. Petersburg's are being written across the country. Colleges and universities are embracing entrepreneurship. Cities and towns welcome incubators, work-sharing spaces, accelerators, startup competitions, and other initiatives to nurture local entrepreneurs. There are nearly 1,000 Small Business Development Centers (SBDCs) housed at colleges and state economic development agencies that provide free business consulting and low-cost training. The Service Corps of Retired Executives, better known as SCORE, is staffed with volunteers who act as mentors to startups.

How about New York City? There are now nearly 210,000 self-employed residents ages 50 years and over, up 19 percent from 2005. These entrepreneurs are launching businesses from their homes and from shared office spaces. The businesses range from offering professional services leveraging their skills and networks developed over the years to artisan food makers like bakers and specialty candies. A recent study by the Center for an Urban Future, a New York City-based think tank, says that chambers of commerce, small business assistance providers, and microfinance organizations that "work with aspiring entrepreneurs report that New Yorkers over age 50 have gone from a sliver of their clients to one-quarter or more."[6]

Take the experience of Senior Planet in New York City. It was started in 2006 by the Brooklyn-based nonprofit Older Adults Technology Services (OATS). Senior Planet's flagship space in Manhattan's Chelsea neighborhood helps people 60 years and older become comfortable with information technologies like computers and tablets. The staff eventually realized that growing numbers of clients wanted assistance in developing their entrepreneurial ideas and learning business-savvy digital skills. Senior Planet started offering courses on entrepreneurship several years ago, and in 2017, it launched the formal Startup! program.

"We realized that people had an untapped power that they really wanted to unleash as they got older," said Alex Glazebrook, Senior

Planet's director of training and technology. "We thought about it and developed an entrepreneurial program that offers a whole medley of skills and activities to get people to unleash their entrepreneurial spirit."[7]

Rachel Roth is an entrepreneur. She walked into Senior Planet one day to see if the staff could help her solve a tech problem: Labels. She needed help making labels for her product, the "delicious and nutritious indulgence" Opera Nuts. "Someone walked me through the process," says Roth. "It was a big thing."

Roth is "older than 65 and under 100." She grew up in Hibbing, Minnesota, the heart of Minnesota's Iron Range and home of singer Bob Dylan when he was known as Robert Zimmerman. A fashion journalist at one point, she also had a long corporate career in marketing in the fashion industry. Roth is also something of a serial entrepreneur. She came up with A Moveable Feast Picnics that offered diners healthy gourmet alternatives to the hot dogs and beans sold at Tanglewood in Lenox, Massachusetts. Rachel's Table was a venture that let people entertain clients in her home. She created Rachel's Guiltless Cakebreads after being diagnosed with high cholesterol.

Her latest venture started in 2012. She devised a confection of dark chocolate and California almonds in a sea salt sauce. An opera lover, she named the product Opera Nuts. Her product is mostly a holiday season item available in some thirty states and four to five countries, including Australia and the United Kingdom. Roth stays engaged with Senior Planet as mentor to other older entrepreneurs. "Senior Planet is very energizing," she says. "It's what you need when you're an entrepreneur."

Other experienced entrepreneurs are well versed in their business, but their marketing skills were honed during the predigital age. Sometimes they need help reaching customers in a wired economy. Like Madelyn Rich, 73 years old.

Rich worked during her career as a bank officer, a paralegal, and a clinical social worker. She always had a side business that drew on her creative talents, especially her love of knitting and sewing. She now supplements her income in retirement with her small design business of accessories, including handbags, totes, mittens, and scarfs. Her designs are "fun, funky, and functional." She develops new products every year to keep existing customers coming back. "You always have to reinvent yourself," she says. Laughing, she adds "I am a small-scale Nike!"

Rich stumbled on Senior Planet during a walk in 2012. She attended classes to learn online skills. She also worked with the Local Development Corporation of East New York (part of the NYC Small Business Technology Coalition) for her website. The day we talked, she had been at Senior Planet in Chelsea getting instruction on improving her facility with Instagram. "Social media isn't my strong point," she says.

Rich isn't making the kind of money she did as a full-time employee. She also has no interest in getting a traditional job. "I would rather eat cat food," she said with a chuckle. "I want to spend time on what I enjoy. I don't need a whole bag of money. If I can supplement my retirement income, I'm happy. And I'm supplementing my income."

The Fueled Collective cosharing workspace in Minneapolis, Minnesota, is hip, the kind of place designed to appeal to millennials. The workspace is housed in the historic trading floor of the Minneapolis Grain Exchange. The 20,000-square-foot facility was mostly built in 1903. The commodity trading boards still line one wall with listed prices. The massive trading floor is now covered with a maze of work tables, white boards, lounge chairs, high-speed wireless, Zen garden, and other modern-day hallmarks of the creative enterprise. (Fueled Collective was previously known as CoCo.)

The design may be millennial-inspired, but walk the floor like I did several years ago and you'll see plenty of gray and white hair. While there, I met with Jeffrey Brown. In his early 70s, Brown has an infectious laugh. The serial entrepreneur claims he's a "failure at retirement." His latest venture is using advanced information technologies to lower the cost to immigrants remitting money back home. He mentors other entrepreneurs and sometimes invests in their businesses. "It keeps me young," says Brown. "It keeps my brain working when I get to interact with all kinds of people, all ages and genders and ethnicities."

Marketer Dan Wallace and designer Kris LaFavor, both in their late 50s, shared space with Brown. The three of them have known one another for a long time, and they often collaborate on projects. They've also gone on "innovation vacations" together, attending South by Southwest in Austin, Texas, and Berkshire Hathaway's "Capitalist Woodstock" in Omaha, Nebraska. "We are always playing off each other," says Brown. (When I talked to them at Fueled Collective, rubber ducky versions of Berkshire Hathaway investing legends Warren Buffett and Charles Munger stared at me the whole time.)

The three no longer work together as a group at Fueled Collective, although they stay in touch. Jeff Brown joined a different coworking space. LaFavor still has a place at Fueled Collective, but with a smaller plan. She carved out a niche for herself in the customer experience journey mapping space in addition to her branding work. Dan Wallace coauthored *The Physics of Brand* and still runs his marketing business out of the old Minneapolis Grain Exchange building.

Wallace believes joining the coworking space was "one of the best decisions" he had ever made. "In particular, it was important because our small band took a chance on being pioneers of a new concept, which attracted diverse people with growth and innovation mindsets," he reflects. "Those relationships and the learning from those experiences continue to support me. I think it's important to take more chances as we age, not less."

The gig economy is also opening new opportunities for older workers to earn an income. Also known as the share economy and on-demand economy, the work is entrepreneurial. You're using your car or your home or your accumulated skills to make some money on the side. The gigs come from a scheduling app developed and owned by a high-tech company. Among the best known brands in the expanding share economy ecosystem are the drive-sharing services Uber and Lyft, the home sharing businesses Airbnb and VRBO and home chore TaskRabbit and the professional service connector Fiverr.

Like co-working spaces, the gig economy seems nearly synonymous with millennials. The reality is that more and more older Americans are participating since online platforms allow for flexible work schedules and earning an income off accumulated assets. A study by the JPMorgan Chase Institute estimates that there are over 400,000 people 65 years and older earning money in the share economy. Looking closely at more than 260,000 anonymized Chase customers who worked with at least one of 30 platforms between October 2012 and September 2015, the researchers found an astonishingly rapid rate of increase. Specifically, the cumulative participation rate growth went from 0.1 percent of adults to 4.2 percent—a 47-fold growth!

Sue Johnson is part of the gig economy. She's in her 70s. Johnson is a former entrepreneur and real estate agent in the Twin Cities. She's a grandmother.[8]

Johnson also drives for Uber to supplement her income. "I've always worked, so I've never developed the retirement skills," she says with a laugh.

A big attraction of this kind of piecework to her is its flexibility. She had worked as a receptionist at a senior center, but she didn't like sticking to a set schedule. Her driving gig allows her to work when she wants. She doesn't drive at night. "It's nice to be able to say yes, I can meet you for lunch, or to be able to be home with a sick grandchild or pick them up," she says. "That's a good thing too."

Johnson enjoys talking to customers and most of her trips are to the Twin Cities airport. She doesn't make much money, but she earns enough to pay for an annual trip with a group of friends and to visit her daughter in Arizona. "Making a little money is probably a good idea," she says. "You don't want to outlive your money."

The job suits Johnson. To be sure, gig economy jobs like hers are controversial. Gig economy work doesn't come with health insurance or an employer-sponsored retirement savings plan. The job is financially insecure for young workers trying to support a family. (Of course, if they're moonlighting for some extra money, fine.) That said, experienced workers like Johnson have a safety net of earned benefits like Social Security and Medicare. The earned-benefit safety net system encourages her entrepreneurship in her 70s.

We may be having something of a self-employment echo from an earlier era. Self-employment at the end of the nineteenth century and early twentieth century was relatively common at retirement age. America was an agricultural economy dominated by small owner-occupied farms. Richard Sutch is an economic historian at the University of California, Berkeley. He notes in an email exchange and subsequent conversation about some of his research the fact that more than one-third of the total labor force in the United States was self-employed in 1900 is hardly surprising. It's the kind of data you would expect with the farm economy of the time. That 24 percent of the nonfarm labor force in the United States was self-employed in 1900 is a revelation, however. But the self-employment rates for the male labor force rose with age from virtually nothing at age 16 to over 30 percent by age 60 in 1900. "Over 30 percent of all working men aged 60 and over were self-employed that year," says Sutch. "These patterns suggest that self-employment was less taxing on one's energy and health than wage labor. Perhaps for many self-employment was a form of 'partial retirement' or phased retirement. . . . The fact that workers at the turn of the twentieth century increasingly moved to self-employment as they aged suggests that self-employment represented a gilded age version of the American dream: work, save, acquire capital, become your own boss."[9]

Sutch adds that less-than-benign factors also account for the embrace of self-employment late in life in the early 1900s. Sometimes self-employment was nothing but disguised unemployment, typified by the rag picker and sidewalk apple seller. Legally sanctioned discrimination and deep cultural prejudices meant older members of some ethnic groups had no choice but to be self-employed, such as Chinese-Americans and Jewish immigrants.

Thankfully, there's Social Security, Medicare, perhaps a retirement savings account, and even a pension to boost the income of the experienced self-employed person these days. Think Sue Johnson!

The desire to own a small business runs strong throughout U.S. history. "What became the United States of America was born of entrepreneurship," Northwestern University economist Louis Cain opens his essay on the subject.[10] "Entrepreneurship has been central to our nation since its inception," writes Scott Shane, professor of entrepreneurial studies at Case Western Reserve in his book on startups.[11] "Entrepreneur. Americans have fallen in love with this French noun, which the dictionary tells us means 'one who manages, and assumes the risks of, a business or enterprise,'" observe historians Robert Sobel and David Sicilia in *The Entrepreneurs: An American Adventure*.[12]

Entrepreneurs are admired. Farmers, merchants, craftsman, artisans, and small manufacturers dominated popular images of business in eighteenth-century America. Nineteenth-century entrepreneurs like Andrew Carnegie, John D. Rockefeller, P. T. Barnum, and Gustavus Franklin Swift helped shape the American economy, much like twentieth-century entrepreneurs Steve Jobs, Bill Gates, Jim Clark, and Sergey Brin. From the eighteenth-century admonitions of Benjamin Franklin through the nineteenth-century rags-to-riches tales of Horatio Alger to the twenty-first-century guidance of Peter Thiel's *Zero to One*, Americans have embraced guides on how to be an entrepreneur.

Immigrants and entrepreneurship are practically synonymous. Highly educated immigrants have been critical to the global success of America's cutting-edge industries. Less-credentialed immigrants have created many smaller businesses in neighborhoods and communities throughout the country, such as restaurants and corner grocery stores. Entrepreneurship is a defining attribute of the American experience.

A survey from the 1950s of industrial workers by two University of Michigan sociologists suggests the cultural pull of entrepreneurship.

The scholars report that many factory workers dreamed of owning a small business of their own. Harvard University sociologist David Riesman reacted to the survey by wondering if the common practice of moonlighting among factory workers wasn't driven by the desire for more money to buy more consumer goods—the traditional explanation.[13]

Instead, he thought, moonlighting might signal the powerful urge to exercise control and creativity over their work. (Riesman speculated that the practice of moonlighting suggested "many factory workers are like the Russian peasants who were drafted into collective farms: they give a minimum quantum of their work to the factory as the peasants did to the farms, and save up their real energies for the 'private plots' of their work outside.") Similarly, studies by sociologists Seymour Martin Lipset and Reinhard Bendix in the 1950s found factory workers wanted to leave the assembly line and become "[their] own boss."[14]

Attitudes like these about entrepreneurship are remarkably durable. What has changed in recent decades is advanced information technologies. The rise of service and information industries make the transition into entrepreneurship increasingly practical, especially for older adults with experience.

Entrepreneurs are a diverse group. Some older entrepreneurs are highly ambitious. They hope to create a durable enterprise that will outlive them. Other older entrepreneurs are looking more for the kind of enterprise that will supplement their retirement income and offer flexible hours.

Count Sharon Emek, veteran insurance industry professional and owner, among the ambitious entrepreneurs. Her story combines many elements of the new unretirement entrepreneurial economy.

Emek had an inspiration in the early 2000s. Concerns were mounting among insurers over the industry's older-than-average workforce. The insurance industry wasn't attracting many replacements from younger generations. Information technologies were making it practical to work from home, including the iPhone which was released in 2007. Putting the two together—the demographics of an aging insurance workforce and high-tech gear—Emek realized that "there's a business opportunity" to exploit.[15]

In 2010, at age 64, she created a new staffing company, Work At Home Vintage Employees LLC or WAHVE. The company finds veteran insurance professionals 50 years and older who would like to phase into retirement. Her staffing agency works with long-time insurance industry workers in the property/casualty side of the business who want to continue earning an income, work from home, and enjoy flexible hours. She later expanded her business model to include accountants. Emek calls WAHVE workers "pretired."[16]

The insurance workers typically put in about twenty-five hours a week. Take-home pay is between $35,000 and $50,000 a year without benefits. The accounting workers earn more, somewhere from $40,000 to $70,000 annually, again, without benefits. Emek would like to expand her business to include other knowledge-based workers.

"They don't have enough retirement money," says Emek. "They may have to stay home to take care of grandchildren while their daughter is getting chemotherapy or help out aging parents. They want to work but they don't want to work nine to five."

Among those insurance industry workers is Judy Bush of Waynesboro, Virginia. Bush enjoyed more than two decades in the insurance business, including account manager with a large book of business. Her last few years on the job were hard after developing a bad back, a condition exacerbated by driving eighty miles in her daily commute to her job. "I was seriously considering filing for disability," she says. "I was 58, and I wasn't ready to get out of the workforce."

Thanks to WAHVE, she works five hours a day from her home office assisting two account managers in Texas on their personal line insurance business. (Personal lines involve home, auto, motorcycles, and the like.) She's familiar with their job, and her task is to provide support services, pulling documents together and entering data, taking on back office processes so that the account managers in Texas can focus on clients. Her "commute" is walking up one flight of stairs to her home office. She and her husband calculate their living standards are about the same, despite fewer hours. The main reason is lower work-related expenses, from gas bills to the dry-cleaning tab.

"It has allowed me to remain productive and stay in an industry I spent twenty-one years developing a career, and it allows me to keep up with changes in the insurance industry," she says.

She has been "WAHVEing" for four years. Her husband is also joining WAHVE on the accounting side. Assuming he gets an assignment, they may decide to move since they can live anywhere so long as it has good internet service. "Wouldn't that be awesome to not be held down to one location because of your job?" she says. "Think of the freedom that would give us."

Where might they go? They own a Virginia farm, but they have their eyes on a couple of places in North Carolina with "beautiful waterfront views." That's cool.

Emek has built an enterprise with management, back office workers, and far flung staffing relationships. Most older entrepreneurs develop much smaller enterprises.

Lifestyle businesses are popular. These small businesses include selling artwork, owning a yoga studio, running a massage business, teaching meditation, and supplying local restaurants with vegetables and spices grown on a small plot of land.

The internet and information technologies have lowered startup costs for these experienced solopreneurs and microentrepreneurs. It's a misconception that entrepreneurs in the second half of life must risk draining their retirement savings to start an enterprise. You shouldn't, and there is no need to do so.

"You won't make a ton of money," says Steve King, founder of Emergent Research, a consulting firm for small businesses based in Lafayette, California. That said, it's relatively easy to "test your business idea" on the cheap these days, he adds. There's no reason to risk retirement savings, home equity, or other scarce savings in pursuit of a business venture. "You take a little risk, and if it doesn't work out, it doesn't work," says King. "If it does catch on, then you grow the business, if that's what you want to do."

■

Parents are going into business with their adult children. Multigener-
ational business startups are one of the more exciting social and economic trends in the U.S. They're also underappreciated.

Surveys repeatedly show that young adults get along with their parents, and vice versa. Multigenerational startups are popular. Boomers
typically have some capital and plenty of experience to bring into the
multigenerational enterprise. Their adult children offer high energy
and are tech savvy. "Most boomers have a much more friend-based,
adult-to-adult relationship with their children than boomers did with
their parents," says Steve King of Emergent Research. "Boomers are
close to their kids, and the kids are close to their parents. It's a big
social shift."

Take Case and David Bloom.[17] They were co-owners of Nashville,
Tennessee-based Tucker & Bloom, a maker of highly crafted mes-
senger bags targeted at the DJ market. David had worked for more
than three decades in bag design, from handbags to luggage. Just
prior to 9/11, he started a job as director of travel products for Coach,
splitting his time between home in Nashville and an apartment in
New York City. In the aftermath of the tragedy, the luggage business
shrank dramatically. He lost his job.

Back in Nashville, he picked up work here and there, setting up
his own bag business. His son, Case, had hoped to go to art school in
New York, but with money tight, he went to college in Nashville and
concentrated his coursework on business. "His logo was so bad. Hor-
rible," laughs Case. "I'd tell him you're doing it wrong. 'Do it like this,'
I'd say. Eventually it became 'we' should do it this way. The business
happened organically."

David handled design and product development of the bags made
in their small factory in Nashville. Case was in charge of brand image
and online sales. Case is also a part-time DJ. "I have a different set of
skills than my father," he says.

Change has come to the business. David has multiple sclerosis
and his deteriorating health finally forced him to retire. Case now

owns the company. He is expanding its product line into other bags, such as handbags. He's negotiating with potential overseas partners since the DJ market is international. Case still consults with his father about bag design. "He's an incredible resource of knowledge," says Case. "When it comes to new product development he has good actionable advice."

Amanda Bates is close to her mother, Kit Seay. They co-own Tiny Pies in Austin, Texas. "We've always had a close relationship, feeding off one another, finishing each other's sentences," says Seay, now in her late 70s.

Seay has retired twice. First, she retired from her job with the state of Texas. She soon unretired to become house director at the Tri Delta sorority at the University of Texas in Austin for a decade. She retired from that position when her daughter approached her about going into business together.

Here's the backstory: Several years before going into business, the Gen Xer Bates got divorced. She was selling real estate in Austin, Texas, but she didn't like her job. Bates got the idea for handheld pies from her son's desire to take pie to school. Mother and daughter started selling small pies based on Seay's family recipes in local farmers' markets in 2011. They now have two retail stores in Austin, one in the south part of town and the other on the north side. "It has been wonderful," says Seay. "The best part of my working life is the time with Amanda."

Seay was initially the baker. Once they hired a professional baker, she largely focused on the catering and wedding planning side of the business. Her daughter runs the enterprise. "The trust is there," says Seay.

Bates agrees. "Yes, the trust is there. If she says something will get done, it will."

At age 77, Seay is thinking about retiring again—her third try! She will take several months off to do some traveling. "I am really trying to retire," she says, laughing. "I am trying to step out when I can."

Bert Weber, age 63, and his son Christian, age 31, clearly get along. When Bert retired from three decades of teaching in Hudson Falls,

New York, he kept himself busy, bringing in an income by consulting with small family farmers for Cornell Cooperative Extension. Like many recent retirees, he was looking for his next chapter. Christian was employed at a small environmental nonprofit in Lake Placid. He liked the job, and the income helped pay down his student loans. But Christian dreamed of starting a craft beer brewery.[18] He had worked at some small breweries in New Hampshire while in graduate school.

Father and son took a long drive in 2012 from South Glens Falls to Salisbury, Maryland. They were biking in the annual Sea Gull Century bike ride along the Eastern Shore of Maryland. They decided to take the plunge and go into the beer business. Common Roots Brewing Company opened for business in 2014. "I liked the concept," says Bert. "I loved the idea of my son for a business partner."

They came up with a plan and successfully applied for a small business loan for $435,000. In 2014, Common Roots Brewing Company opened in South Glens Falls. Three years after its debut, the venture has twenty employees, and it's on track to sell 5,000 barrels of beer, ten times more than its first year. (Bert's wife and Christian's mom now keeps the books for the business.)

"It has been so much fun to work together on projects, to see how passionate he is about the work," says Bert.

Adds Christian: "We quickly learned what our strengths were, and we support each other."

The members of the Bruch family also support one another. Their improbable business story begins about a decade ago, when the family decided to open a retail store following a lunch conversation at a restaurant in Hudson, Wisconsin. Hudson is a small river town along the banks of the St. Croix River with an historic district and plenty of restaurants. The lunch included Elizabeth, a part-time college professor and, at the time 65 years old; her husband, Dan, a retired pastor, 70 years of age; and two of their children, Sarah and Angela, ages 37 and 43, respectively. They debated what they could do to lean against an increasingly polarized society. They hit on the idea of a retail store that sells sustainable products with bipartisan appeal.

Sarah's sister Angela wrote the business plan. The Purple Tree opened in Hudson six weeks after the luncheon agreement, with the family putting up some $20,000. (Purple is a mix of red and blue.)

The family has always been close, so they have consistently found ways to work things out. "We don't always agree," says Sarah, the only family member working full time at the Purple Tree. "But we have managed to successfully agree to disagree, and we have been able to reach compromises. We always find a way to talk things out."

Elizabeth (the Mom) works at the store part-time. She's clearly having a lot of fun with the enterprise. "I will always be one of those people working in retirement," she says. I guess I am a working-in-retirement person."

How about Dr. Samuel Lupin? Back in 2004 when he was 66 years old, he dropped his private medical office practice in Brooklyn, New York. He became an old-fashioned solo practitioner making house calls on his elderly patients. Dr. Lupin wanted a more flexible schedule to help care for his critically ill daughter. She died a year later.

He stuck with his practice of treating patients in their homes. When he was nearing age 70, his grandson Daniel Stokar approached him with a business proposition: to tether modern telecommunications to old-fashioned medical visits for the frail, home-bound elderly. Intrigued, Dr. Lupin agreed to delay his long-planned retirement at age 70 for six months, while Daniel developed the Brooklyn-based venture.

Daniel's father Ari—a computer whiz—was also part of the business. He developed its information technology system. The multi-generational enterprise Housecalls for the Homebound operates in all five boroughs. The business treats homebound elderly patients. Dr. Lupin is its medical director. He stopped making house calls. "We are on the leading edge of value-based care," says Daniel.

"What about that retirement plan from seven years ago?", I asked.

"I may just stay the way I am for the foreseeable future," Dr. Lupin replied. "It is such an unbelievable pleasure to see the project as it evolves and continues to expand."

Little wonder this three-generation enterprise was recognized by Encore.org in 2015 with the Purpose Prize for Intergenerational Collaboration (sponsored by The Eisner Foundation).[19]

Technology isn't the only major force in the economy boosting prospects for second-life entrepreneurship—including multigenerational entrepreneurship. Another transformation supporting the creation of new businesses by experienced workers is the rise of craft industries and artisan businesses. Artisans combine time-honored techniques and individual creativity with modern technologies.

Craft work blends purpose and a paycheck. People in craft industries often talk about how much fun they're having creating products and building their business. The traditional barriers between leisure (fun) and work (hard) crumble. "Craftsmanship names an enduring, basic human impulse, the desire to do a job well for its own sake," writes sociologist Richard Sennett in *The Craftsman*.[20]

Merit Shalett worked for two decades as associate director of the Contemporary Arts Center New Orleans, a multidisciplinary performance space. A new director came in and Shalett, after helping with the transition, felt it was time for a change. Several years ago, at age 61, she joined her husband and then 31-year-old son at Faubourg Farms, a sustainable straw bale urban farming operation in two locations in the Big Easy. (The produce is grown in straw bales that naturally feed the plants as they decompose.) Faubourg Farms primarily grows hardy greens like kale, arugula, and pak choi (a Chinese cabbage also known as bok choy), all of which they use in their small-batch recipes. "We've always valued good food," she says. "It's exciting that so many people are beginning to embrace the culture of co-ops and urban farming here in New Orleans."[21]

She also developed Faubourg Farms' flagship product, "Mom's Dressing." When they first began selling their produce at farmers' markets, they wanted to entice customers by sampling their organic greens with their family salad dressing. "Mom's Dressing" is a lemon vinaigrette recipe using locally foraged Meyer Lemons as the primary ingredient. They had been working at expanding into the wholesale business with grocery stores. But the family members were dismayed by some of the compromises they would have to make with ingredients and packaging to succeed in the wholesale side of the industry.

Forget making concessions. Shalett and her son, during one of their periodic business meetings, decided to shift the emphasis of the business in 2018. (Her husband weighs in on the business from the sidelines.) They would no longer try to break into the wholesale business. Instead, they would continue their focus on farmers' markets and put greater effort into their "pop-ups." The pop-up menu offers customers a choice of three salad bowls, ten toppings, and Mom's Dressing on the side. This way, they can keep their ingredients local and rotate them depending on the season. She's excited about the new direction. She also loves working with her son. "It's the best," she says.

Now 65 years old, Shalett has developed a consulting business on the side that draws on her skills developed at the Contemporary Arts Center. Companies hire her to set up events, including some VIP gatherings in California. "I am still holding my own with the younger people," she says, laughing.

For a long time it seemed that artisans were artifacts, largely driven out of business or sidelined with the rise of efficient mass production in the nineteenth and twentieth centuries. Yet the new generation of artisans and craftspeople—mostly small businesses and often founded and staffed by people in the second half of life—have emerged in recent years as a potent economic force. The Intuit Future of Small Business Series notes that these small craft businesses will reach much bigger markets than their historic predecessors, thanks to advanced technologies. They'll partner with larger firms when it makes sense. Most importantly, artisan business will attract a highly skilled labor force that wants to learn a craft, including many workers in the second half of life.

Richard Sennett, sociologist at New York University and at the London School of Economics, is something of a philosopher of craft. In his thoughtful exploration of craft in the modern era, he observes that craft is a practical activity, but the work also provides meaning and engagement. "Competence and engagement—the craftman's ethos—appear to be the most solid source of adult self-respect, according to many studies conducted in Britain and the U.S.," Sennett observes in an essay. To be sure, he goes on to note, mastering a craft isn't easy. "But most people have it in them to become good craftsmen. They have the capacities to become better at, and more involved in, what they do—the abilities to localise, question and open up problems that can result, eventually, in good work. Even if society does not reward people who have made this effort as much as it should, in the end, they can achieve a sense of self-worth—which is reward enough."[22]

Perhaps the dominant image for those looking for purpose and a paycheck in the second half of life is participating in the craft economy. The activity is entrepreneurial and creative. Not every experienced worker will find an artisan job or start a craft business. Far from it, of course. But the aspiration among so many older entrepreneurs and experienced workers reflects the deep desire that the returns to labor reflect quality, community, and creativity; that our work makes a difference—leaves a legacy—even if only in small ways.

"Hot dog stand" memories pull people from their unretirement into entrepreneurship. I met the "hot dog man" years ago at the Pearl Street Mall in downtown Boulder, Colorado. A somewhat rakish-looking man with his white mustache and white hair hanging over his collar, he was doing a brisk business selling Chicago hot dogs from his cart.

You couldn't miss him. His voice boomed in cadence, "Hot dog, hot dog, hot dog, Pepsi, Pepsi, chips, chips." A long line snaked across the plaza as people lined up for their Chicago dogs, including me.

Later that afternoon, when the crowd had died down, we got to talking. Eddie Ermoian grew up in Chicago's Armenian community, not far from Wrigley Field. He used to hang out on game days with the Armenian hot dog sellers who worked the street corners outside the baseball stadium.

"My mother used to say, when other kids wanted to be firemen or cowboys or policemen or whatever, I wanted to have a hot dog stand," he says, laughing.

Ermoian worked for a beer company for some four decades. He married, raised a family, and eventually owned a piece of a beer distributorship. When he retired at age 57, he remembered his dream of owning a hot dog stand. He took some savings, bought a cart and opened Fast Eddie's World Famous Hot Dogs not far from the Boulder County Courthouse.

"Everybody always has a hot dog stand in the back of their mind," he said.[23]

For Sylvia Burgos Toftness, her "hot dog stand" was a farm. When she was in her late 50s, Toftness found herself commuting sixty-five miles each way from her home in rural Wisconsin to her public relations job in downtown St. Paul. During those long drives, she thought about what she and her husband, Dave, a chiropractor, might do next (what I call their unretirement years).[24]

Fond family memories pushed her toward the idea of owning a sustainable farm. Her grandparents grew up on a small farm in Puerto Rico before moving to Manhattan as young adults. Toftness was raised in the Bronx, but during the summer, her extended family spent weekends at a Latino collective on Staten Island called "Spanish Camp." Many families had large gardens. Her grandmother grew tomatoes in their small yard.

When Toftness graduated from college, she left the Bronx behind and headed to Minnesota for a career mostly in media, public relations, and nonprofit work.

She knew she wanted farming in her life, but she didn't know what it would look like. When her husband suggested retiring to an old, small farm, she was determined it would be a working business enterprise. Her husband responded, "Everyone who goes into farming ends up destitute."

To prevent that outcome, she and her husband took farming classes, learned from nearby farmers, and established a realistic budget. After much planning and education, at age 60, they bought a small herd of cattle and started raising grass-fed, grass-finished beef on some eighty acres of land. Toftness makes additional income teaching baking classes in her kitchen and preparing three-course, linens-and-fine-china, Cowgirl High Teas once or twice a month. "It's about providing an opportunity for visitors to experience what sustainable agriculture, and real food prepared tastefully, are all about," she says.

Her husband continues with his chiropractor business in the nearby town. They didn't put their retirement savings at risk either.

"We didn't want to run out of money. The aim was to break even, and we have done better than that," she says. "The farm has a mission. We are stewards. The cattle must be treated well. The land must be treated well."

The farmhouse is nestled into a small ridge on one side of the farm. The barn is a good walk away on the other side. The cattle with a white band in their middle have been bred for the cold climate of the upper Midwest. The work is physical.

When I visited the farm, we walked out into the fields. Sylvia had to feed the calf Annie with a giant milk bottle. Annie was ill, and she had been abandoned by her mother. While feeding Annie, Sylvia tells stories about breaking ice in the water trough several times a day during one very hard winter, and how voracious hawks defeated their efforts to raise chickens on the property. Her enthusiasm for what she is doing is clear.

What would she recommend if someone thought farming might make for a good encore career? She would have them think first about their life goals. Take the time to write down the key points about the day and the life they want to live. Here are some of her suggested questions:

- Do you want to wake at 5:00 a.m. or ease into the day?
- Do you like spending weekend afternoons wandering bookstores?

- Is it important to you to travel and visit friends a few times a year?
- Do you want to attend sports events or recitals with the young relatives in your family?
- Do you like to be able to travel to foreign countries at a moment's notice?
- Do you want to be able to periodically upgrade your vehicles and home?
- Do you want to be able to interact with customers on a daily or weekly basis?

"Answer these quality-of-life questions first. Be brutally honest," she says. "The answers are your base values and needs. Once you have these in front of you, then you can explore the types of farming that will support your needs and goals. Deciding on the farming product or technique first could lead to financial strain and hurtful frustration."

Good advice for anyone thinking through a major transition. What really stuck with me as we drove away from her farm in rural Wisconsin was how she defined retirement during our conversation. "For me, retirement doesn't mean stopping. It means shifting," she says. "It means now I get to do something else I really want to do."

That's a good definition of the movement to rethink and reimagine the opportunities opened by increased longevity.

7

Doing Well by Doing Good

Life teaches you how to live it, if you live long enough.

—TONY BENNETT[1]

Michael Butler, age 60, wants to make the world a better place. Specifically, he is creating Novocognia, the chronic kidney disease education specialists. Novocognia will help at-risk minority populations identify, manage, and achieve better health results for all stages of chronic kidney disease. "That is my elevator speech," says Butler.[2]

Butler grew up in Florida and moved to New York in his early 20s. His career was in the health care industry, including EKG technician and sales representative for a pacemaker company. For the past nine years, he has been a kidney dialysis patient. Like many dialysis patients, he went through an early difficult period with the demanding three-times-a-week treatment. "Dialysis is an art form," he says. "There is a steep learning curve for the nephrologist and the patient."

The experience pushed the East Village resident to become a certified patient advocate. He also learned he had another skill—public speaking. Butler was in a nocturnal dialysis program. It's a slower, longer treatment that takes place at night while sleeping. He was invited to speak at industry conferences and gatherings about living with dialysis and his experience with nocturnal dialysis. "I'm not a public speaker," says Butler. "But this resonated with me. It all came together."

Butler is concerned about rising numbers of minorities needing dialysis and well-documented disparities in their treatment. The people he sees at the dialysis center he attends in New York City seem younger to him, in their 30s and 40s. He was also concerned at how little people knew about dialysis when they came to the treatment center. "They know nothing when they come to the dialysis center," he says. "I'm thinking, why aren't they getting help? I felt compelled to do something."

He was still mulling over what to do when he signed up for the entrepreneurship class at Senior Planet in Manhattan. "Immediately, I had my 'aha moment,'" he says. "Let me start a business and address health care disparities felt by minority populations."

He is working with lawyers to get his enterprise set up. The legal advisors are recommending a hybrid nonprofit and for-profit business model. He has two mentors from SCORE, the Service Corps of Retired Executives. These veteran executives volunteer to help small businesses owners start and grow their enterprise. One of his SCORE mentors is knowledgeable about nonprofits and the other is well-versed in branding. He has signed up several board members. "I am surprised at myself," he says. "I am not a business person."

He is passionate about the project. When I talked to him in the summer of 2018, Butler was still refining the business plan. He was spending time trying to understand the nonprofit world better. The initial focus of the kidney disease education initiative to minority communities will be workshops, seminars, and (eventually) online education. He plans on starting the outreach efforts with minority churches, where he has good connections. He'll also reach out to schools. His instructors will include his fellow dialysis patient advocates.

Older people share a strong desire to see that they have made a difference when they look back on what they've done through the years. "Most do not fear dying nearly as much they do the prospect of having lived a meaningless life," write Richard Leider and David Shapiro in *Work Reimagined: Uncover Your Calling.* "We want to have made some 'small dent' in the world."[3]

Lots of "small dents" are being made in the longevity economy. The lure of social entrepreneurship is strong in the second half of life. These are for-profit and nonprofit companies started by entrepreneurs and explicitly designed to do good. A similar entrepreneurial mind-set is behind an even larger movement of older adults retiring from their professional and for-profit careers into encore careers at nonprofit organizations. Older adults are active volunteers. The annual economic value of volunteer activities for adults 55 years and older is $75 billion, estimates the Corporation for National and Community Service.[4]

These mission-driven efforts add value to the economy and society. Social entrepreneurs draw on years of experience and skill to connect the dots in new ways to address social problems. Older workers looking for second careers and postretirement jobs (often part-time and flexible schedules) are bringing their insights and knowledge into the nonprofit sector. Volunteers are passionate participants in the social mission of nonprofit organizations and religious institutions. "Volunteering and paid work produce better physical and mental health," says Linda Fried, dean of the Mailman School of Public Health at Columbia University. "People need purpose. They need a reason to get up in the morning."

David Campbell is something of an accidental social entrepreneur. He enjoyed a forty-year-plus career in the high-tech industry as an executive. He retired in 2004 at age 63. During lunch with a close friend in Boston shortly after retiring, their conversation turned to the Indian Ocean tsunami that had recently wreaked havoc in Thailand. He decided to help.

He wasn't quite sure how he could best assist rescue efforts. Campbell flew to Bang Tao in Thailand and set up a base at a hotel that survived the tsunami. He picked the hotel because it had a working internet connection, and he quickly learned he could be useful by coordinating efforts of other volunteers. He took that experience to run a similar volunteer effort following Hurricane Katrina in 2005.

Campbell created All Hands Volunteers in 2005. The nonprofit organization sends thousands of volunteers to disaster zones around the world. The volunteers pay their way and, in return, All Hands deals with the logistics. Campbell drew on his experience as an executive in the high-tech industry. He understood the power of the internet to make connections, and he had managed partnerships and diverse workforces during his career. (Campbell was a recipient of the 2014 Purpose Prize for Future Promise. The Purpose Prize highlights the achievements for the common good by people 50 years and over.)

"It's like starting a small business," he says. "If you talk to someone who opened a restaurant, it's really challenging to get through the first five years. We proved we could be effective."

Campbell is a big believer in transparency in an organization and in testing out ideas. Try something. Get feedback from people. Work on the idea and improve it. "Any social entrepreneur has to think through who is their target audience and how will you reach them," says Campbell.

In 2017, the organization merged with another nonprofit, the Happy Hearts Fund founded by supermodel Petra Němcová in 2005. She too was in Thailand during the 2005 tsunami and lost her fiancé to the devastation. Happy Hearts was created by her to work with communities hit by natural disasters. The two organizations collaborated in Nepal to build disaster-resilient schools following the devastating earthquake in 2015. They merged in 2017. The new social enterprise is called All Hands and Hearts—Smart Response.

Anne Patterson's story echoes Campbell's, although she embraced the for-profit business model rather than nonprofit. Now in her early 60s, she also had a long high-tech career, including stints at Hewlett

Packard, Next, and 3Comm. She and her husband were sailing in the Caribbean, and she fell in love with a solar oven manufactured by the Solar Oven Society, a nonprofit organization started by Mike and Martha Port.

Based in St. Paul, Minnesota, the oven and its assembly were designed by retired 3M engineers. The oven's target market was developing countries, and it offered the promise of cooking with sunlight instead of wood. The smoke from wood fire cooking is bad for health. Patterson learned that, after some dozen years, the Ports wanted out of the grind of running the nonprofit. The business was essentially shut down. Patterson and a small group of investors bought the solar oven business in 2012 and renamed it Solavore (which in Latin means "devour the sun").

Remember the Remington electric shaver commercials starring Victor Kiam and his famous catchphrase, "I liked the shaver so much, I bought the company." Patterson laughs. "I feel like Victor Kiam—I liked the solar cooker so much, I bought the company."

Solavore is no longer a nonprofit. Instead, it's a limited liability company (LLC). In her encore career, Patterson sees Solavore as a social enterprise with a triple bottom line: Profit, purpose, and planet. The goal is to distribute the solar ovens in the parts of the world still using wood fires. The solar oven is environmentally friendly, and it's much healthier than wood fires. The oven is large enough that families may want to run a small side baking business to supplement their income, adds Patterson.

"We pledge to use profits to remain independent and self-sustaining while pursuing our ultimate aim, solving social and environmental problems," Patterson says. "Like Newman's Own and the shoemaker Toms, the profits of the company will make sure our ovens are deployed in regions of the world where people are still cooking with wood fires."

Patterson, age 65, plans on transitioning out of company leadership by the end of 2018. But the social enterprise will continue its triple-bottom-line mission.

Turning a social enterprise idea into a thriving organization isn't easy. Encore.org is an enterprise based in San Francisco and founded by the social entrepreneur Marc Freedman. He is a pragmatic proselytizer for people in the second half of life to engage in strengthening the common good. Freedman realized long ago that increased longevity offered an aging population the incredible opportunity to work at social change during an "encore career." Articulate, with a self-deprecating sense of humor, Freedman has pushed his optimistic vision redefining the last stage of life in books, columns, speeches, conferences, fellowships, and various social enterprise initiatives.

At one of those conferences, I attended a panel on social innovation. I learned about the catchphrase "stagnation chasm" during the session. Social entrepreneurs raise a small amount in philanthropic dollars to test out their idea. The program succeeds in the real-world experiment. The social entrepreneurs find it difficult to get additional investments to take their project to the next level. The social venture seed money is no longer interested in the nonprofit (the idea works) and yet the nonprofit is too small to attract interest from larger funders (taking the idea to scale).

I've witnessed a version of the stagnation chasm watching the remarkable efforts of three social entrepreneurs in south Florida. They're struggling to transform antiquated views on aging in their respective communities. Bevan Gray-Rogel is founder and president of Encore Tampa Bay in Tampa. Gray-Rogel has more than three decades of experience in organization and leadership development.

Catherine "Kitty" Preziosi founded Boomer Breakthrough in Davie, Florida, a town near Fort Lauderdale. She has been a consultant in organizational development for much of her long career. She is also a partner in a consulting firm with her husband, a professor of management at the Nova Southeastern University's Huizenga College of Business and Entrepreneurship.

Rosemary Nixon spent most of her career as a financial advisor. She retired in 2010, but soon became certified as a retirement coach and started working with people on nonfinancial aspects of retirement. She also created the nonprofit organization Encore Palm Beach County. "My vision for Encore Palm Beach County is that we become the one place people over 50 can go to find what they need to contribute to their continued engagement with life and purpose," she says.

Each has held conferences to get the message out about encore careers. They've solicited local business, political, and philanthropic leaders. They've networked nationally with like-minded national organizations. They hold workshops and host community conversations.

Gray-Rogel, Preziosi, and Nixon have helped many people in their communities find meaning and money in the second half of life. Their efforts have fallen short of their ambitions—so far. Encore Tampa Bay still operates on a shoestring budget that makes it tough to fulfill its goal of promoting positive aging and connecting talent in the second half of life in the community. Encore Palm Beach County largely relies on "sweat equity" and funds from events to stay in business. Nixon has sharpened its mission to focus on helping people connect to new work opportunities. She hopes that new mission will attract some funders.

Preziosi shut down Boomer Breakthrough. She has shifted her efforts to chairing the advisory council of the South Florida Institute on Aging, an ambitious nonprofit with more than fifty years of history working with older adults in Broward County. The idea informing Boomer Breakthrough lives on through the South Florida Institute on Aging.

That said, these three social entrepreneurs are making a difference. Their energy and ambition are impressive (and contagious). They're helping to make the encore glass more than half full in south Florida. They're succeeding in so many ways. Better yet, there are efforts like theirs happening all over the country.

These grassroots activities remind me of the opening lyrics to the Buffalo Springfield song, "For What It's Worth": "There's something happening here. What it is ain't exactly clear."

It's becoming clearer every day that the second half of life is being reimagined, with work at the core of the new vision.

The desire to live one's values is why older adults flock to encore careers with nonprofits. In a thoughtful interview with the Minneapolis-based certified financial planner Ross Levin, cofounder and president of Accredited Investors Wealth Management, he remarked that it's common for clients nearing the end of life to talk about what they wish they had done. The conversations are always along the lines of "I wish I had done more with the kids when they were younger," says Levin. "It's never 'I wish I had bought a Mercedes.'"

The late historian Daniel Boorstin described America's nonprofit organizations as "monuments to community." Nonprofit organizations "originate in the community, depend on the community, are developed by the community, serve the community, and rise or fall with the community," he added.[5]

These monuments to community are remarkably diverse, ranging from tiny soup kitchens to science museums to multinational behemoths. The sector employs about one in every ten American workers, not including volunteers. Most nonprofits are the equivalent of small businesses. They don't have human resource departments, let alone information technology help desks. These nonprofits reflect the passions of their entrepreneurial founders.

The transition into nonprofit work in the second half of life can be difficult. At a talk several years ago at a community center outside Phoenix, a man in the audience had everyone in stitches relaying his tale of self-inflicted woe in navigating the shift from the for-profit sector to the nonprofit world. He was a self-described "know-it-all." He had a good corporate career managing information technology systems. When he retired, he wanted to take his skills into a nonprofit—to make a difference.

Here's how I remember he told his story. (We were all laughing hard.) He got a job at a local nonprofit and in short order loudly informed his new colleagues that they were doing information technology wrong. He was thanked for his insights and asked to leave. He went to another nonprofit. He quickly announced to everyone that the nonprofit wasn't managing its IT right. Once again, he was shown the door. Chuckling, he said that he joined the gig economy driving a car to make some money and get out of the house while he rethought his approach toward working at a nonprofit.

Terry Araman of Phoenix, Arizona, made the transition much more quickly. "After four days of retirement, I said: 'This isn't going to work for me,'" he says.[6]

Araman was an Army medic for three years, serving in Vietnam with the 9th Infantry Division in the late 1960s. He subsequently had a two-decade career as a manager in the semiconductor business, retiring in 2006 at age 59 from Motorola/Freescale Semiconductor by taking a buyout package. To stay busy after his four days of retirement, he volunteered at the Human Services Campus for the homeless run by the Lodestar Day Resource Center in Phoenix. "Volunteering was part of my life," he says.

His job? Working in the mailroom. He went from management in the high-flying semiconductor business to the low-rung of the mailroom. He loved the change. "By starting out at that level, I got the chance to talk to the homeless," he says. "I really got to know the clientele, the homeless community."

I met Araman while giving a talk at Helpings Café, the café, catering service, and food market created by the social enterprise UMOM New Day Centers. The Helpings Café generates funds and job training for the homeless. My talk largely dealt with encore careers. Araman at one point got up and made an impassioned plea for anyone thinking about making an encore career transition to spend time volunteering on the lowest rung of an organization. He made a compelling case based on his own experience.

"Volunteering is a great way to find out if you are a good fit for the organization," he advises. "So many things have to match up. Your skills and abilities. The culture. Will they work with you with flexibility and time?"

Araman's six-month volunteer stint in the mailroom led to a part-time paid position at the front desk for the shelter, including most weekends. His next paid position came in 2007, doing development work for Lodestar. "These shelters built for the homeless are done on a shoestring budget," he says. "Toilets are always getting clogged, and I became expert at unclogging them. I am proud of that."

During this time, Araman learned about the many homeless veterans in town. The next year, he started helping, without pay, fourteen veterans at the Men's Outreach Shelter on Madison Street in downtown Phoenix. The veterans had formed a self-help group, managing their own space. Their initiative led him to create the Madison Street Veterans Association (MSVA), a pioneering peer-group organization for homeless veterans with Araman as executive director. One of the reasons he wanted to work with homeless veterans is he became homeless for several months after leaving the military in 1970. "I am sometimes reluctant to admit that I was homeless, but I have learned that it can help other veterans if they learn of my personal experience navigating the challenges of homelessness," he says.

Catholic Charities Community Services Arizona recently became the nonprofit's parent organization, renaming it MANA (Marine, Army, Navy, Air Force) House. At age 68, Araman stepped down from his operational duties. But since February 2017, he has been back working as a consultant with Catholic Charities Community Services. He remains very active in the veteran community as legislative director for Unified Arizona Veterans and legislative coordinator for Vietnam Veterans of America, Arizona.

Here's another example of making a difference. Samuel Samelson, age 78, lives in Sarasota, Florida. He is the former chief executive officer of ExCell Home Fashions, a large supplier of shower curtains, bath mats, table linens, and the like to major retailers such as Walmart and Bed Bath and Beyond. He worked at the company for thirty-six years before retiring some fifteen years ago. He and his wife Susan moved to Sarasota some twelve years ago. "Retirement to me has meant the opportunity to get involved in things," he says. "I keep busy, pretty much. One of the best ways for not getting old is staying busy."

Samelson is a good example of using skills honed over the years in business to make a difference in the community during the unretirement years. The story runs along these lines.

He and his wife started taking classes at the Lifelong Learning Academy when they settled in Sarasota. The small nonprofit organization offered affordable classes and seminars on a broad range of topics. It wasn't long before Samelson shifted from student to board member to chairman of the board. Several years ago, he used his expertise to help engineer a merger of Lifelong Learning with the Ringling International College of Art and Design, the local visual arts school. Samelson's work wasn't done. Not long after the merger, thanks to a grant from the Bernard Osher Foundation, a San Francisco-based philanthropic organization, the lifelong learning institution was renamed the Osher Lifelong Learning Institute at Ringling College. Samelson is chairman of its Advisory Council. "That's what I have been doing," says Samelson.

Actually, there's more. There are some forty to fifty lifelong learning schools in the region, other than religious institutions. These lifelong learning programs vary in size and they were in need of a united public voice. Samelson got involved in creating the SunCoast Alliance for Lifelong Learning (SCALL). The Alliance trade organization supports the lifelong learning schools in the Florida communities of Sarasota and Manatee Counties. Samelson is vice president and treasurer of SCALL.

He's also a certified mediator in the Florida court system. He started a local chapter of YPO, a well-known meeting platform for chief executives. "Keep involved," he says.

That's how you make a difference.

Samelson doesn't need an income-earning job. But for many people, volunteering is a savvy way to find a new career or job later in life. Volunteers learn how an organization operates. Volunteers may still believe in the nonprofit's mission, but by helping they can also figure out if they admire management and staff. They get a chance to see which of their skills translate best into what a nonprofit organization needs. "Volunteering is critical to making the transition," says David Garvey, director of the Department of Public Policy's Nonprofit Leadership Program at the University of Connecticut.

Still, there remains a need for institutions and networks that would ease the transition for those looking to promote the common good in the second half of life.

There are heartening examples. Encore.org started the Encore Fellowships Network. The program helps private sector professionals take their talents into the nonprofit community and social purpose ventures. The program is basically a matchmaking service between Fellows looking for nonprofit work and nonprofits needing particular skills to fulfil their mission. The Fellowship ends after 1,000 hours (usually six months of work spread out over the course of a year). The Fellows may stay with the nonprofit or take their experience elsewhere.

Other matchmaking services include Experience Matters in Phoenix, Metro Volunteers in Denver, and NYC Service in New York City. Among online resources, VolunteerMatch.org and Idealist.org are helpful.

Volunteering is how many people give back. An intriguing variation on volunteering is the emergence of what might be called the "stipend economy." The job comes with a small amount of money. The stipend isn't nearly enough to live on (not even close). But paying even a small stipend seems to encourage organizations to take their "volunteers" more seriously and vice versa.

ReServe is a good example. ReServe specializes in bringing 55-plus professionals to local nonprofit organizations, public institutions, and government agencies. The talent is often drawn from the ranks of professionals, such as lawyers, doctors, nurses, teachers, and accountants. They work for a small hourly stipend, well below their market value during their main career. The job is typically for ten to twenty hours a week. The average contract lasts less than a year. (ReServe is a subsidiary of Fedcap, a larger nonprofit headquartered in New York that offers an array of services—education, workforce development, occupational health, and economic development.)

Obviously, money is not a big factor in joining ReServe. Participants are looking for a challenge and a way to give back. An accountant is certainly good at math and maybe likes kids. A stint as a tutor is a possibility. A marketing professional might find his or her skills in demand at a government agency struggling to get its public service message out.

AARP Experience Corps is another stipend enterprise. The organization now has nearly two thousand volunteers ages 50 and over in twenty-three cities working with more than 30,000 students in elementary schools. Volunteers work ten hours or more a week. They receive a stipend of around $200 a month and an approximately $1,200 tuition education award.

Mary Mabry enjoys her Experience Corps work at a small charter school in southwest Minneapolis. She tutors third graders in reading several times a week for a few hours. Mabry is a psychotherapist who has held numerous jobs over the years, such as working with families and their children, guidance counselor, university administrator, and prison teacher. "Education is at the core of everything I do," she says.

Mabry is a cancer survivor. She joined Experience Corps several years ago once she was better. She loves the children. Tutoring is a way for her to give back. Her passion and commitment are infectious. "We are here for a reason," she says. "To share with them that they will do better and not make the same mistakes as we did."

Marc Freedman of Encore.org was a cofounder of Experience Corps early in his career. He is fond of quoting his mentor, the late John Gardner, who had a long and distinguished career. Gardner's achievements include serving as president of Carnegie Corporation and head of the Carnegie Foundation for the Advancement of Teaching; Lyndon Johnson's Secretary of Health, Education, and Welfare during the heyday of the Great Society; and founder of

Common Cause. Freedman often quotes from a talk Gardner gave in his late 80s.

"All my feelings about the release of human possibilities, all of my convictions about renewal are offended by the widely shared cultural assumption that life levels off in one's 40s and 50s and heads downhill, so that by 65 you are scrap heap material," Gardner said. "What I want," Freedman recalls Gardner saying, "is a long youthfulness of spirit. It doesn't seem much to ask—but it is everything."[7]

Mary Mabry has that youthfulness of spirit. And yes, it is everything.

Management (Increasingly) Embraces Experienced Workers

I'm going to die. So why can't I do everything? And what is this idea that I worked all day yesterday, so I'm tired today? I've never believed that.

—MAYA ANGELOU[1]

Older entrepreneurs are in the vanguard of rethinking work and aging. Small businesses are receptive to hiring experienced workers and mentors. Larger employers are starting to look at older workers with greater appreciation. The revolution rolls on.

For years, human resources conferences held panels on how organizations should adjust to the aging of the boomer workforce. In many respects the conversations stopped there. The need to do something wasn't pressing during the high unemployment years of the Great Recession and slow recovery. Management had its choice of workers eager for a job. Inaction is giving way to action with the tighter labor market. Progress in larger organizations may be slow compared to smaller businesses and the startup culture. But the movement is going in the right direction and, more recently, is gathering momentum.

The shift in attitudes doesn't add up into a cultural revolution—yet. For example, advertising budgets remain youth-obsessed, despite some recent notable exceptions. Rather than sudden enlightenment, management seems to realize it can lose business or embrace experienced workers. "There is a demand for workers, and more and more jobs will have to be filled by older workers," says Eugene Steuerle, economist at the Urban Institute. Economics matters.

Age-friendly initiatives are spreading. There is greater effort spent on retaining experienced workers, often with variations on phased-retirement programs. Management is beginning to realize that, to achieve hoped-for returns from diversity strategies, the initiatives should include experienced workers. Mentorships are seen as valuable for transferring skills and knowledge to younger generations of workers.

Take the experience of Ultra Machining Company (UMC). It's a half-century-old family-owned business in Monticello, Minnesota, about 30 miles from the Minneapolis/St. Paul International Airport. The precision machining operation was started by its founder in his garage. Its approximately 165 employees produce machined products for a variety of industries, including medical, aerospace, and energy. Business is booming, but the pipeline of skilled machinists is thin. Management is aggressively recruiting younger workers through partnerships with community colleges and apprenticeship programs.

In the meantime, management accommodates the needs of its older machinists so they don't retire early. One way to keep older workers around is to invest in automation. Robots and similar machines reduce the physical strain of the job. "They don't take as big a toll on the body as it used to, when they had to actually manually crank machines and move things around," Chief Executive Officer Eric Gibson told *Enterprise Minnesota*, a trade magazine. "And we're trying to work with them."[2]

The German automaker BMW offers a valuable lesson for U.S. companies and older workers. Back in 2007, the head of BMW's 2,500-employee power train plant in Dingolfing, Germany, worried about assembly line productivity with the aging of the population and workforce. Along with two BMW colleagues, an experiment was launched, according to the *Harvard Business Review* article "The Globe: How BMW Is Defusing the Demographic Time Bomb." They transformed an assembly line by staffing it with its future workforce in 2017 (average age of 47). The 2017 line was nicknamed the "pensioners' line." Listening to worker suggestions on the pensioners' line, management made about seventy changes. The investments were largely targeted at limiting physical wear and tear, such as wooden flooring and orthopedic footwear, special barbershop-like chairs at workstations, adjustable tables, and the installation of flexible magnifying lenses. The total investment was about $50,000.

"What did BMW get in return? The line achieved a 7 percent productivity improvement in one year, equaling the productivity of lines staffed by younger workers," write the authors of the *Harvard Business Review* article. The ten defects per million quality target was consistently beaten, and absenteeism dropped below the plant average. "BMW now touts the 2017 line as a model of productivity and high quality in its internal communications."[3]

The BMW story reinforces the insight that the main barrier to unleashing the power of experienced workers is management attitudes. The draw on corporate resources was minimal, especially for a company the size of BMW. What's $50,000 to a manufacturing company with global revenues of $111 billion in 2017?

Experienced workers also appreciate flexibility on the job. For example, more than 78 percent of respondents to the Center on Aging & Work at Boston College reported that having access to flexible work options contributes to their success as employees to a "moderate" or "great extent." Flexible work options contribute to overall quality of life to a "moderate" or "great extent," as reported by 90 percent.[4]

Here is a list of suggested workplace innovations for management to embrace that would increase workplace flexibility. The list was compiled by the Center on Aging & Work at Boston College:[5]

Flexibility in the Number of Hours Worked. Examples include: part-time work, part-year work, job share, phased retirement, and having input into overtime.

Flexible Schedules. Examples include: frequent requests for changes in starting/quitting times, occasional requests for changes in starting/quitting times, compressed work week, schedule that varies from typical schedule, choices about shifts.

Flexible Place. Examples include: being able to work from home/remote site, or being able to select or periodically/seasonally change the work location (if the employer has more than a single worksite).

Options for Time Off. Examples include: paid leave for caregiving/personal/family responsibility, extra unpaid vacation days, paid/unpaid time for education/training, paid/unpaid sabbatical, and paid time to volunteer.

Other Options. Examples include: control over the timing of breaks and allowing employees to transfer to a job with reduced responsibilities and reduced pay, if they want to.

Notice anything? Every one of these options for greater workplace flexibility that would help organizations recruit and retain experienced employees are also attractive to younger generations.

Considering the efficient and easy-to-use networking and mapping technologies developed by on-demand ride services and home-sharing companies, it shouldn't be too difficult to build platforms that overcome traditional hurdles with flexible schedules within organizations.

There are programs worth highlighting that embrace flexibility and experienced workers. The pharmacy giant CVS Caremark ran for years a widely admired optional snowbird program for its older workers. They could transfer to different CVS pharmacy stores on a seasonal basis. CVS ended that program and substituted a broader menu of flexible options for its employees, ranging from telecommuting to job sharing. Marriot's Flex Options for Hourly Workers gives older employees the opportunity to learn new skills to transition out of physically taxing jobs at the hospitality giant.

Bon Secours Virginia Health System in Richmond, Virginia, has taken several steps to retain older workers. Pension payouts are calculated off the five highest-paying years of service rather than the last five years of service; health insurance includes part-time employees; and the company's daycare centers are open to employee grandchildren. The utility Consolidated Edison in New York offers career-long training opportunities to keep mature workers, as well as elder-care referral services.

Herman Miller is the global commercial office manufacturer based in Zeeland, Michigan. Miller is best known for its office chairs, like the Aeron. The company's products are manufactured in the United States. Like most manufacturing companies, Miller has an older-than-average workforce. Management doesn't want to lose its older employees' skills and knowledge too quickly. The company instituted two programs with built-in flexibility. In one program, workers get to take six to twelve consecutive weeks off during the year. Employees aren't paid during that time, but they keep their benefits and length of service toward their pension. The program is open to all employees, but management has found most participants are in their 50s and older.

The other program is its "flex retirement" plan for employees 60 years and older with at least five years at the company. The retirement decision is irreversible. Participants in the program start the retirement process two years ahead of schedule, gradually reducing their hours as their retirement date approaches. They keep full-time benefits during the two years. Their take-home pay is cut to reflect the fewer hours. Vacation time is prorated. The key requirement of the flex retirement program is that participants must pass on their knowledge to their successors.

Jake Boeve retired at age 68 in 2014. He was nearly a forty-nine-year veteran of Miller. Boeve started out on the production line right after high school, worked his way up into supervisory roles and, for the last fifteen years of his career, he was in charge of information technology inventory management. When he entered the flex retirement program, he worked four days a week the first year and three days a week the second year. The last several months, he trained people to take his place. When I talked to him several years ago to learn about his experience with the program he summed it up this way: "It was awesome," he says.

The transition helped him get into a retirement mind-set, he added. Boeve has a huge backyard, and he enjoys yardwork. He'll look for volunteer opportunities now that he is retired. He'll spend time with his children and grandchildren. He and his wife like to travel. "You have to be physically, mentally, and financially ready for retirement," he says. "I would highly recommend flex retirement."[6]

Formal and informal, these phased retirement programs are concentrated in industries with older-than-average workforces, such as manufacturing. They're also popular in industries with a skilled workforce and high demand, like nurses in health care. Phased retirement programs recognize that older workers want to continue working and using skills developed over the years. But experienced workers often desire to put in fewer hours and enjoy greater flexibility. The details of various phased retirement programs vary greatly, but the basic trade-off remains the same.

"Phased retirement allows you to dip your toes into the shallow end of the retirement pool," says Jessica Klement, legislative director of the National Active and Retired Federal Employees Association. "You get to test it out."[7]

Another trend gathering momentum is management welcoming back former employees in their retirement years for part-time work and seasonal jobs. Odds are that the number of "boomerang" retiree programs will expand, especially among larger companies with deep pockets. Older workers are a deep well of skills to tap. The talents of recent retirees are well-known to managers. Former employees are comfortable with an organization's culture.

A well-known boomerang program is run by Aerospace Corporation, based in El Segundo, California. Aerospace occupies a unique business niche: The independent nonprofit organization provides technical analyses and assessments for national security and commercial space programs. The company has approximately 3,700 employees, many of them highly skilled engineers, scientists, and technicians who provide a variety of services for rockets and satellites. The company's primary customer is the U.S. Air Force Space and Missile Systems Center.

Many Aerospace employees possess specialized knowledge. In the 1970s, management found many of its retirees were coming back to Aerospace to help on various projects. But they were working for other contractors. In 1985, the company launched its Retiree Casual program to bring order to an increasingly chaotic situation. Instead, the company now taps into their knowledge and expertise when needed.

The casuals (love that term, don't you?) can work up to 1,000 hours a year. They don't accrue any more benefits (and retirees get health insurance from the company.) Most people make an equivalent sum to their previous salary, prorated to their part-time status. There are usually about three hundred casuals in the program. The casuals allow management to keep better control over staffing.

Establishing a boomerang retiree program like Aerospace involves a substantial commitment of resources, including systems for navigating complex labor market rules and pension law. Most returning retirees must wait several months before they can come back to their former employer, and they're often limited to 1,000 hours a year. This is why managements are increasingly turning to outside firms like Kelly Services, Manpower, and other talent recruiting companies to manage their boomerang program's nuts-and-bolts. For instance, Blue Cross/Blue Shield of America has its "Blue Bring Back" program. Managers can request the services of a retired former employee for an assignment. The program is managed by Kelly Outsourcing and Consulting Group.

One of the more intriguing outsourced boomerang organizations is the independent consulting firm YourEncore. The firm was created in 2003 when P&G, the Cincinnati-based consumer products behemoth, and Eli Lilly, the Indianapolis-based pharmaceutical giant, asked consultant John Barnard to come up with a way management could draw on the knowledge and expertise of their retired employees. Boeing quickly joined the venture, which subsequently expanded to other companies, mostly in the food, consumer product, and life sciences industries. YourEncore acts as a matchmaker between corporations looking for expertise to deal with pressing problems and skilled retirees' occasional challenge for part-time income.

Boomerang employees can be seasonal. For example, package deliveries boom during the holiday season. The United States Postal Service posts on its website an invitation to "letter carriers, clerks and motor vehicle operators who have retired within the last few years to come back and help us deliver holiday cheer." UPS supplements its regular workforce of some 440,000 with nearly 100,000 seasonal workers to handle the holiday surge. UPS averages some 18 million packages a day—about 6.5 percent of the GDP (gross domestic product)—a figure that about doubles during the holidays. (I find these numbers incredible.) The company has learned over time that its retirees are a valuable resource. They come with twenty-five to forty years of experience at the company. They can hit the ground running during the holiday rush, saving UPS millions of dollars.[8]

The company recently changed the name of its retiree relationship department into the alumni group. The name change reflects a significant shift in the company's perspective on retirees. The old attitude reflected the traditional approach. Employees worked hard. When it came time to retire they could move on with their benefits. The alumni network idea reflects the desire to maintain closer relations with its retirees. Not only are they invaluable workers during the holiday season, but UPS has learned tapping into its retiree network is a way to increase its community volunteer initiatives.

Among those alumni is Bill Simomowicz. For more than thirty years, he drove the iconic UPS brown truck delivering packages in the Grand Marais area (Minnesota) on the north shore of Lake Superior, a small harbor town with a vibrant arts and crafts community. Simomowicz retired in 2012, but after two years of steering clear of the company, he joined its holiday season workforce from Thanksgiving to Christmas. He typically put in six- to eight-hour days during the busy holiday push. "UPS actively went after its retirees," says Simomowicz, in his early 60s. "It's pretty easy work. And there is light at the end of the tunnel."

The public sector has its boomerangs. Many states offer public employee retirees the opportunity to come back part-time, including California. The federal government is rolling out its phased retirement program. Federal employees who sign up for the program work part-time. They collect half their salary and half their accumulated retirement annuity. Phased retirees must dedicate 20 percent of their time at work mentoring younger employees. (The federal government's phased retirement rollout and participation rates have been slower than expected.)

Perhaps most important, management realizes that the biggest value of boomerangs lies in teaching the formal and informal ropes of the business to younger generations of workers. Mentoring is popular with three generations in the workplace—and sometimes more. The lure of mentoring at work was nicely captured by the late Warren Bennis, professor of management at the University of Southern California, and Robert Thomas, director of research at the Accenture Institute for High Performance in *Geeks & Geezers: How Era, Values, and Defining Moments Shape Leaders*. (In their tongue-in-cheek title, *geeks* are young leaders and *geezers* are older leaders.)

"Our geezers understand, as we all should, that the successful old can lead the way as we deal with the inevitable challenges of finding an exciting, useful, healthful place in a culture that continues to despise and fear old age," they write. "Building and maintaining networks across generations, organizations and cultures is a way to learn continuously and to leverage the insights of people who have a genuine interest in your growth and success."

The tiremaker Michelin North America is based in Greenville, South Carolina. The company has its Returning Retirees Program. Among its participants is Beulah Webb. Webb was 59 years old when we talked. She retired in 2015 after putting in thirty years on various assembly line jobs at Michelin. Her retirement involves rooting for her beloved Clemson Tiger football team and, most important, spending time with her grandson. "I love spending time with him," she says. "He makes everything all better."[9]

Through the tire maker's eleven-year-old Returning Retiree Employee program, she puts in some thirty hours a week as a facility training manager for wage production employees and operators at the Michelin Rubber Mixing Facility in Sandy Springs, South Carolina. Michelin has four generations working in its plants. She values the program for its "flexibility," she says. "I really enjoy what I am doing. It's like living the best of both worlds."

She likes the people she works with and trains. "Most of my career I have been from one end of Michelin to the other," she says. "I gained a lot of knowledge here at Michelin, and I like imparting knowledge. The expertise I gained while employed at Michelin, I'm passing on to new employees."

That's quite a legacy to leave behind during the so-called retirement years, isn't it?

9

Taking Lifelong Learning Seriously

In spite of illness, in spite even of the arch-enemy sorrow, one can remain alive long past the usual date of disintegration if one is unafraid of change, insatiable in intellectual curiosity, interested in big things, and happy in small ways.

—EDITH WHARTON[1]

The annual Milken Global Conference at the Beverly Hilton in Beverly Hills, California, is the brainchild of the financier Michael Milken. The conference brings together the global elite from government, business, finance, and philanthropy for several days of discussion in the spring. The theme of the 2017 conference was "Building Meaningful Lives."

On my way to the conference, my 50-something Latino ride-share driver told me that he had been a long-haul trucker for some fifteen years. He made good money as a trucker. He liked the job. But he was driving a car to be with his family more. The ride-share money wasn't good, but it paid some bills while he thought about his next chapter. "Life as a trucker is hard on family," he says. 'But you can't just sit around and watch TV."

Certainly not with a daughter in college and a son about to start his freshman year in college. What might he do next? A semiprofessional soccer player in his youth, he was thinking about becoming a junior high and high school soccer coach. He would need to pick up a certification to qualify, which was fine with him. He was drawn to coaching for his encore career.

Our conversation was appropriate considering the panel session I attended titled, "Unbound: Retraining the American Workforce." The session started off with a short video highlighting the speed of job market change, thanks to accelerating automation and globalization. The first panelist was Ellen Hughes-Cromwick, former chief economist at the U.S. Department of Commerce. She set the tone for the session with her passionate call for an "all hands on deck" mind-set when it comes to training initiatives. "This topic really matters," she says.

"We have an archaic belief that learning is over at age 22," observed Shernaz Daver, another panelist and chief marketing officer at Udacity, the online learning company. "The process of learning is lifelong. We're living longer. We need to work longer."

Jamie Merisotis, chief executive officer of the education-focused Lumina Foundation, echoed her sentiment. "It no longer works to get an education, get a job and retire," he said. "It's lifelong learning."

The catchphrase "lifelong learning" is something of a cliché. But it's the right perspective. Education in the United States is frontloaded. Investments in education are high from elementary school through college. After age 22, according to the White House Council of Economic Advisers, both public and private contributions to education spending fall "precipitously." Employers do spend on worker education, but the total sum is less than 10 percent of the amount spent by private and public parties on education at age 18.[2] The sense of urgency apparent at the Milken conference isn't widely shared, especially when it comes to educating, training, and retraining experienced workers.

Too bad. All the evidence is that experienced workers would benefit from greater investment in their human capital. Certainly, the experience of Hans Anderson supports the importance of lifelong learning. He was the oldest student in the master's degree program in the management of technology at the University of Minnesota. The degree is a joint program run by the College of Science and

Engineering and the Technological Leadership Institute. Anderson joined the part-time program in 2013 at age 70.

He also got his degree on the cheap. He earned his master's degree for $10 a credit, thanks to Minnesota's Senior Citizen Education Program (SCEP). That compares to the typical charge of more than $1,800 per credit for the graduate degree. If you live in Minnesota and are 62 years or older, you may audit courses at the University for free or take courses for $10 per credit. You still pay for any fees or materials.[3]

Anderson had a long career, mostly in the high-tech field. Education has been important to him throughout his career. He got his undergraduate degree from the University of Wisconsin, Madison, with a degree in electrical engineering in 1969. He got his MBA from the University of St. Thomas in Minneapolis in 1991. He worked for a variety of companies, mostly in sales, including such legendary companies as Intel, Fairchild, and National Semiconductor. He ran for mayor of Bloomington, Minnesota, and lost with 32 percent of the vote. He developed a currency trading program with a friend. He was also a contract worker with a global technology company while getting his degree.

Anderson needs an income. The father of five children, he and his wife made a deliberate decision to invest in their children's education. "Family comes first," he says. "It took the resources we would have saved for retirement." They have no regrets about their choice.

He felt he needed to upgrade his tech management skills to get his next job. He was right. He got a management job immediately after graduating from the program with a local high-tech company. Reflecting on his experience, Anderson says he enjoyed his time at school. "There isn't a student in the class who couldn't be my child. I am older than my professor," he says. "I keep up with all of them. I support all of them. And they tell me I give them a different perspective on life."

The degree also paid off when he was laid off from his last job in Minneapolis. He and his wife returned to their hometown of Wakefield, Michigan, in the Upper Peninsula region. The idea was to embrace retirement. Instead, he got a job as engineering manager at

Burton Industries in Ironwood, a town about twelve miles from home. "I am 75 now and as productive as I ever was," he says. "I am finding value daily in what I do and satisfaction in my current position."

Postsecondary education in the second half of life can be invaluable for launching a new career or taking a new job. Getting a two-year or four-year degree isn't common. Instead, the demand is stronger for certificates. They typically involve a shorter time commitment. The certificate signals to potential employers that you've learned a skill.

Postsecondary certificates are growing rapidly. Postsecondary completions increased by 33 percent from 2009 to 2011. The labor market analytics company Emsi calculates annual completions exceed 1 million. These degrees are awarded by community colleges, technical colleges, and vocational schools.[4]

Industries and companies can also offer certificate programs. Sandra Kollath got a company-specific certificate to propel her career transition. I met Kollath through her daughter and my colleague at Minnesota Public Radio, Annie Anderson. "You should interview my mom sometime," she told me. "She's a professional nanny, but she's changing careers. She's getting a certificate to become a certified quilting instructor."[5]

Really? From nanny to quilter. I had to learn more.

Kollath and her husband had owned a small resort with cabins on a lake in Minnesota. She was widowed when Annie was 10 years old. That's when Kollath started quilting. Her sister signed her up for some quilting classes to get her out of the house. "Little did we know she had touched off a passion," Annie says.

Kollath became a professional nanny. She describes it as a well-paying job for someone like her, without a college diploma. She loved the job, but it was wearing. "I had been a nanny for fifteen years, and then in the last year, it was like 'I got grandkids. I want to be with my grandkids,'" she says. "Annie would call me up and say, 'Can you watch the kids?' And I would say, 'No, I have to go watch someone else's kids.'"

At age 58, she felt it was time for a change. She also wanted to have more fun. She was making quilts with other women in classes she attended. "I decided this is what I want to do. I want to work with women who are hilarious, and after working with toddlers all the time, I wanted some adult interaction."

She still needed an income. Her idea was to shift from quilting hobbyist to quilting teacher. The interest in quilting is strong and the opportunities to teach have expanded. Kollath loved a quilting method that allows less experienced sewers to create complex quilts. The patterns are designed by QuiltWorx. She wanted to become a certified instructor for the company.

She enlisted her daughter and partner who has an MBA to research the company. Was Quiltworx a scam? No. Would the certificate pay off? They figured with travel to Montana for classes, plus tuition, the certificate was going to cost Sandra $15,000. That's more than double the average cost of the typical certificate program. Still, the certificate would pay off in 18 months or less. Could she pay the approximately $15,000 cost without going into debt? Check. With an MBA in the family mix, they hashed out a business plan. Kollath was already teaching some classes since she had enrolled in the certificate program.

"I thought I'd like to teach, but I had no idea it was that much fun. The day just flew by," she says. "The thrill of seeing [the students] excitement at succeeding at something they want to do. And they hold it up and you can just see the look on their face. 'Oh! I just love this! It's perfect! Ahh!' I'm looking forward to having that in my life, three to four days a week."

Kollath is already planning for her later years. She'll travel with her partner in an RV to different parts of the country when he retires. "I can be teaching at a quilt store and we can bring our camper and I can teach during the day and he can fish," she says. "You can quilt indefinitely."

America's colleges and universities haven't exactly rolled out the welcome mat to older learners. They're still focused on young undergraduates and slightly older graduate students. Typical offerings for the 60-plus crowd are geared toward retirees eager to take the

Renaissance Art or History of Science class they missed (or slept through) decades ago. These enrichment classes are intellectually stimulating and meet a need. They aren't useful to older workers looking to launch their second or third acts.

There are intriguing signs of innovation, however. Efforts are under way to push colleges closer to an intergenerational career-and-job oriented model. The future isn't here yet—far from it. But maybe the future is starting to pound on the hallowed school doors.

"We are only at the beginning," says Philip Pizzo, founder and head of Stanford University's Distinguished Career Institute, a program geared toward encouraging encore careers for successful professionals: "Let's think this through together and develop more and different programs tailored to the community the institution serves—public universities, private colleges, and community colleges."

Two higher education pioneers in encore careers are Phyllis Moen, sociology professor at the University of Minnesota, and Kate Schaefers, consultant, executive coach, and volunteer state president of AARP Minnesota. They're cofounders of the University of Minnesota Advanced Careers Initiative launched in 2017. Moen is founding director and Schaefers is its executive director. The program at the land grant university is designed to help people—called fellows—in the second half of life segue into a new career with a social purpose. "The fellows want jobs and work. They want to do meaningful work, often in a nonprofit," says Moen.

Adds Schaefers: "People do want to give back. They want that social impact in the next phase of their life."

Ten fellows between the ages of 50 and 72 joined the first class of the two-semester program. The 2017–18 program fee was $7,500. The next class of twenty fellows was charged $15,000 each. Fellows are on campus at the University of Minnesota Twin Cities for the first semester. They attend classes with undergraduates and participate in seminars and discussion groups. (No tests and grades, though.) The program matches fellows with nonprofit organizations, social enterprises, and public institutions that could use their skills. The second semester, fellows volunteer half-time for four months at a nonprofit or similar social purpose enterprise. They return regularly to campus to share with other fellows their experiences with their applied project with a social impact organization.[6]

Moen and Schaefers say they've learned that the title "fellow" offers an identity for those spending time in a higher education institution to change careers. The fellows support one another, and those relationships are important to the experience. "They're no longer on their own," says Moen. "They all get cards that they're a fellow at the Advanced Careers Initiative at the University of Minnesota."

A shorter program with similar ideals is Encore!Hartford headquartered at the University of Connecticut. The four-month transition training program comes with a price tag of almost $4,000. The target market is unemployed corporate professionals over age 50 looking for a managerial career in the nonprofit sector, public agencies, and government. Someone going through the program may have a network in engineering, insurance, or some other industry, but their contacts among nonprofits is limited.[7]

Among its graduates is Archie Elam of Stamford, Connecticut. He's on his third transition. Now in his early 60s, Elam is a 1976 graduate of West Point. His two-decade Army career included acting as head of operations for the 18th Airborne Corps 24th Infantry Division in the first war in Iraq. The organization was composed of 36,000 troops with hundreds of tanks, artillery, and other instruments of war. The Army sent him to get an MBA at Duke University's Fuqua School of Business, a degree that launched his private sector career in 1996. He worked as a manager at General Electric, United Technologies, Accenture, and elsewhere, mostly focused on Six Sigma (a collaborative program for boosting performance by cutting waste), running customer relations management (CRM) systems, and overseeing other large-scale operations.

His next act? He remains active with West Point, especially with its diversity initiatives. He's also commander of the Fairfield County branch of Connecticut Veterans of Foreign Wars. He's responsible for twenty posts and almost 2,500 veterans. The father of two daughters keeps an eye on opportunities in the nonprofit sector. "The stuff you volunteer for, you care about, you do for free and then one day you realize you can get paid to do something you care about," he says. "How cool is that!" Very cool.[8]

Other university-based programs are targeted at elites. For example, centers for encore careers at Notre Dame, University of Texas, Stanford, and Harvard cost north of $50,000. The fellows at these centers have enjoyed highly successful careers, and they are looking for a second act.

Still, there's no reason why the blueprints developed by high-end centers like these can't be transferred with some modification to less expensive institutions and more inclusive missions. "There is no one path or blueprint. We're all trying to figure it out," observes Moen of the University of Minnesota. "We're all in this together."

In an essay published in the *Journal of the American Medical Association*, Stanford's Pizzo captures an ambition shared by Moen, Schaefers, and other multigenerational university pioneers:

"Rather than allowing mid- to later-life transitions to become a loss of opportunity, it seems reasonable to develop strategies to reimagine our sense of purpose in ways that might be transcendent to one's past," he writes. "This is tied to the question of whether the 'university of the future' can become a place for intergenerational learning and teaching, fostering new pathways for those in midlife to make their lives more meaningful and productive while at the same time mentoring and advising those beginning the life journey."[9]

That's the dream. My guess is that colleges will transform themselves into multigenerational institutions with a core mission of lifelong learning and engagement, working with adults of all ages looking to gain the skills and knowledge they need to work well into late life. Instead of alumni, colleges and universities will have lifelong learners. Colleges and universities—especially community colleges—will be part of the lifelong learning infrastructure. They will offer "students" multiple entry and exit points throughout a lifetime, abandoning a singular focus on the young. The reforms will take time to unfold.

"To remain competitive, and to give low- and high-skilled workers alike the best chance of success, economies need to offer training and career-focused education throughout people's working lives," the *Economist* magazine stated in a special report on lifelong education. "Lifelong learning is becoming an economic imperative."[10]

Contrary to popular stereotypes, experienced workers are receptive to additional training. More than eight in ten workers ages 45 to 64 say the opportunity to learn something new is critical to their view of an ideal job, according to an AARP Work and Career Study survey. More than seven in ten responded that job training is an essential element of that ideal employment. The evidence is compelling that training targeted at experienced workers pays off for the worker, the employer, and the wider society.[11]

That's the striking conclusion of a study by scholars Matteo Picchio and Jan C. van Ours of Tilburg University in the Netherlands. Like the rest of Europe and the United States, government and business leaders worry about an aging population in the Netherlands. The Dutch had one of the lowest employment rates of experienced workers among European countries. In 1992, the employment rate of people 55 to 64 was 28.7 percent. Following a series of policy reforms designed to encourage later retirement, the employment rate of experienced workers rose to 52.6 percent by 2009.[12]

Picchio and van Ours explored whether it paid to invest in these experienced workers. Their answer is an emphatic yes. Company-provided training improves employability as "training leads to retaining." Their data strongly supports the notion that "older workers who receive training are more likely to remain employed," they note. The scholars call for government policies to encourage employers to invest in offering older workers training to encourage the public policy goal of longer work lives. "Our research findings suggest that on-the-job training may be an important instrument to achieve this goal," they conclude.

The impact of training could be strongest among lower-income women. That's the conclusion of a study by four scholars on training older workers in Germany. Germany also has an aging population (much older than the United States). German companies have an incentive to invest in training to convince older workers to stay on the job. The scholars found that older women, especially low-wage older women less financially secure than men, (on average) are more likely to see fatter pay packages from participating in employer-sponsored training programs and delaying retirement.[13]

Fact is, it isn't hard to find good examples of experienced workers benefitting from additional education and training in Europe, Singapore, New Zealand, and elsewhere Unfortunately, both corporate and government investments in training in the United States are lackluster in comparison.

The proportion of workers receiving employer-sponsored training dropped by 42 percent between 1996 and 2008. Corporate spending on training as a share of gross domestic product (GDP) went from a mere half a percent in 2000 to a pitiful one-third of a percent in 2013, according to the Information Technology and Innovation Foundation.[14]

Those numbers include all workers. The situation for experienced workers is worse. Corporate training programs tend to ignore older workers. The Department of Labor's Taskforce on the Aging of the American Workforce notes that employer-provided training declines with the age of the employee. For instance, workers between the ages of 25 and 34 received an average of thirty-seven training hours per year, compared with nine hours per year for employees over 55 years of age. Management's perspective is relatively straightforward. Why bother? They'll retire soon.

I've always found this assumption somewhat puzzling. Young people change jobs frequently as they look for the right organization and career for them. They should move around for promotions and opportunity. Workers who are 60-something and happy with an organization's culture and the specifics of their job are likely to stay longer. They're less interested in bouncing around to find their calling.

Employers have hiked their training budgets in response to the tight labor market in recent years. However, the rates of spending remain too low for an economy defined by technological change and global competition. In any case, the U.S. government isn't heeding the training and retraining message either. The combined spending on training programs by federal, state, and local governments was less than 0.5 percent of GDP in 2015, according to the White House Council of Economic Advisers. "Look at the government budgets," says Christopher J. O'Leary, economist at the W. E. Upjohn Institute for Employment Research in Kalamazoo, Michigan. "They're puny."

O'Leary is one of three authors of the report, "Selected Public Workforce Development Programs: Lessons Learned for Older Workers." Their research emphasized that existing federal and state programs to help workers pay for education and training don't focus on the needs of older adults. For example, no government job centers providing employment services and assistance have dedicated staff members specializing in job development and job placement for older workers, they report.[15]

"Over the past twenty years, older workers have become a significantly larger percentage of total jobseekers," the authors write. "Nonetheless, this group continues to constitute only a small percentage of workers receiving reemployment services from the public workforce development system."

The demand for training is much higher than the opportunities for learning new skills. That story clearly emerges at the East Side Neighborhood Services in Minneapolis. The organization runs several antipoverty programs, including a Senior Community Service Employment Program (SCSEP). It's the only federal program targeted at bringing low-income, unemployed, older Americans into full-time employment. I spent some time there to learn more about the program for a column I was writing. I came away impressed with the mission and the dedication of the people involved in the program, from management to participants.

Here are the basic details: Program participants must have an annual income less than 125 percent of the federal poverty guideline (less than $15,175 annually for an individual). They get job training and, to encourage on-the-job learning, participants are assigned a part-time training assignment, usually with a community-based organization. They're paid the federal, state, or local minimum wage—whichever is highest—while in the program. Participants can stay with SCSEP for up to four years. The program is operated through eighteen national organizations, such as Senior Service America, Inc., and AARP.[16]

The goal is to enhance their work skills and eventually find permanent, full-time, and unsubsidized jobs. Most participants have spotty employment histories. Some had careers that tanked after a job loss, health problems, and other setbacks. "It's so important that we can provide them with opportunities," says Macey Wheeler, former program director for East Side's SCSEP. "They want and need to work."

Vanessa Willis, who is in her early 60s, is an example. She worked at many jobs over the years, including at the department of corrections, teaching and substitute teaching. Laid off in 2012, she tried to get another job but her deteriorating health didn't allow it. She has had a hip replacement, back surgeries, and heart ailments. She did get a job working one day a week as a receptionist at an assisted living facility in Minneapolis. But she wanted a full-time position. She signed up for East Side's SCSEP program. Her part-time training assignment was at a conflict resolution center as receptionist and data entry. Her training boosted her computer, résumé writing, and job search skills. She also took a conflict resolution course, training that unexpectedly opened a new chapter for her.

Finding a receptionist position tough to land, Willis returned to substitute teaching at Columbia Heights High School north of the Twin Cities two days a week. She supervised students in a classroom being disciplined for a variety of reasons. She used insights gained from her conflict resolution training to engage the students. The principal was impressed, and Willis became a full-time specialist with the school's Check-and-Connect, a dropout prevention program.

"Isn't that wonderful!" says Willis. "I wake up every morning looking forward to my work. The training I got prepared me for the job I'm doing."[17]

That's not all. She also got a job at the Hubert H. Humphrey Job Corps Center working with young adults ages 16 to 24. She helps them achieve their job and career goals. They call her Ms. Willis, Grandma, Mom, and other affectionate names, she tells me. She has a saying that she repeats to the young people: "Gratitude is the right attitude to take you to the aptitude that you desire to be in life." She adds, "I love that!" She has meaning and money on the job!

Unfortunately, SCSEP has been underfunded for a long time and is occasionally put on the chopping block. According to the Center for Labor Market Studies at Northeastern University, an estimated nine million people between the ages of 55 and 74 were eligible for the program—some one hundred times the number of people served by SCSEP. "Older adults too easily become invisible, yet we know that they have more to give back," says Susan McCauley, chief performance officer at East Side.

Clearly, the United States needs to devote more resources on training and retraining workers. Experienced workers are too often left behind when they lose their jobs and benefits. For instance, workers with more than twenty years' experience typically earn wages almost a quarter less than they had been making previously. The new job often doesn't come with health insurance and retirement savings benefits.

The potent combination of globalization, the digital economy, and the aging population strongly signals that the traditional neglect of training is an enormous mistake. With training, "the worker is better off," says Lee Branstetter, faculty director of the Center for the Future of Work at Carnegie Mellon's Heinz College. "A more educated workforce speeds the rate of innovation and stronger economic growth. But to do this we need to spend more on training."

Adds Paul Magnus, vice president for workforce development at Mature Services in Akron, Ohio: "And, yes, older workers can still learn. Maybe they take it in differently. But they have had to learn new things all their life."

There is no shortage of policy recommendations. For example, the federal Trade Adjustment Assistance program established in the 1960s could be overhauled. The program is supposed to provide retraining and financial support for workers who lose their job to international competition. But the Trade Adjustment Assistance program is inadequately funded and hard to qualify for. The history of the program shows that displaced experienced workers were largely on their own to deal with the downside of a job loss.

The program could be redesigned into the Trade, Technology, and Policy Adjustment Assistance Act. The new act would help all workers displaced by technology, trade, or government policy (for example, defense base closures), recommends the Information Technology and Innovation foundation. The program would need to be well-funded to help displaced workers. The program will fail if it's funded on the cheap. "However, the program might be reformed to provide stronger incentives for workers to take shorter-term training where appropriate, to enroll in training more quickly after a layoff, and to get back into the labor market more expeditiously," suggests Robert Atkinson, head of the foundation.[18]

The motivating idea behind a proposal like the Trade, Technology, and Policy Adjustment Assistance Act is to develop institutions of learning and training that ease the transition to another job or occupation or career over a long-lived life. A Darwinian "you're on your own," except for brief access to unemployment insurance, isn't enough.

What President John F. Kennedy said in 1963 still holds true: "Denial of employment opportunity to older persons is a personal tragedy," he said. "No economy can reach its maximum productivity while failing to use the skills, talents, and experience of willing workers. Rules of employment that are based on the calendar rather than upon ability are not good rules, nor are they realistic."[19]

A little training and additional education will help turn the wisdom in those few sentences into reality.

The Personal Finances of Aging—
Don't Despair

*Aging today has become an improvisational art form calling
for imagination and willingness to learn.*

—MARY CATHERINE BATESON[1]

For years, I contributed to *Businessweek* magazine's annual retirement guide. These special reports were rich in information and
insight. Retirement meant saying goodbye to colleagues for the
last time. Retirement planning largely focused on savvy investing
strategies and smart asset allocation decisions during the working
years. The basic idea with these special reports was to help readers
figure out how best to manage their 401(k), IRA, and other retirement savings plans. The big question was, "What is my number?"—
the elusive sum that tells people at retirement that they have enough
in savings to maintain their standard of living without running out
of money.

How well Americans are prepared financially for their retirement
years is fiercely debated. The Society of Actuaries reviewed the vast
and contentious literature on the topic of retirement adequacy and
I think hit the right note in their conclusion: "After careful consideration of this body of research, it is clear that the U.S. retirement

system lies somewhere between crisis and serendipity," note the authors of the report.[2]

The "crisis" involves segments of society that are highly vulnerable to falling living standards in their elder years, including the disabled, widows, and people with careers that didn't come with retirement benefits. More than a third of private-sector workers lack access to an employer-sponsored retirement savings plan. In essence, the people most likely to live off a low income in retirement had low-income no-benefit jobs throughout their work lives.

That said, the research also "shows that a large majority of Americans are on track to support a reasonably comfortable retirement," according to the actuaries. Retirement won't be a financial disaster for a majority of older Americans. Recent calculations into income by two U.S. Census Bureau researchers finds that, in 2012, median income for householders 65 years and older was 30 percent higher than previously thought. The revised gain is from $33,800 to $44,400. The poverty rate for the 65-plus population fell from 9 percent to 6.9 percent.[3]

Another in-depth study finds financial insecurity has declined among retirees. The percentage of retirees living on the minimum wage or less has been cut in half over the past thirty years. The share of households living at or below the minimum wage in 1989 was about 28 percent of retirees. The rate had fallen to just 15 percent of retirees by 2016. "American retirees are living longer, healthier, and wealthier lives than at any other point in human history," write Matt Fellowes and Lincoln Plews in their report, "The State of Retirees."[4]

Then why do so many of us feel financially unprepared and vulnerable? Pin part of the blame on the rise of 401(k)s, 403(b)s, and similar defined contribution retirement savings plans. The value of retirement portfolios is subject to the whims of the market, as well as contribution decisions and investment choices made over the years. You can't eliminate the uncertainty.

Retirees don't know how long they will need to live off their retirement savings—five years, twenty years, or thirty years? The apprehension largely reflects the realization that there is no way of knowing in advance how much is enough to maintain a lifestyle let alone future medical bills. There are so many more "known unknowns" than "knowns" with retirement savings (to borrow a phrase popularized by Donald Rumsfeld, former Secretary of Defense during the George W. Bush administration).

Working longer reduces the risk of not having enough. Near-retirees and those in the second half of life have an opportunity to bolster household finances by working longer. Older parents can shore up finances once they become empty-nesters. "We don't have a retirement crisis because people can be flexible," says Bruce Wolfe, former head of the BlackRock Retirement Institute and now principal at management consulting firm C.S. Wolfe & Associates, during a talk at Columbia University. "People can control their spending."

Most people now realize it isn't realistic to expect that they can save enough over a thirty- to thirty-five-year career to live off savings (plus Social Security) for another two or three decades. Less appreciated is the fact that they're shifting preparation for the retirement years from a financial market-based perspective to a household-centric model.

The foundation of this household-centric model is maintaining an income off the knowledge and skills developed over the years, what economists call *human capital*. People are embracing entrepreneurship, self-employment, encore careers, and other work arrangements. These jobs often offer some degree of flexibility, making it easier to, say, manage caregiving responsibilities and travel goals while still bringing in an income.

The entrepreneurial enterprise or the late-life job blurs the traditional personal finance divide between preretirement lifestyle and postretirement lifestyle. A small but telling example: A common assumption in the retirement literature is that people will cook most of their meals at home. They now have the time, and cooking saves money. Yet mature adults are going out frequently. One reason may well be that they're continuing to earn an income. For example, between "the first year of Bill Clinton's administration and the middle of George W. Bush's presidency, senior citizens' restaurant spending rose from 27 to 38 percent of their food budget, far surpassing the increase among shoppers under 45," writes Derek Thompson of the *Atlantic*.[5]

The family is a vital part of the household-centric retirement planning perspective. The American family has changed dramatically over the past half century. Marriage rates are down, and the ranks of single parents are up. The Pew Research Center estimates that about 40 percent of Americans have at least one step-relative in their family.[6] But a changing family structure doesn't mean the bonds of relationships are broken. Research convincingly tells the story that aging boomers and their relations are engaged with one another. "Although the demise of the American family has been lamented throughout the Baby Boomers' lives, most Baby Boomers are actively involved with members of generations above and below them," observe four scholars in an article published in the *Gerontologist*.[7]

Intergenerational relationships are durable. "Grandmothers and grandfathers looked after children when mothers returned to the workforce, provided emotional support to parents and children when marriages fell apart, received step-children with open arms and offered financial assistance to family members enduring economic hardship," writes historian Katherine Anne Otis.[8]

One of the more impressive signs of strong family ties is the more than 44 million caregivers helping their aging elders. The RAND Corporation calculates that family caregivers spend an estimated 30 billion hours per year caring for older family and friends. The annual cost of this informal caregiving—measured by estimating income lost during the time that unpaid caregivers spend on eldercare—is $522 billion. Replacing that uncompensated family care with unskilled paid care at minimum wage would cost some $221 billion. Replacing family members with skilled nursing care could cost $642 billion annually.[9] The AARP came up with comparable numbers on the economic value of unpaid caregiving—approximately $470 billion.[10]

The extended families in the Asian, Latino, and other minority communities are especially engaged in supporting their aged parents.

Some cultural traditions emphasize parents should prepare for their elder years by investing in their children's education rather than in the capital markets. Professor Bruce Corrie is director of the Planning and Economic Development Department for the City of St. Paul, Minnesota. He was a long-time professor of economics at Concordia College in St. Paul before moving over to city government in 2018. Corrie immigrated to the United States from India in the early 1980s to get his doctorate at the University of Notre Dame. "My parents never saved for retirement," he reflects during a conversation at a local coffee shop. "The goal was to get us children where we needed to be. They saved money for our education."

Among the more moving interviews I've had in recent years was with Bee Yang. A remarkable man, I met with him for a PBS Next Avenue column.[11] Yang is a Hmong song poet, with seven children and six grandchildren. Warm, friendly, he's somewhere in his 60s. When he registered as a refugee of war with the United Nations in Thailand, he chose January 10, 1956, for his birthday, but no one really knows his actual birthdate in Laos.

Whatever his age, Yang is a survivor. He fled his village in war-torn Laos in 1975, lived in the jungle for the next three years, married the love of his life, reached the safety of the Bin Vanai Refugee Camp in Thailand in 1979, and came to St. Paul, Minnesota, in 1987.

We met at Swede Hollow Cafe, an appropriate setting since this St. Paul neighborhood has long been home to waves of immigrants. Yang's work in America involved a series of low-wage factory jobs handling machinery. His wife, Chue, also worked. They scheduled their jobs so that a parent was always home with the children. Chue's shifts were in the day and his at night. "In coming to America, everything changed," he says. "The life here has been difficult."

His last manufacturing job ended in 2012 when management abruptly laid off its workers when they tried to unionize. "My heart broke," says Yang. "There are no more days for me in manufacturing. My hands have lost their durability. I can't hear well. They don't hire men like me anymore."

Yang's words are strong and direct even through his daughter's translation, the writer Kao Kalia Yang. The story he told me that day was a powerful narrative about a difficult life of pain, loss, and poverty. His story is also about love, resilience, and family. He and his wife now live in a small house in Canon Falls, about forty miles south of St. Paul. He has chickens. She has a garden and a mushroom patch. They take care of the grandchildren. He's an elder in the community, the person with the experience and the wisdom to help resolve disputes. "He has always supported my rebellious heart. That's his gift to me and my siblings," says Kao Kalia Yang. "And he's a wonderful grandpa," she adds.

He also creates Hmong song poems. At Hmong gatherings, he is called on to sing his poems. His daughter Kao Kalia Yang wrote a moving book honoring his life and art, *The Song Poet*. Here is how his daughter describes his song poems in her book: "In perfect pentatonic pitch my father sings his songs, grows them into long, stretching stanzas of four or five, structures them in couplets, repeats patterns of words, and changes the last word of each verse so that it rhymes with the end of the next," she writes. "He is a master at parallelism, the language is protracted, and the notes are drawn deep and long. The only way I know how to describe it as a form in English is to say: my father raps, jazzes, and sings the blues when he dwells in the landscape of traditional Hmong song poetry."[12]

Some of his song poetry reflects the many losses of the community, such as the hurt survivors feel for family members who didn't make it out of Laos alive. There are song poems yearning for a better life and a better humanity. "I see my songs are for the children of the future," says Bee Yang. "The children in the lifeline I won't know and won't touch. Life is like a spool of thread."

He has received recognition for his song poetry. AARP Minnesota and the networking nonprofit Pollen named him as one of fifty Minnesotans over age 50 making a difference in the community in 2017. Yang is rich in family, community, and connections.

"All my life I have lived without a safety net. And now, I must be there for the children. There is no retirement from parenting. So I try to be what they need me to be every single day," he says. "In my life, what I have learned about money is that it's unreliable. I have always been poor. I gave all my money to our kids so that they could eat and learn. They are my 401(k)."

We're all richer because of that legacy.

The classic image of retirement income is the three-legged stool. The legs are retirement savings, personal savings, and Social Security. The metaphor is too limited, however. Work is another leg, including entrepreneurship and self-employment, bridge jobs and encore careers, part-time work and flexible schedules. The home is another asset to add. Some 80 percent of people 65 years and older are homeowners (with 41 percent carrying a mortgage). Family and friends are another critical part of the safety net. In a conversation with Meier Statman, the savvy finance professor at Santa Clara University, he proposed an alternative metaphor to the three-legged stool: the many-footed centipede.

"I just helped my daughter buy a home. And if, God forbid, I needed her help later on, she would help me out," says Statman. "Centipedes may be a better metaphor than the three legs of a stool."

OK, Statman's centipede image probably won't gain popular currency in the retirement literature. But the many-footed centipede metaphor (centipede literally means 100-footed) better captures the more multifaceted and flexible household-centric prospects for aging Americans in the traditional retirement years. Earning an income is at the core of the centipede metaphor of finances in the traditional retirement years. "There is no need to live in fear that you are going to be penniless in retirement," says Statman. "Most people grow up reasonably responsible financially."

The household gains from working longer relieve much of the retire-ment gloom. The income punch for the typical retiree largely comes from delaying filing for Social Security. Economists John Shoven, Gopi Shah Goda, and Sita N. Slavov illustrate the gains from delay. They calculate that the optimal age for a single woman born in 1951 to claim Social Security is 70. Her expected income is 17.8 percent greater than if she had claimed at age 62. For a man born in 1951, the comparable numbers are age 69 and 12.6 percent increase in expected income. For two-income couples, the target age to claim is 70 for the primary earner born in 1951 and age 67 for the secondary earner born in 1953. The gain in income is estimated at 17.1 percent.[13]

The practical personal finance implications of calculations like these are considered in "The Power of Working Longer," a scholarly paper by four economists, Shoven and Slavov, as well as Gila Bronshtein and Jason Scott. They looked at various scenarios for people nearing retirement. They found that the employees who work just one month longer can get the same increase in their retirement income as if they had increased their 401(k) contributions from 6 percent to 7 percent of pay (with a 3 percent employer match) over a decade. Of course, many people will work longer than one month.

"The results are unequivocal," the scholars write. "Primary earners of ages 62 to 69 can substantially increase their retirement standard of living by working longer. The longer work can be sustained, the higher the retirement standard of living. For example, retiring at age 66 instead of 62 increases living standards by about one-third."[14]

Here's another calculation with a similar message, this time from the Center for Retirement Research at Boston College. If the typical worker starts saving for retirement at age 25 rather than age 45, she cuts her required savings rate for a decent retirement by about two-thirds. Computations like that are behind the standard advice to start saving for retirement early rather than later. (The conventional advice is good. Start saving early.) The Center notes, however, if she delays her retirement from age 62 to age 70, she also cuts her required savings rate by two-thirds.[15] In other words, there is no reason for despair if you find yourself age 62 without much in savings.

One more calculation. This comes from Alicia Munnell, head of the Center for Retirement Research at Boston College. A leading expert in the retirement field, she looked into the old age financial prospects of the millennial generation. Millennials lag previous generations at the same age in building wealth. They graduated into a hostile job market. It is taking them longer to land on a career that comes with employer-sponsored benefits. They're less likely to own a home than previous generations and more likely to be saddled with student loans.

Yet she doesn't conclude her review issuing dire jeremiads about millennial living standards when they reach retirement age. Instead, she highlights the "powerful lever" of working longer. "In fact, my research shows that the vast majority of millennials will be fine if they work to age 70," she writes. "And although it might sound odd, it's historically normal in another sense: Retiring at 70 leaves the ratio of retirement to working years the same as when Social Security was originally introduced."[16]

Household finances are important, of course. Savings matter. But the finance-centric question of "Do I have enough in savings?" and "What is my number?" are the wrong questions to ask, at least in the beginning. That's what Charles Turpin told me when he was 80 years old and sent me an email on safe withdrawal strategies in retirement.

"There are studies conducted by trained psychologists where they interviewed seniors living in assisted care facilities. One of the areas explored was what do you most regret not having done? The most common answer was 'not taking enough risks,'" wrote Turpin. "Perhaps the right question to ask is not 'What is a safe spending meter?' but 'What do I want from my remaining life?' and 'What risks am I willing to take to fulfill that want?'"

What a wonderful question: What do I want from my remaining life? For many in their 50s and 60s, the defining question is what kind of work offers both purpose and a paycheck when nearing the transition into "retirement."

Take this representative email I got:

My dilemma revolves around the meaningfulness of work. . . . I've been a nurse since 1976. I left my school health center job one year ago to retire at 60. Within six months, I began working part-time at a family planning agency. . . . It is difficult to have much-needed skillsets and just put them in a box and walk away from meaningful careers. . . . My first choice would be to work outdoors, in nature, doing something related to the environment or biological research . . . but I have no skills there and not much to offer but my time and willingness to learn. I need permission, I think, to leave the first career behind.

Her stage of life is a time for testing, for experimenting to see what works and, just as important, what doesn't. She might want to take her skills into a different environment, perhaps by becoming an emergency medical technician in a park system or leading ecotravel expeditions. She'll figure it out.

Parents have an opportunity to improve household finances when they become empty-nesters. Kids are expensive to raise. Since 1960, the U.S. Department of Agriculture has published its Expenditures on Children by Families (better known as the Cost of Raising a Child). Middle-income, married-couple parents of a child born in 2015 should anticipate spending between $12,350 and $13,900 annually (in 2015 dollars)—or $233,610 on child-rearing expenses from birth through age 17. Lower income families can expect to spend an average of $174,690 and well-off parents $372,210. These projections don't include the cost of college.[17]

Kids eventually leave home and start their careers and households. Empty-nesters find themselves with extra cash flow. Scholars at the Center for Retirement Research at Boston College illustrated the possibility by creating a married couple raising two kids and making $100,000 annually. They're contributing 6 percent of salary to a 401(k). The simulation suggests that when the kids leave the home to launch their own careers, the couple could set aside 18 percent of earnings into the 401(k)—a 12 percentage point hike. Says financial planner Ross Levin of Accredited Investors Wealth Management: "The key is you need to grab what has been going to the kids and put it toward you."

To be sure, households aren't heeding his advice or setting aside anywhere near 18 percent of earnings. The evidence is that empty-nesters are increasing their contributions by only a fraction. Still, households may change their behavior in the future, especially with work in the second half of life becoming routine. The realization that there is time to save for retirement later than commonly assumed should influence how we think about managing savings over the lifecycle. For many young adults, saving for retirement is hard as kids demand more of the household income. What is underestimated is the ability to save in the second half of life.

"The bottom line, though, is simply this: perhaps it's time to stop guilting parents in the 30s and 40s about not saving enough and recognize the savings opportunity for empty nesters in their 50s and 60s," writes Michael Kitces, director of research at Pinnacle Advisory Group, a private wealth management firm headquartered in Columbia, Maryland. "Because telling parents to save 10 to 20 percent of their income during the child-rearing phase may be unrealistic, and telling empty nesters to save 10 to 20 percent of their income may underestimate their ability to save and get their retirement on track."[18]

Older adults often have other ways to free up cash flow, especially by spending less or embracing frugality. Thrift is where the real gains in living standards often lie. It's well documented that people spend less on stuff as they age, including clothes, jewelry, and furniture. People in their 60s and 70s engage more with experiences, like travel, taking art lessons, and volunteering in the community. These activities often cost less than the price tag of accumulating material goods. Thrift is about quality, not quantity. Frugality involves the pursuit of creativity and experiences, not purchase of things at the mall. Frugality doesn't mean a lower standard of living—far from it.

Certainly, that's what a survey by the mutual fund company T. Rowe Price suggests. Among the people surveyed who had retired in the previous five years, many reported that their households were living on less than the 70 percent to 80 percent of their preretirement income that financial planners assume they need. Four out of ten were living on 60 percent or less. Despite their reduced incomes, these retirees said they're satisfied with how they're doing and agreed they "don't need to spend as much" as they did before. For instance, 65 percent like spending less and see it as newfound freedom.

Some people may be too cautious with their retirement money, at least among those with retirement savings. That's the clear implication of a Blackrock Retirement Institute report, "Spending retirement assets . . . or not?" The study found that after seventeen to eighteen years in retirement median retirement assets were down only some 20 percent on average. Specifically, for the wealthiest group ($500,000 and above) the draw down was 17 percent. Medium-wealth households—$200,000 to less than $500,000—had spent down their retirement assets by 23 percent. The lowest wealth households—less than $200,000—were down 20 percent.[19]

These results echo findings from a Vanguard Center for Retirement Research study. The researchers found that for retirees with at least $100,000 in household wealth, about 40 percent of withdrawals is saved (usually in a money market account or its equivalent).[20]

Similarly, an article by four scholars published in the *Journal of Financial Planning* found a substantial "consumption gap" for retirees with financial assets at the median level and above. These retirees could have spent more—significantly more for well off households—than they did without running out of money.[21]

The spending caution is understandable. No one wants to exhaust their savings in their elder years. Retirees don't know how long their money must last. Another major factor behind spending hesitation is uncertainty over late life medical bills.

Medical expenses are extremely difficult to estimate beforehand. While most people 65 years and older are enrolled in Medicare, the universal health insurance program for older Americans doesn't cover many long-term chronic health care needs and services. A handful of economists investigated medical expenses not paid for by Medicare for people age 70 and over. They found that the 70-plus population incurs an average of $122,000 in medical costs paid out-of-pocket, by private insurers or by the state/federal Medicaid program. Some elders face substantially higher costs, however. Out-of-pocket medical bills for 5 percent will be more than $300,000, and 1 percent will see their medical expenses total more than $600,000. The scholars found that luck—really, bad luck—was a major factor behind the small percentage saddled with large bills.[22]

Hence, the importance of the centipede financial approach to the elder years. Financial prudence suggests when it comes to planning for the elder years we need to save more, invest in our human capital over our lifespan, plan on earning an income well into the traditional retirement years, and borrow less to own things (one definition of frugality or thrift). In my experience, people underestimate how much they can cut back on spending without compromising their quality of life. Top of the expense-reduction and risk-lowering list is getting rid of debts, another way of raising household savings. Of course, when it comes to the financial centipede a key decision is where to live. While popular images of the retirement years is picking up stakes and moving to an adult community in a warm climate, the data supports the notion that staying put in the local community is the trend of today and tomorrow. The main economic and social trends—especially the desire and need to work longer—is both pushing and pulling older adults toward aging in their current community (or nearby).

Older Americans are mostly homeowners. About 80 percent of people 65 years and older own their home. The share of retirees reporting that they have moved is down. Specifically, the number of retirees who say they moved within five years after retirement has fallen from a high of 23 percent in 1980 (when the data series started) to 15 percent in 2015. "Perhaps more tellingly, even when retirees do move, they are most likely to move within the same county," write Fellowes and Plews. They also find that older Americans increasingly live in the suburbs of major cities (like Los Angeles or Phoenix) or in city centers of less crowded cities (such as San Antonio or San Diego).[23]

In other words, older Americans are increasingly choosing to stay near family, friends, familiar cultural attractions, and employment opportunities. The value of community—the local community— has been rediscovered by an aging population. One of the most important values is networks developed over the years by older adults that can be tapped to start a business or to find a job. The network of colleagues, friends, acquaintances, and other relationships are invaluable when trying to develop a vision for the next chapter. Once you've figured where you might find meaning and money, the network can help you to land the job.

Another reason people are more reluctant than before to move far away is the desire to "age in place." An AARP survey had 55 percent of respondents 50 years and older strongly agreeing that they would like to stay in their current residence for as long as possible. Another 21 percent somewhat agreed with the goal.[24] In other words, 76 percent favored staying in the home, if possible.

Aging-in-place is an attractive idea, but it isn't necessarily the best idea, at least once older adults reach their early-to mid-80s. Long-term care expenses typically begin around age 80. It's also a time of life when social isolation is a growing concern. That's why many experts believe people should think more about aging-in-community rather than aging-in-place. "How much does aging in place become stuck in place? You don't want to be lonely," says Robyn Stone, Senior Vice-President of Research at Leading Age.

The trend is toward greater choice. Cohousing, cooperative housing, home sharing, shared residences, multigenerational complexes and other communal living arrangements are growing in popularity. These living arrangements have largely operated on the fringes of the aging housing market, but they're heading into the mainstream.

Whatever the housing arrangement, work in the later years will help redefine these communities. That's one major takeaway from a conversation with Robert Kramer, founder of the National Investment Center for Seniors Housing and Care (or NIC) based in Annapolis, Maryland. We met on a short bus ride in San Francisco during a conference on aging. Kramer has witnessed numerous changes in the housing industry for older Americans since he first got involved in the business in the early 1980s. He made a passionate case during our brief bus ride that the industry would be transformed in the future.

I got back in touch with him to learn more. He is in his unretirement, after turning over the CEO post at NIC to a younger colleague last July. Kramer is now the nonprofit organization's senior advisor with the charge of figuring out how the aging of the population might impact the senior housing business. "We're entering a time of disruptive innovation. The basic business model and system will be radically disrupted," he says. "My job is figuring out the people and the idea trends that will disrupt the sector in a positive way."

Kramer's ideas fit well into the themes of the work-longer movement. The language of retirement is "I'm done," he says. "You disengage from society." The language of boomers entering the retirement years these days is very different, he adds. "It's 'what do I want to do next?'" says Kramer. "Boomers won't retire. They will transition."

He draws an analogy to his father-in-law, a member of the World War II generation. The glass is always half full to his father-in-law. The war was the defining experience of that generation. Many are still glad to have "three hots and a cot"—military slang for three hot meals and a place to sleep. In sharp contrast, the defining years for boomers was college. Boomers believe the elder years should be a time of engagement, enrichment, experience, and enjoyment. Good meals and a safe place to sleep aren't enough. "It's an engagement model. It's the purposeful years," says Kramer. "Boomers won't want to be in an age ghetto."

What really grabbed my attention was this prediction of his: He expects 40 percent to 50 percent of residents in older American retirement housing complexes will be working in the future, launched on their second and third careers. His projected percentages may be too conservative.

Outside of a wealthy sliver of society, you can't get rid of the financial uncertainty about the elder years. Nevertheless, near-retirees should focus less on safe withdrawal strategies and devote more time to asking, "What do I want to do next that will bring me purpose and a paycheck?" The mantra of finding meaning and money in the second half of life is a major reason why the retirement years will turn out better for many people than a quick glance at retirement savings levels would suggest. It's also why as a society we should pay much greater attention to improving the quality of work over the lifespan for everyone and less on financial imbalances in the earned-benefit system of Social Security and Medicare/Medicaid.

Gains from a Multigenerational Society

> Impossible is not a fact. It's an opinion. Impossible is not a declaration. It's a dare. Impossible is potential. Impossible is temporary. Impossible is nothing.
>
> —MUHAMMAD ALI[1]

Sometime back in the early 1970s, I was caddying for my older brother and father. We were joined by a pair of 60-something businessmen. My brother was a college graduate, former Navy lieutenant, recent Harvard Business School graduate, and card-carrying boomer. The businessmen complained nonstop for several holes about boomers like my brother. They were entitled. Boomers didn't listen. They didn't understand corporate loyalty. They refused to work hard. They wanted to get promoted fast. The businessmen said they avoided hiring boomers like my brother. I didn't feel sorry for my older brother very often (after all, he's my older brother), but for several holes he was a good sport putting up with their crude generational prejudices.

Boomer stereotypes are nasty and silly. My brother enjoyed a good career. Boomers are probably now better known for spending too many hours on the job rather than too few. These days, I hear plenty of similarly ignorant stereotypes about millennials. They're entitled. They're lazy. They don't show corporate loyalty. They don't work hard. They want to get promoted too fast. Seriously? C'mon. Let's put an end to this nonsense.

Unfortunately, a large industry stokes the concept of intergenerational warfare. Consultants feast on offering expert advice on how companies can prevent generational strife from destroying productivity.

"The popular press has had a field day alerting human resource (HR) and talent management professionals to the looming generation gap at the workplace. The stories invariably begin something like this: 'For the first time in history, four generations will be in the workplace at the same time,'" writes Marion White of the University of North Carolina Executive Development program. "Most reporters then describe the gap and its potential adverse impact on the workplace. In many cases, it isn't merely described as a gap. It's a crisis, a war, a chasm so deep that it threatens our organizations' very futures."[2]

The evidence is more than compelling that systematic and sustained intergenerational conflict at the workplace is mostly nonsense. Her analysis of generational studies by various researchers concluded the generation gap narrative had little scientific merit. Instead, the various studies she reviewed emphasized the shared commitments across the generations, including "work-life balance, opportunities for advancement, learning and growth in their jobs."

Perhaps most important, generational stereotypes limit the potential contributions of different people at different ages in the workplace, hurting "collaboration, production, workplace relationships, and individual self-perception."

Researcher Brenda Kowske of the Kenexa Research Institute looked into twenty-four years of workforce survey data on the generations. Her analysis also emphasized the workplace commonalities among the generations at the same stage of their career.[3] "However, at the end of the day, the vast majority of employees in the United States are subjected to certain rules about being at work, prescribe to the same value proposition of work-for-compensation and similarly engage in our consumer-driven economy," she writes.

Survey research by the IBM Institute for Business Value also suggests the three generations desire the same thing from the workplace. The Institute surveyed millennials, Gen Xers, and baby boomers and found that the three generations shared common work goals, such as making a positive impact on the organization, helping to solve social and environmental problems, working in teams, and dealing with a diverse group of people.[4]

A study commissioned by McDonald's in Britain in 2009 by scholars at the Lancaster University Management School to look into the performance of 400 of its restaurants echoes these results. The study found that customer satisfaction levels were on average 20 percent higher in outlets that employed kitchen staff and managers over 60. These results reflected the benefits of a multigenerational rather than age-segregated workforce. The older workers demonstrated a work ethic and had skills, while the younger workers responded well to their older colleagues.[5]

The Great Places to Work organization has produced lists of the best places to work in partnership with *Fortune* magazine since 1998. In 2016, it surveyed 230,000 employees at 620 organizations for its Best Workplaces for Millennials, Gen Xers and Baby Boomers. What it found was that all three generations value pride, a sense of community, and honest, competent leadership. For example, there was no meaningful difference in the top reasons respondents from the three generations said made them give extra at work: A workplace that is cooperative, friendly, caring, and welcoming. The differences in the workplace among employees have more to do with their stage of life—just starting a family versus coming home to an empty nest—than their generation.[6]

Think about Barbara Beskind. She got a job at the San Francisco-based design firm IDEA in 2013 in her late 80s. At age 92, in 2016, she became a Design Fellow. She commutes by train to the IDEA offices in downtown San Francisco from her San Mateo retirement community every Thursday. Beskind has had numerous careers, but her primary job has been as an occupational therapist, including two decades in the Army. She helps teams of designers working on products targeted at older adults.[7]

"It isn't about designing for an older population," says Gretchen Addi, who hired Beskind at IDEA, in an interview. Addi, age 67, is now a design consultant continuing her passion for aging as a design opportunity. "It's designing for the population that will be older," she says. "We need to have multigenerational engagement."

Here's another sign people should abandon their generational conflict lens: millennial family caregivers. One in four of the nation's 44 million family caregivers is a millennial, according to the AARP Public Policy Institute report, "Millennials: The Emerging Generation of Family Caregivers."[8] Millennial caregivers pay a substantial price for caregiving. The AARP study found that 73 percent of millennial caregivers work and more than half of them say caregiving has interfered with their jobs. They've received warnings about performance, turned down promotions, and taken other actions that could jeopardize their long-term financial security. AARP figures millennials pay an average of $6,800 a year in out-of-pocket costs to meet their caregiving responsibilities—a higher percentage of income than other generations.

Much more unites the generations in the workplace and in society than divides them, especially when it comes to jobs and careers. There are differences, of course. New parents have different worries than someone negotiating a phased retirement package. Powerful generational memories differ, too. The Civil Rights movement, Vietnam War, and 1968 are memory touchstones for me. For millennials, their knowledge about these historic events comes from books, movies, and perhaps a college class. Among their defining moments are 9/11, student loans, and graduating into the Great Recession.

Still, when it comes to work everyone on the job wants the chance "to have a go" for purpose and a paycheck. The common desire across generations is "can I make a good living and do something that is meaningful," says William Shutkin on a conference panel about encore careers when he was president of Presidio Graduate School in San Francisco.

The rise of intergenerational conflict—think Social Security, greedy geezers, and the silver tsunami—is a common political refrain in Washington, DC. Robert Samuelson, economics columnist for the *Washington Post*, wonders why generational warfare isn't breaking out.

"An enduring puzzle of our politics is why there isn't more generational conflict. By all rights, younger Americans should be resentful," he writes. "Although the 75 million baby boomers (people born from 1946 to 1964) are flooding into Social Security and Medicare at about 10,000 a day, there's no clamor from the young to shift some of the programs' costs from themselves to the elderly. (Social Security and Medicare are financed with current taxes and general funds, generated mainly by workers.) Why?"[9]

The tactic of stoking generational warfare became popular among advocates for privatizing Social Security in the early 1980s. The kids versus canes rhetoric is now standard operating procedure whenever Social Security and Medicare cuts come up. Yet once again the idea that one generation's gain is another generation's loss is flatly false. The ageist view that older Americans will selfishly vote their material self-interest as a block ignores the rich diversity of elders, with differing financial resources, work histories, family relations, educational attainment, and mental and physical health.

Let's change the narrative about relations between young and old away from conflict and toward intergenerational interdependence. Here's how Marc Freedman, head of the social venture Encore.org, captured the power of generational connections and the common good in his book *How to Live Forever*:

"We now know that engaging olders to support youngers, to connect to them in meaningful ways, is one of the routes to well-being in later life. An extensive body of research on purpose, generativity, relationship, and face-to-face contact makes it plain: engagement with others that flows down the generational chain will make you healthier, happier, and likely longer-lived," writes Freedman. "It's the real fountain of youth. Likewise, when we think of what younger people need, the answer looks a lot like the assets of the older generation, today and into the future."[10]

The evidence is overwhelming that the conflict narrative doesn't work outside the political arena. Study after study, poll after poll, finds that support for Social Security is multigenerational. Here's just one example. When asked about the long-term future of Social Security, 71 percent of registered voters surveyed by the Pew Research Center said that benefits shouldn't be reduced in any way. Clear majorities of both Democrats (72 percent) and Republicans (68 percent) opposed benefit cuts, according to Pew. (Among Trump supporters, 73 percent were against reducing Social Security benefits.)

In fairness to columnist Samuelson, while he raised the generational warfare puzzle, he answers it with savvy insight: The generations like each other.[11]

Young adults get along better with their parents than boomers with their parents at comparable ages. "And when we asked adults of all ages which generation has the better moral values, young or old, about three-quarters of the young said the old. (The old agreed.)" writes Paul Taylor, author of *The Next America* and the former executive vice president of the Pew Research Center. "It's hard to imagine the Baby Boomers saying the same back when their coming-of-age rallying cry was: "Never trust anyone over 30."[12]

Years ago, during an interview with Steve King, cofounder of Emergent Research in the Bay Area, we talked about our parents and our kids. We're both boomers. We love our parents. But if our parents had raised the idea of going into business together, both of us would have fled the room. "Are you insane," King says, laughing at what would have been his immediate response. "That was a common reaction."

Yet both of us said we would leap at the opportunity to go into business with our own children. Our children are building their own careers and the idea isn't practical, at least not at the moment. But the prospect is fun to think about. "Baby boomers are close to their kids," says King. "I would go into business with my kids in a heartbeat. They're smart. They're involved. I like them."

The stronger bonds between the generations is heartening.

Intergenerational interdependence often starts at home. Multigenera-tional living is making something of a comeback in the United States. A record 64 million Americans or 20 percent of the U.S. population lived in multigenerational households in 2016, according to Pew. That's up from a low of 12 percent in 1980.[13]

The return of multigenerational living partly reflects the wave of immigration over the past four decades. Living under one roof is more common among immigrants, especially Asians and Latinos. The aging of the population is another factor. Living with parents saves time and money and, increasingly, childcare services as adult children become parents themselves. The average cost of full-time care for one infant in a childcare center ranges from 7 percent to 17 percent of state median income, depending on the state, for a married couple. The average cost of center-based infant care is greater than 27 percent of median income for single parents in every state.[14]

Saundra Plett and her husband, Dwight Miyake, grew up in extended families in small towns in the central valley region of California. The longtime educators lived in Fresno. She was a Montessori teacher, a teaching consultant, and a university instructor in early childhood education. He taught music in elementary school. Their only child, Emily, is a lawyer in Washington, DC. When she had her first child, Dwight and Saundra found themselves flying out to DC whenever possible. They started to wonder if they should take early retirement and move closer to their grandson (and, shortly, granddaughter).

Saundra and Dwight had deep roots in the central valley. They knew the cost-of-living difference between Fresno and DC meant going from a comfortable lifestyle with ample disposable income to a tighter budget. They had many conversations with their daughter and Aric, their son-in-law. "We opened up a serious conversation. How do we make this work?" says Saundra. "We had several months of in-depth conversations. We talked to financial people, real estate people."

They sold their California home, and their daughter and son-in-law sold their home in Alexandria, Virginia. Everyone moved to a three-story house in Takoma Park, Maryland. Dwight and Saundra comfortably live on the lower floor. Their daughter and her family are on the top floor. The main floor is shared living space.

The economic benefits of multiple generations living under one roof are striking. Pooling financial resources among the generations is a smart way to lower the overall cost of home ownership. That's before considering built-in childcare and easy monitoring when aging parents turn frail. Shared ownership allows young adults to build up savings and the older generation to draw down less on their retirement savings. "It has worked out better than I thought it would," says Saundra.

The retired teachers are both in their early 60s. Dwight works full-time at Trader Joe's as the "wine-guy." He loves helping people find the right wine and, very important, the job comes with health insurance. Saundra is the full-time householder in their multigenerational family, caring for the kids. She has run a small Montessori at Home program in the house for several neighborhood children.

The economics works for them. "We don't have as much money as we would have had if we had stayed in California. We were to the point of paying off our house, and our retirement income would have been higher," she says. "But if you gauge standard of living by being able to be with family and things like that, it's a real good trade. Plus, there are cultural things to do in DC that we didn't have in California." As Dwight and Saundra age, they'll be able to rely on Emily and Eric to take care of them—the circle of life. "Emily was kind of concerned about us being on the West Coast and her being on the East Coast. She wanted to be able to keep an eye on us as we got older," says Saundra. "Now we're playing a big role taking care of the grandchildren, and later on, who knows who will be taking care of whom."

That's reassuring and financially savvy.

Multigenerational homes may well become a common living arrangement in the future. Mother-in-law apartments, granny flats, garage apartments, and other "accessory dwelling units" (the arid social science designation) are increasingly popular with "sandwich generation adults" responsible for raising young children and minding aging parents. The sharing of responsibilities also makes it easier for everyone to do their work and pursue their careers.

Volunteering is also a multigenerational affair. Linda Meadows, 50-something, is with the AmeriCorps Reading Partners program at Cherry Hill Elementary in south Baltimore, a low-income, mostly African-American, neighborhood. Meadows tutors students in reading in the school library. Her husband is an Episcopal minister, and she has spent most of her peripatetic career in administrative and program development jobs, often in higher education. When they left Connecticut last year for his new job in Silver Spring, Maryland, Meadows decided to give tutoring a try. She started at Cherry Hill last August, and she delights in her students.

"Learning is a wonderful thing. They have to be able to read and comprehend what they read," she says. "I like to encourage young people. They need to be told they can do it."

Meadows convinced Michael Cobb—her 31-year-old son—to apply for the program when he moved with them from Connecticut. He liked Baltimore when he got his graduate degree in African-American studies at Morgan State University a few years ago. Cobb is the Reading Partners site coordinator for volunteers at the Furman L. Templeton Preparatory Academy, a charter elementary school in the Sandtown-Winchester neighborhood in west Baltimore. "How about that," laughs Linda Meadows. "I recruited my son. Yes, I did. I was so happy he joined Reading Partners."

There is evidence that the generations reinforce one another in volunteering. That's a conclusion drawn from a research study by a team of scholars at the Lilly Family School of Philanthropy at Indiana University–Purdue University Indianapolis. They tapped into a database of more than 13,000 people developed over the past decade to investigate the charitable behavior of three generations—grandparents, parents, and adult children.

Among their findings: Parents who volunteer are more likely to have children who volunteer. Specifically, for a 1-percentage point increase in parental volunteering incidence, the odds of the child volunteering increase by 0.8 percent.[15] "The narrative seems to be about clashes across generations," says Una Osili, professor of economics and director of research at the Lilly Family School of Philanthropy. "What we actually found is that there is a lot of shared interest."

That's the inspiring case with the Bancroft family. Ann Bancroft is in her 60s. The famed arctic explorer lives in St. Paul, Minnesota. She remembers the conversation that influenced her volunteerism with Wilderness Inquiry well. In 1986, she was some two weeks away from the North Pole. She was the only female member of the Will Steger International North Pole Expedition and the first woman to cross the ice to the world's northernmost point. Her fellow explorer and dogsledder Paul Schurke asked what she planned on doing when the expedition was done. He suggested she hook up with Wilderness Inquiry, at the time a small nonprofit housed in a garage in southeast Minneapolis. Wilderness Inquiry takes people with disabilities into the wilderness, such as kayaking the Apostle Islands on Lake Superior. Bancroft took his advice and she has been involved with the organization as staffer and volunteer since then. "I am a lifer," says Bancroft.

Wilderness Inquiry became a family affair. For instance, her mother joined the volunteer board and her father took photos for the organization. Her siblings got involved. They shared the organization's passion, which strengthened them as a family and their ties to the wider community.

"We have all learned it a million times," says Bancroft. "It is so much more rewarding to give than to receive. The engagement benefits all of us."

I've attended many conferences on aging in recent years. The panel discussions I attend focus on a work or entrepreneurial challenge confronting people in the second half of life. Yet the conversations outside these formal sessions always revolve around the realization that our ideas to increase economic opportunities for older adults also improve prospects for younger generations (who will get older). We should embrace the diversity that comes from people of all ages and backgrounds dealing with one another and learning from one another at the workplace and in our communities. Age segregation on the job and in the workplace is wrong.

"The wisdom of older and experienced individuals, combined with the fresh thinking and new paradigms of younger generations is clearly a smarter way for all of us to move forward to solve current and future problems," says John Tarnoff, a veteran of the entertainment industry and career coach. "Relegating anyone to the sidelines for any reason serves no purpose."[16]

A far richer framework is to focus on generational interdependence among entrepreneurs and workers from different generations. Each generation has something to offer other generations. Life isn't a zero-sum game. Just ask Antoinette Edinburgh Williams.

She was 93 years old when I met her in 2017. She owned the Edinburgh Williams Beauty Salon on Bruxelles Street in the Gentilly neighborhood in New Orleans. The salon appears small from the outside, red brick with clapboard siding on the top third. While I was standing on the opposite corner from the salon making sure I was at the right place, she opened its door and welcomed me in. The salon is spacious and warm inside. Williams is spry, quick with a smile and a story. I almost didn't notice the cane she uses for balance.

One of the joys of journalism happens when you meet remarkable people at unexpected moments. (This time it was for a PBS Next Avenue column.)[17] Williams is one of those people and so many of the themes of this book come together with her story. She has been in the hair salon business ever since she graduated from high school. Her mom decided Williams would go to beauty school to learn a trade. She later became a social worker, a pioneer among African Americans in segregated Louisiana. She also graduated from Xavier

University of Louisiana with a degree in fine arts in 1957. She taught art in schools for a long time.

Her late husband was a social studies teacher, school principal, and deacon at their church. They bought the salon some forty years ago to serve the community. "When people walk through the door, they should feel that they are getting something they can't get elsewhere," she says.

Reflecting on her years in the salon business, she is particularly proud of the stylists she and her husband taught the basics of running a business, talented hairdressers who eventually left to start their own salons. "We wanted to give young people an idea of what it's like to run a business," she says. "A salon is a vehicle, a way to be independent and they learned what it is to serve people."

Among the inspired entrepreneurs is her niece Kim, in her early 40s. Kim got her undergraduate degree at the University of Houston and an MBA from Howard University. She worked at Ford Motor Co. for five years before returning to New Orleans. She works for an affordable housing developer and rents property. She's restoring a historic New Orleans classic double camelback shotgun house from the 1850s. She's raising her teenage daughter.

Kim worked at her aunt's salon when young. She is taking over the business. "I was sweeping the floors and emptying the ashtrays when I was 9 years old," says Kim.

Her aunt chuckles. "She has been around the business all her life."

Change is coming with the transition. Kim is adding more stylists, as well as a nail technician and receptionist. She's brought items to sell in the salon, such as candles, soaps, and purses. She hopes to develop her own line of hair products.

What Kim won't change is her aunt's commitment to community. The Gentilly neighborhood was badly flooded during Hurricane Katrina in 2005. The salon shut down. Williams and her husband lived in Baton Rouge for eight months. But they came back and rebuilt, reopening the salon in 2007.

Talking with them around a simple foldout table in the back of the salon, drinking water out of plastic cups, it's obvious how much each is looking forward to their next chapter. "Kim is taking it another direction," says Williams. "I am good with that. It's a whole new ballgame."

Intergenerational interdependence shows up in the growing popularity of mentoring. YPO is a global community of more than 26,000 chief executive officers in 130 countries. The organization is putting greater emphasis on creating mentoring opportunities for its members with other executives, including an online matching program. A YPO survey showed that more than half of its members were interested in being mentored, and more than half of their peers in the network reported that they were interested in mentoring.

The social enterprise Encore.org launched its Generation to Generation campaign in 2017. The initiative aims to get at least one million people over age 50 to dedicate time, talent, and experience to improving the lives of young people. In its first year, the campaign was joined by more than 130 organizations, including AARP, Big Brothers Big Sisters, and Girls Inc.[18]

"In launching the Generation to Generation (Gen2Gen) campaign, we are working to shine a light on this growing phenomenon, inspire others to join in, and find strength in numbers," writes Freedman. "We hope to build a society where older people standing up for younger ones becomes both the expectation and the norm in later life. Our rallying cry: a better future for future generations."[19]

Mentoring is hardly new. Socrates and Plato. Ralph Waldo Emerson and Henry David Thoreau. Maya Angelou and Oprah Winfrey. Yoda and Luke Skywalker.

An impressive body of scholarly research supports the benefits of mentoring for both the mentor and the mentee. For example, mentors can help younger people establish career goals. They open their work-based networks to the younger generation. Students who meet regularly with their mentors are 52 percent less likely than their peers to skip a day of school. At the same time, mentors learn about the interests of the younger generation, staying up with trends in technology and society.[20]

"The past twenty years have been a golden age of mentoring research," says Ellen Ensher, professor of management at Loyola Marymount University in Los Angeles and author of *Power Mentoring.* "People realize that mentoring is something that is relatively low cost and high reward."

Mentoring at the workplace isn't only for white-collar employees and young professionals. Skilled blue-collar workers like plumbers, electricians, construction workers, and similar trades often find their work engaging. Experienced blue-collar workers often shift to mentoring the next generation in their craft when it comes time for them to move into their unretirement.

Mentoring is at the core of New Century Careers, a Pittsburgh-based nonprofit organization. New Century offers several entry-level machinist apprenticeship programs, including the certified National Tool and Machining Association. An entrepreneurial enterprise, New Century is developing a robotics apprenticeship program. It's also testing out a social venture that would involve students doing simple machining jobs for companies that might bring in some new revenue. Students range in ages from right out of high school to retired military. They also have a preapprenticeship qualification class in the jail. Most students are in the 24-to-30-year-old range, although there are some mid-career students looking for a new gig.

"The students might have been homeless, in and out of jail," says Paul Anselmo, cofounder and executive director of New Century. "We want them to do better."

New Century is on the other side of the Monongahela River from downtown Pittsburgh. Once over the bridge and heading toward New Century, one side of the road is a steep cliff and on the other side industrial buildings run down toward the river. Down one flight from street level at New Century is a large open floor covered with substantial machines—lathes, milling machines, computer numerical control machines, and other tools of the trade.

Anselmo's office is large and plain, nothing fancy. Comfortable for holding meetings. The paintings on the wall are of a coastal town near Naples. Anselmo remarked when we met that he would turn 64 in a few weeks. He felt he was about two years away from retirement. The job is intense, and he would like to spend more time with his eight grandchildren. "I want to slow down," he sighed. "But I don't know how to do that."

I met several machinists ranging in age from their 50s to 80s passing on their craft to the younger generations. The instructors loved the art of machining. They're all part-time instructors. Everyone wanted the younger generation in the program to succeed as machinists so that they could get a job, own a home, and support a family. The American Dream is alive and well among the older machinists and their students at New Century. "They had a great life and they want to pass it on," says Anselmo.

Lou Pavsek is a cofounder of New Century Careers' Manufacturing 2000 program and he continues as an apprenticeship instructor. His career has been fascinating, including eleven years machining at Westinghouse and serving as a votech teacher for twenty-five years until retiring in 2013. His three children are "his life." With his gray hair flowing over his collar and his gravelly voice, Pavsek looks like the motorcycle fan he is, traveling the countryside on his Harley. He's made the late-summer pilgrimage on his Harley several times to Sturgis, South Dakota, for the Motorcycle Rally, the world's largest motorcycle gathering. "All my kids call me Mr. P," he laughs. "I love the students."

He sees opportunities for the students. The demand is there. "I see nothing but jobs out there," says Pavsek. "You just have to find the right job for the right person. That's one of the hardest things to do, finding the right job for the right person."

Paul Urban is 81 years old and a lifelong machinist. He's a big man with a square face and close-cropped hair. He looks like the basketball player he was in high school and the weightlifter he became when he was 19 years old. He stopped weightlifting when he was 57 and could still bench press 345 pounds. Urban has had two knee replacements. He volunteers at the hospital where he had his operations to encourage people with hip and knee replacements to exercise and follow their recommended regimen.

Urban worked at the machine shop owned by his father-in-law from his first marriage for much of his career. But they got divorced after thirty years of marriage and three kids. He had a "wonderful second marriage." He also knew that he was starting from scratch financially and that he would have to work. His second wife died from cancer after thirteen years of marriage. Paul lives on Social Security and earnings from his part-time job at New Century. He never expected to be an instructor.

"Just because you've reached a certain age, I don't think you're done having an influence on society," he says. "I love the teaching. There is no better feeling in the world than to teach the students how to run a machine and get a job."

He takes the students on field trips to visit different companies. His students say he makes machining look so easy. He tells them that is "sixty years of experience." He's also taught for New Century in the county jail. Our conversation turns sober when he talks in detail about the four students he worked with who overdosed from drugs. He tears up telling their stories. "A lot of them eventually get out and get jobs, get work," he says. "That's a good feeling."

Urban has three children and several grandchildren. A yearly highlight is when he and a woman friend head off in September to Myrtle Beach, South Carolina. They attend an annual ten-day party held in lounges with names like Fat Harold's and Pirate's Cove, clubs and block parties, dancing the night away to the sound of shag music. (Shag music, also known as Carolina beach music, is a blend of rock, R&B, and pop music from the 1950s and 1960s.) "We call it spring break for seniors," he says, laughing.

Joe Abraham, 78 years old, swears a lot. He keeps apologizing for swearing, but it's a habit. He teaches students the four-week National

Institute for Metal Working Skills course on the computer. He has three children, all working in the medical field in Pittsburgh. He and his wife moved from rural Pennsylvania to be closer to their children. He works (partly) to pay his #^@**@@ property taxes.

Joe has a mechanical engineering degree. He worked as machinist for Rockwell International for fifteen years, ran a mill for four years in West Virginia (a commute of 140 miles round trip, so he only came home on weekends) and fifteen years as high school teacher. He retired in 2008, and he works part-time at New Century. "I love it, honest to God," he says. "The students, when they come in here, they get intimidated. I tell them, stick with it. If you don't understand it, I'll get you through it. Don't be embarrassed. Don't think I don't make mistakes."

Joe has another gig. He goes to flea markets to buy and sell stuff. One time he bought a lot of DeWalt drills, the ones with the trademark yellow and black colors. The drills didn't come with batteries, so he got them for $2 each. He sold them for $10, a "steal" if you had the right battery at home. "I don't like to say I'm old," says Joe. "I'm always active. You have to enjoy life."

Bruce Thompson is 64 years old. When we met he handed me his 1977 graduation certificate from the Westinghouse Air Brake apprenticeship program and his 1978 U.S. Steel identification button. Thompson was only the second African American to go through the four-year Westinghouse program. "The civil rights movement opened doors," he says.

Thompson worked at U.S. Steel from 1978 to 1983. A master machinist, when the mill closed, he got work at different shops in town. He is a full-time machinist during the day and teaches part-time in the evening at New Century. "I like the program. I like to see the results," he says. "Lots of good stories."

He plans on retiring in two years at age 66 and filing for Social Security. He is training his replacement for his current employer. Thompson's replacement is 70 years old. "I said, 'How many years are you planning on working?'" says Thompson. His future replacement replied, "Until about age 75."

That's a sentiment to celebrate.

12

Reimagining the Common Good

There is nothing to be afraid of. On the contrary. The future holds in store for us far more wealth and economic freedom and possibilities of personal life than the past has ever offered.

—JOHN MAYNARD KEYNES[1]

I n the conclusion of their book *Life Reimagined: Discovering Your New Life Possibilities*, authors Richard Leider and Alan Webber address the millions and millions of people creating new prospects and opportunities in the second half of life.

"It's a movement that is reimagining more than fifty years of accepted practice and conventional wisdom about the trajectory and purpose of our lives. This movement does away with outdated boundaries, irrelevant conventions, and unproductive expectations. It challenges a system that has emerged to tell us how society expects us to live our lives. . . . In a world that's changing, it's time for us to change—to take on our deepest fears and take hold of our greatest aspirations. It's your movement. It's your move."[2]

Millions of people in the second half of life are taking up their challenge. But individuals can only do so much, even when numbered in the millions involving every ethnic group and income level. The goals and ambitions of the grassroots movement need to be translated into norms and institutions, products and services, laws and regulations that support the transformation.

Major transitions are never easy. Shifts in organizational behavior and institutional development unfold over long periods, measured in decades. There is no magic wand that dramatically overhauls outdated practices and hidebound stereotypes, particularly in a society as deeply divided politically as the United States. The work-longer movement has gathered enough momentum to be unstoppable. We've turned the corner on rethinking the aging S-curve. Question is, will the pace of change be fast (my hope) or slow (the risk).

What might slow progress? Reform could slow to a crawl as political entrepreneurs in Washington, DC, and state capitals stoke nostalgic anger among supporters rather than negotiate legislation that would improve economic security and economic opportunity for their constituents. Business elites could stay solely focused on maximizing shareholder profits, reluctant to invest money and time into developing worker skills for the new economy. Public intellectuals could indulge in endless arguments over the fine points of moldy debates, unwilling to boldly grapple with unsettling new public policy trade-offs (because there are always trade-offs).

The Trump administration isn't helping. The administration seems locked in nostalgia rather than grappling with the future.

However, several powerful forces are pushing for change. High on the list is financial insecurity, heightened thanks to the pincers of globalization, technological change, and political gridlock. The haunting fear in many quarters is that too slow a pace of social change will only deepen the dark disillusionment of those feeling left behind.

On a more positive note, experienced workers are joining the ranks of entrepreneurs. Growing numbers of people in the second half of life are looking for both purpose and an income. Their willingness to innovate and their admirable "can-do" spirit are redefining old age in America.

To paraphrase the earlier quote from Leider and Webber, "In a world that's changing, it's time for politicians, policymakers, and leaders of organizations to change—to take on our deepest fears and take hold of our greatest aspirations."

The need for a major overhaul in America's earned-benefit programs is obvious. Thomas Fisher is the director of the Minnesota Design Center at the University of Minnesota. He's an enthusiastic prose-lytizer for the gig economy. The keynote speaker at a conference on the emerging share economy, Fisher drew a vivid, optimistic vision of a future defined by the rise of a high-tech version of the traditional village economy. Collaboration trumps competition. The pursuit of experience replaces the desire to own things. Consumers become producers, and vice versa. Workers enjoy flexible jobs and multiple careers. Sounds good, right?

A member of the audience skeptically wondered, isn't the gig economy more of a worker dystopia, offering low wages, no benefits, and job insecurity? "We are in the early Industrial Revolution phase once again, and like then there is a lot of inequality," Fisher replied. "We'll need to develop laws and public policy to handle it."

Fisher was right. The gig economy has garnered huge attention, even though the actual number of workers involved is relatively small. The gig economy is simply part of a much larger trend toward a contingent or independent workforce, including freelancers and in-dependent contractors. The labor market challenge highlighted by the gig economy is how best to ensure that all workers of any label—gig, contingent, part-time, full-time, temporary, self-employed, and fledgling entrepreneurs—enjoy the kind of earned-benefit safety net that provides financial security and encourages risk-taking.

Is even the thought of reform a pie-in-the-sky belief? I hope not. The United States has made major social transformations before despite formidable obstacles. In the late nineteenth century, most workers la-bored long hours at hazardous, arduous jobs. They didn't get regular vacations, let alone pensions in the elder years. Job insecurity was an inescapable part of working life. Strikes were common and often violent. Mass production companies had little use for older workers. Business wanted younger workers to speed up the assembly line.

The foundation for the modern earned-benefit safety net—the one we still live with—was largely built from the Great Depression through the early post-World War II years. The modern safety net represented a vast improvement in economic security.

Some of the key legislation included the 1935 Social Security Act, which provided support to the elderly and disabled during the Great Depression, and laid-off workers got some financial relief with unemployment insurance. The Fair Labor Standards Act of 1938 included a national minimum wage and overtime rules. In 1965 Medicare offered universal health care to those 65 years and older while the joint federal-and-state Medicaid program has been a safety net for the poor. The Civil Rights Act of 1964 banned employment discrimination on the basis of race, color, religion, sex, and national origin. The 1967 federal Age Discrimination in Employment Act protected older workers from discrimination in hiring, firing, and other conditions of employment. The Employee Retirement Income Security Act of 1974 (ERISA) strengthened pension and health insurance protections.

Big business played a critical role in knitting the new social compact. Large companies like General Motors, General Electric, and U.S. Steel reached relative industrial peace with labor starting in the 1950s. The negotiated agreements with labor allowed corporate executives to maintain their authority over business operations and capital allocation. Management agreed in return to share more of the wealth with employees and offer greater job security.

"The new social contract emerging between employer and employee in the United States represented a dramatic departure from the punishing past," writes Rick Wartzman in *The End of Loyalty: The Rise and Fall of Good Jobs in America*. "It was forged between men and women—some of them unionized, some of them not; some of them blue collar; some of them white collar—and corporations such as Kodak, GM and Coca-Cola and GE. These four giants, as well as thousands of other large businesses, would affect job security, pay, benefits, and worker engagement through this compact."[3]

The landmark deal of the new compact was the five-year contract negotiated between General Motors and the United Auto Workers in 1950. The contract guaranteed autoworkers a substantial pay increase, plus improved life, health, and pension benefits. The so-called Treaty of Detroit symbolized America's employer-centric approach for providing retirement, health, and other benefits to employees and their families.

The employer-centric role in benefits was something of a historical accident. The Stabilization Act of 1942 allowed President Roosevelt to freeze wages and salaries, which he promptly did. The Act exempted health insurance and pension benefits from the freeze. Labor markets were tight during the war with so many people serving in the military. Management retained and attracted workers by boosting compensation with improved benefits. The United States came to rely on employers to offer employees and their families health insurance, pensions, and other benefits after the war. A good career meant getting a job at a company with benefits.

The U.S. economy grew rapidly in the two decades following the Treaty of Detroit. Smokestack America dominated the world economy. Young men (and it was mostly men at the time) could graduate from high school and make a good living on the assembly line. Worker wages rose smartly. Families bought cars and homes. Long-term employees could plan on spending their elder years in retirement. The pursuit of leisure became the defining activity of old age for the first time in history (outside the wealthy). The popular image of old age in the media became golf in the afternoon and barbecues on the patio in the evening. Shuffleboard, anyone?

I've never managed to get too romantic about the grand bargain. The Treaty of Detroit system largely excluded blacks and women. Small businesses didn't participate, and many workers never labored at a company with benefits. The ranks of the poor were far larger than commonly believed at the time. Nostalgia for the traditional pension reward for thirty years of service has obscured the fact that the full benefit was enjoyed by only about 12 percent of the workforce. Most workers weren't on the job long enough at one place to qualify. A laid-off worker lost more than wages. His family no longer had health insurance.

Nevertheless, the 1950s through the early 1970s was a time when the American Dream seemed within reach to more people than ever before. The modern image of middle-class life—education, career and home, retirement and leisure—was shaped during this era.

The earned-benefit safety net system started eroding in the 1970s. U.S. companies stumbled with auto, steel, electronics, and machine-tool industries losing market share and profits to international rivals based in Europe and Japan. U.S. productivity growth faltered. The Treaty of Detroit broke down. Private sector unions fell into long-term decline. Companies outsourced jobs to low-cost regions of the United States and abroad. The rise of the maximizing shareholder value ideology among executives and investors built a corporate culture that "explicitly elevated shareholders above employees," writes Wartzman.[4]

The economy didn't fall into long-term decline, as many end-of-empire commentators at the time feared. American companies were in the vanguard in high-tech industries, from software to biotech to the internet. U.S. multinational corporations invested in building robust global supply chains and remained formidable international competitors. Workers with college diplomas and advanced degrees did well. Women transformed the paid labor force by entering in record numbers. Highly educated immigrants were a dynamic presence in cutting-edge industries. Less educated immigrants revitalized neighborhoods.

However, the labor market changed incrementally and, in many respects, not for the better. Wages adjusted for inflation grew slowly for most workers. Access to company-sponsored benefits shrank. The notion of a "job for life" became a relic. Management loyalty to its workforce ended with the strategic embrace of mass layoffs. Workers on the wrong side of international trade competition or high-tech innovations were mostly on their own when they lost their jobs.

Employers retreated from offering employees generous retirement, health, and training benefits. Managements that continued offering these core benefits redesigned them so that employees absorbed much of the financial risk and cost.

The classic example is pensions. During the Treaty of Detroit era, large companies offered their employees traditionally defined benefit pension plans. The employer bears all the investment risk and commits to a fixed payout of money, typically based on a salary and years-of-service formula. In essence, the employee continued to get a regular payment from the company, this time called a pension rather than a wage.

To cut costs and reduce future financial obligations, managements retreated from pensions and substituted defined contribution plans like 401(k)s. The 401(k) puts all the risk on employees. They must decide how much to invest and where to invest it (within the choices offered in the plan).

Similarly, since the early 2000s, employers have pushed their employees into high-deductible health plans where employees shoulder much more of the cost of care. The proportion of workers who received employer-sponsored training dropped by 42 percent from 1996 to 2008.[5] Employees often have to take the initiative and the expense on their own to get additional training.

Most small businesses never offered their employees benefits. The Government Accountability Office estimates only 14 percent of small employers—businesses with fewer than 100 employees—offered some type of retirement plan.[6] The Kaiser Family Foundation reports that some 54 percent of companies with three to forty-nine employees offer health insurance coverage, down from 66 percent about a decade ago.[7]

Fewer workers are covered by the traditional job arrangements. Although estimates vary widely, somewhere between 15 percent and one-third of workers probably fall into the "contingent" worker category. The contingent workforce includes temp workers, on-call workers, contract company workers, independent contractors, self-employed individuals, standard part-time workers, and gig economy workers. Contingent workers aren't eligible to participate in an employer-sponsored retirement savings plan and health insurance plan. Contingent workers don't enjoy much of the government's safety net, such as unemployment insurance and minimum wage protections.

America's employer-based benefits system is an anachronism for an economy buffeted by international trade, high-tech innovation, and growing numbers of workers in the second half of life. Why should families lose benefits when the worker gets laid off? Why shouldn't new entrepreneurs in their mid-50s and early 60s have easy access to affordable benefits like health insurance and retirement savings?

The changing nature of work and increased longevity are pushing people toward multiple jobs, fluid careers, and on-demand tasks. Older workers want to stay attached to the job market longer, perhaps in phased retirement, semiretirement, part-time work, and flexible schedules. Workers need economic security—adequate retirement savings, good health care, training programs, and the like—designed for more mobile careers and jobs.

"Policy should facilitate people's ability to change job, occupation, or entire line of work at various points in the life course, even if the switch is simply to something different, rather than something better. This calls for counseling, mentoring, and perhaps several sabbaticals (every adult, not just parents of newborn children, should have access to several one-year paid leaves)," writes Lane Kenworthy, sociologist at the University of California, San Diego. "It also means eligibility for pensions, unemployment insurance, sickness insurance, parental leave, holidays, and other nonwage benefits should be contingent on employment, but not on the particular job or employer you have."[8]

Kenworthy has the right framework. The Treaty of Detroit can't be restored. Tying core quality-of-life benefits to employers with sufficient resources to afford them doesn't make sense. But you can't just leave people to their own devices. The insecurity is too great.

The fundamental insurance principle for the new economy is for benefits to be portable, "available to all workers, that continue from job to job, and across multiple jobs at once," write Shayna Strom and Mark Schmitt in "Protecting Workers in a Patchwork Economy."[9] Think Social Security. Social Security records stay with workers as they change jobs, shift to part-time work, join a small business, start their own company, and participate in a phased retirement program.

A portable and universal benefits system will encourage greater entrepreneurship, increased job flexibility, and longer work lives. A portable safety net creates more opportunities for older Americans to choose from part-time work, gig economy jobs, and phased retirement programs.

"We need to create a new narrative. We need to redesign our social protections for the new economy and increased longevity," says Linda Fried, dean of the Mailman School of Public Health at Columbia University. "We all need these social protections, but they will work better for our new reality if they are not employer-based."

The new narrative calls for understanding that a better safety net en-courages industriousness and risk-taking. That's what research and common sense tell us. The Global Innovation Index is compiled by the global business school INSEAD in Fontainebleau, France, and the World Intellectual Property Organization (the latter a specialized agency of the United Nations). Switzerland was ranked first in 2018 with the Netherlands, Sweden, United Kingdom, and Singapore following in that order. The United States came in sixth, followed by Finland, Denmark, Germany, and Ireland.[10]

Notice anything about the top ten list? Except for the United States, these countries offer their citizens universal health and retirement benefits.

Closer to home, a fascinating set of studies by economist Gareth Olds documents how social insurance encourages entrepreneurship.

(Olds did the research while professor at the Harvard Business School's entrepreneurial management program. He's currently senior economist in Nike's Global Supply Chain Innovation group.)

Specifically, Olds examined the Supplemental Nutrition Assistance Program (SNAP), better known as food stamps. The food stamp program was expanded in the early 2000s by loosening qualification standards. His research shows that food stamps reduce one kind of risk—lack of food for the family. The result was to encourage another form of risk-taking—entrepreneurship.

"Newly eligible households are 20 percent more likely to own a business as a result of the policy, driven by an increase in new firm birth of 12 percent," he writes in *Food Stamp Entrepreneurs*. "These tend to be high-quality firms: the marginal effects were particularly strong for incorporated ventures, with the probability of owning an incorporated business increasing by 16 percent as a result of the policy. The expansion of SNAP also increased the length of the work-year by 2.5 percent and the work-week by 5 percent relative to the baseline, a labor supply increase equivalent to 1.1 million full-time workers."[11]

His conclusion? "Finally, I find that the results are driven entirely by newly eligible nonenrollees, suggesting the presence of a large population of would-be entrepreneurs held back by uninsured risk." Think about that.

Olds arrived at similar results with an investigation into the State Children's Health Insurance Program. SCHIP provides health insurance to moderate-income families with children. Looking at the period from 1992 to 2011, he found that both self-employment rates and new business formation rose among SCHIP-eligible households compared to those moderate-income households just above the eligibility cutoff level.

"The program also increased the self-employment rate by 15 percent, the number of incorporated firms by 36 percent, and the share of household income derived from self-employment by 12 percent, indicating that these are relatively high-quality ventures," Olds writes in *Entrepreneurship and Public Health Insurance*. "The increase is driven largely by a 12 percent rise in firm birth rates and a 26 percent increase in the birth rate of incorporated firms."[12]

A similar insight comes from an examination of whether eligibility for universal coverage under Medicare affected entrepreneurship rates. A 2011 Kauffman-RAND Institute for Entrepreneurship Public Policy study found the business ownership rate for men at age 64 to be 24.6 percent. Business ownership for men jumps to 28 percent when over age 65 and qualified for Medicare. "The availability of affordable health insurance for the self-employed has an important impact on whether individuals are likely to become entrepreneurs," conclude the authors.[13]

One last example, this time drawn from an academic paper presented at the eighteenth annual meeting of the Retirement Research Consortium in Washington, DC: "How Does Retirement Behavior Respond to Drastic Changes in Social Security Rules? Lessons from the Norwegian 2011 Pension Reform." But the story told by economists Christian Brinch (Norwegian Business School), Ola Vestad (University of Chicago and Statistics Norway), and Josef Zweimüller (University of Zurich) is illuminating, especially about how to encourage older workers to stay employed.[14]

Norway overhauled its private sector pension system in 2011. In the pre-reform era, workers covered by a pension scheme called AFP could retire between ages 62 and 67. Benefits were subject to a strict earnings test (means testing). Filing could be delayed up until age 67, but there was no financial reward to waiting. Filings understandably clustered around age 62. The other pension scheme—non-AFP workers—allowed for claiming benefits starting at age 67.

In the post-reform era, both AFP and non-AFP workers came under the same system. Everyone can claim benefits starting at age 62 and up to age 75. Pension benefits aren't means tested. The pension benefit improves with delayed filing. The economists found that many AFP workers continued to file at age 62. The non-AFP workers also embraced earlier filing now that the option was available to them. Among AFP workers, the fraction claiming at age 62 was about 30 percent pre-reform and above 50 percent post-reform.

Here's the kicker: The scholars noted a substantial drop in the fraction of AFP workers choosing to stop working. The fraction employed at age 62 increased by about 12.5 percent, corresponding to an increase in employment rates of 20 percent relative to pre-reform employment rates. In other words, growing numbers of experienced Norwegian workers were both filing for their pension and continuing to work. The traditional connection between the decision to take a pension and to stop working was severed.

"The most important lesson is when you remove the earnings test and give people flexibility over when to start their benefits, people are much more likely to continue working past their early retirement date," says Professor Vestad in a subsequent interview. "People seem to appreciate the opportunity to take their benefit and continue working." Think phased retirement.

What might a portable benefits system look like? Here are several key reforms I believe will encourage greater entrepreneurship and labor force participation among all workers, including those 50 years and older. The fundamental principle is universal, portable, and earned benefits. A key aim is to encourage employment throughout the lifespan, including for those who want to keep working in their 60s, 70s, 80s, and on.

When it comes to proposing major public policy reforms I've tried to keep in mind the lesson of the dog and the Frisbee. Seriously.

At the annual symposium for central bankers in Jackson Hole, Wyoming, in 2012, British finance regulator Andrew Haldane and Bank of England economist Vasileios Madouros gave a talk, "The Dog and the Frisbee." The economists noted that the act of catching a Frisbee is incredibly complex. It takes Ph.D.-type calculations to decode the underlying dynamics. Yet catching a Frisbee is relatively easy. Even dogs can effortlessly grab Frisbees out of the air.[15]

What is the secret to the dog's success—and ours? Keep it simple, they say. "For studies have shown that the frisbee-catching dog follows the simplest of rules of thumb: run at a speed so that the angle of gaze to the frisbee remains roughly constant. Humans follow an identical rule of thumb," they said.

What does this have to do with policy? The economists used their example to argue against the understandable impulse of legislators and regulators to create complex rules when dealing with complex problems. Instead, they advocated for embracing simplicity. Keep reforms simple.

Collectively, the reforms I'm going to briefly suggest draw on deep wells of research. The policy shifts are designed to benefit all generations, rather than a single generation. Encouraging and rewarding work is critical. My list is far from comprehensive. You may emphasize different policy choices.

What I'm trying to do here is take up Linda Fried's challenge and suggest some plot lines to "create a new narrative" for society to take advantage of the opportunities created by increased longevity.

Embrace full employment. *Full employment* **is a catchphrase from an-**other era, popular during the 1950s and 1960s. The ambition foundered on the double-digit inflation rates of the 1970s. Economists and policymakers became convinced the only way to keep inflation down was to tolerate higher rates of unemployment. Although most economists didn't quite put it this way, the belief was that too strong economic growth and too low an unemployment rate drove the overall price level higher. A reserve army of unemployed and underemployed workers helped keep inflation down.

Full employment is typically defined as somewhere between 1 percent and 2 percent unemployment, a figure that reflects the normal ebb and flow of the workforce as people leave jobs seeking better opportunities. A full employment economy in the United States is realistically somewhere between 3 percent to 4 percent unemployment for an extended period, a level reached only a handful of times during the past half century.

What about the fear of inflation with full employment? The relationship between employment and inflation is tricky. Here's the basic idea behind the fear that low unemployment leads to higher prices. In the economy, worker preferences, job changes, labor market institutions, and other factors add up to a "natural" rate of unemployment. When the unemployment rate drops below its natural rate, the result is high and accelerating inflation. The theory was popular on Wall Street and among policymaking economists. The only real question was what was the nonaccelerating inflation rate of unemployment—or NAIRU? In the early 1990s, the consensus pegged NAIRU at around 6 percent. Yet the unemployment rate fell from 6.5 percent at the end of 1993 to 4 percent at the end of 2000. Inflation stayed tame and workers saw sustained wage gains.[16]

The late economist Robert Eisner called the concept of NAIRU the "greatest misconception of all." The data doesn't support the idea that low unemployment leads to higher inflation. "Can I guarantee that measures—short of war—to reduce unemployment to 3.4 percent will not increase the rate of inflation? No!" he says in *The Misunderstood Economy*. "Can anyone be sure it will increase inflation, let alone by how much or that the inflation will continue accelerating? I daresay no."[17]

The greater willingness of management to embrace experienced workers has accelerated during the relatively tight labor market of recent years. As former U.S. Treasury Secretary Larry Summers puts it, "The best social policy is a high-pressure economy in which firms are chasing workers rather than workers chasing jobs."[18] That's what a full-employment economy does for workers, including those in the second half of life.

Training and retraining programs. There are plenty of models to learn from and adopt for U.S. circumstances. The "flexicurity" programs of the Nordic nations are intriguing. The widely admired Danish system combines ease of hiring and firing employees by management (the flexibility) with extensive labor market training and education policies (the security).[19] New Zealand overhauled its apprenticeships programs so that participants, regardless of age, get the same level of support and the same level of subsidy. The demand among older workers to join workplace learning programs is strong.[20]

The most ambitious initiative comes from Singapore. In 2015, the island nation launched its SkillsFuture Singapore or SSG. It's a lifelong learning program with many elements. The government initiative is closely linked with employers. It offers Singaporeans tools for developing and adapting career skills over time, including broadly defined digital skills. Lifelong learning is supported with a combination of tax credits for individuals, employer tax breaks, and grants.

The training courses are targeted at four stages of life: School, early career, mid-career, and the "silver" years. "These policies range from internships for those in their schooling years, to retraining schemes for those in their silver years," writes Robert Atkinson of the Information Technology and Innovation Foundation.[21]

Any model would need to be adapted to U.S. circumstances. Unions play a much bigger role in the economies of Denmark and New Zealand. The Singaporean government's civil service labor force—the highest paid in the world—is unusually competent, well-educated, and civic minded. Still, the need for lifelong learning in the United States remains, and older workers are a force for change.

Family-friendly flexibility. Here's a startling statistic to think about: Most of the income gains middle-class families have achieved since 1970 come from the rise in women's earnings. Put somewhat differently, the White House Council of Economic Advisers calculates that America's economy is $2 trillion or 13.5 percent larger since 1970, thanks to the increased labor force participation rate and hours work by women. Fathers have been taking on more family caregiving responsibilities at the same time. (You can imagine from these numbers the economic kick that could be produced by more people working well into the traditional retirement years.)[22]

The gains are under stress. Young parents struggle to cope with the costs of childcare and time away from work to raise a baby. Older adults find it hard to balance work and caregiving responsibilities for aging parents. Some companies offer their employees generous benefits to meet their caregiving responsibilities, such as extended time off, flexible schedules, telecommuting, and the like. Most don't, and the government doesn't help much with childcare expenses or eldercare responsibilities.

The lack of family-friendly policies is a major factor behind the decline and stagnation of America's female labor force participation rate since 2000 for the 25-to-54-year-old group. The United States used to be a leader with one of the highest rates of women working among the OECD (Organisation for Economic Co-operation and Development) nations. The United States has dropped to around average while France, Canada, the United Kingdom, and Japan have shown strong gains.[23] The United States is the only major nation without maternity and paternity leave. The United States also doesn't have a universal long-term care system. Medicaid is the public long-term care option but it's a means tested program. Childcare and eldercare expenses take a toll, emotionally and financially. The social insurance system needs updating to offer greater support for family caregivers.

Boost Social Security. Social Security is America's most successful earned-benefit program. Nearly every wage earner pays taxes into the Social Security system. Social Security helps keep millions of America's older people out of poverty. Social Security isn't broke. Social Security isn't in crisis. Social Security won't go bankrupt. Social Security will be there when millennials retire.

Yes, the Social Security Board of Trustees reports that the Social Security Trust Funds, the main source of funding for Social Security benefits, will fall short in 2034.[24] In other words, if Congress and the White House do nothing and allow that grim moment to come, Social Security recipients will suffer reduced benefits by nearly a quarter. The system will have enough money coming in from payroll taxes to fund about three-quarters of scheduled benefits until 2090—hardly a desirable result, but far from bankruptcy.

The lack of legislative action bolstering Social Security's finances and reassuring future beneficiaries that their Social Security checks will be there is a national disgrace. The earlier the books are balanced, the better. Odds are that any significant effort to shore up Social Security won't happen until the financial deficit looms. The divide over solutions between conservative and liberal politicians is too wide to bridge without the deadline of an imminent funding shortfall. (I say *politicians* because survey after survey reports that Social Security is popular with a majority of Republican and Democratic voters from all demographic age groups.)

At a conference of retirement experts in Washington, DC, several years ago, Nobel laureate and MIT economist Peter Diamond gave a savvy overview of Social Security's history and finances. Toward the end of his talk he dealt with the question of when Washington would act to shore up Social Security, "Is the last minute inevitable?" he rhetorically asked. "I fear the answer is yes."

What's behind the shortfall? A major factor is the increase in income inequality since the last Social Security overhaul, the 1983 National Commission on Social Security Reform. (It's better known as the Greenspan Commission after its chairman, Alan Greenspan.) Specifically, the Greenspan Commission established that the Social Security payroll tax applied only to earnings up to a certain ceiling. The cap was set so that 90 percent of all earnings from jobs covered by the program were below the ceiling. The cap is adjusted for inflation annually. (For example, in 2018, the cap was $128,400.) The rise in income inequality means that only 83 percent of earnings are below the cap.

Simply restoring the coverage balance back to 90 percent would extend the date of trust fund exhaustion to 2050. Hiking the cap to $250,000 extends the day of fiscal reckoning to 2077. The Trust fund lasts until 2090 if the ceiling is eliminated and the Social Security tax rate is applied to all wages. "Again, the projections for the distant future should not be taken too seriously, but they indicate that on present assumptions, eliminating the ceiling on wages subject to tax would basically resolve Trust Fund concerns for the foresee-able future," writes Frank Levy, a retired economist from the World Bank.[25]

Social Security is the main retirement program for most workers. The administrative costs are low. Private savings plans like 401(k)s aren't working well enough to provide for old age. The history of retirement savings over the past half century strongly suggests the simplest, most effective way to help maintain living standards in the elder years is to boost Social Security payouts.

"One should not underestimate the advantages of our time-honored Social Security systems," said economist Axel Börsch-Supan in an interview at the Stanford Center on Longevity. "When I was younger, I was much more fervent in the direction that the bulk of old age income should be from personal savings, and now I am more skeptical after having seen all of these failures in the capital market. We need a mix with a substantial role for Social Security.[26]

Remember, keep it simple.

Universal retirement savings plan. That said, policymakers should also make it easy for individuals to save for their retirement. A major flaw with the current employer-centric system is about one-third of pri-vate sector workers don't have access to an employer-sponsored re-tirement savings plan. There is no shortage of savvy proposals for establishing a universal retirement savings plan. The basic idea usu-ally involves attaching an IRA or 401(k)-type account to Social Secu-rity accounts.

For instance, Gene Sperling, former director of the White House National Economic Council under President Clinton and President Obama, has a version of a universal 401(k). Lower- and middle-income Americans would receive a dollar-for-dollar matching credit for up to $4,000 saved annually per household. Higher-income households would get at least a 60 percent match. The match also would be avail-able through IRA contributions for the self-employed and those tem-porarily not working.[27]

Teresa Ghilarducci, economist at The New School for Social Research, and Tony James, president of Blackstone, the money-management behemoth, have proposed Guaranteed Retirement Accounts.[28] Their plan requires that any employer without its own 401(k) participate in and contribute to a government-sponsored plan. The Auto-IRA proposal by economists J. Mark Iwry and David John would make retirement savings automatic for workers not covered by an employer-sponsored retirement account.[29]

Any of these ideas would go a long way toward eliminating a major inequity in the retirement savings system.

Universal health care coverage. Health insurance is controversial, un-fortunately. Health insurance plans should reflect the needs of a mobile workforce. The Obama administration's Affordable Care Act (ACA) took a step toward improved portability with its insurance exchanges. Individuals and families, regardless of their employment status, had access to comprehensive and affordable health coverage. The Trump administration and its Republican allies in Congress have slashed and nicked the pillars of the ACA without quite destroying it. The negative impact of the anti-ACA initiatives is mostly felt by the 50-to-64-year-old group. Their insurance premiums are going up and, in too many cases, making health insurance unaffordable.

Health insurance should be comprehensive and portable in the new economy. Most health experts have argued as much in recent years. The politics of transition are daunting. Nevertheless, changes in the economy and society should push employees and employers to embrace personal and portable health insurance. Employees would be freer to look for jobs that excited them without worrying over health benefits. Employers could get out of the draining and divisive business of managing their employee health insurance plans. There are plenty of systems to learn from and adapt to U.S. circumstances, such as the universal health insurance programs in Switzerland, Germany, and the Netherlands.

■

Raise wages of lower-income workers. The rewards to work need to go up, especially for lower-income workers. Education and training comprise one path to pursue. So are more immediate policies to boost household income and encourage employment.

A good option is to expand the Earned Income Tax Credit, or EITC. The EITC was signed into law in 1975. The anti-poverty program rewards work. The focus of the program is helping low-income families with children. The amount of the credit varies by marital status and the number of dependent children. The program is effective.

The problem with the EITC is that it essentially ignores adult childless workers, even though many live paycheck to paycheck. Lane Kenworthy, professor of sociology at the University of California, San Diego, recommends boosting the EITC to include single low-income adults. He would also pay it well into the middle class. Rather than phase out the benefit, he would simply turn it into a flat benefit indexed to average compensation.

"It is a very good program, supplementing the incomes of households with low earnings while encouraging employment," writes Kenworthy. "If the benefit were tied to average wages, it would rise over time in real terms, helping to stem the widening gap between growth of the economy and growth of household incomes."[30]

Nobel laureate Edmund Phelps favors an alternative solution: tax credits targeted at employers to encourage them to hire low-wage workers. The subsidy adds dollars-per-hour to the worker's wage. The biggest subsidy goes toward the lowest paid workers and eventually phases out. The advantage of the wage subsidy is that it appears to the worker as a higher wage. Let's say the worker was making $10 an hour and the subsidy boosts the wage to $12 an hour. It doesn't matter if he works part-time or full-time. He gets $12 an hour. But to the employer, the cost is still $10 an hour.

Wage insurance is another benefit that mitigates the downside of a volatile economy. Take a 50-year-old truck driver living in an isolated rural community in Tennessee. He loses his job to automation (perhaps the self-driving truck). He gets another job at a local big box retailer, but the new job comes with a wage cut. Wage insurance would kick in and, for the next two years or so, reduce the wage cut in half. It's an incentive to take that new job.[31] "We need to invest more in training," says Lee Branstetter, director of the Center for the Future of Work at Carnegie Mellon. "But wage insurance could be more helpful for the older worker."

I could go on, but you get the basic idea.

That said, there is one popular idea not on my suggested agenda: Universal basic income. The idea behind universal basic income is everyone gets periodic income payments with no conditions attached to the money beyond citizenship. The amount suggested for universal basic income payments in the United States typically runs in the $10,000 to $13,000 a year range.

The concept has attracted conservative and liberal supporters in the United States, although for very different reasons. For example, conservative theorist Charles Murray of the American Enterprise Institute promotes a $13,000 universal basic income (with $3,000 of that amount dedicated to buying health insurance). In return, he wants to scrap all antipoverty and social-welfare programs.[32] More liberal proponents of the idea don't buy that aspect of his proposal. Instead, they see a universal basic income as an additional payment stream to combat poverty and lean against inequality.

Silicon Valley billionaires like Mark Zuckerberg of Facebook and Elon Musk of Tesla are big fans. The tech elite openly worry about mass unemployment with the spread of automation and algorithms. Rather than deal with political fights and complex details of universal health insurance, universal retirement savings and the generation of meaningful jobs, universal basic income is seen as simple way to stave off revolution (while buying highly secure properties in New Zealand, Montana, and other remote outposts just in case).

Numerous pilot experiments in universal basic income are being tried in places like Canada, Finland, and Scotland. In California, Oakland has an experiment with a small-scale pilot, as does Stockton in the Central Valley. The details of experiments tried over the years have varied considerably, but in general they're limited to small groups of low-income people. These experiments are valuable and hopefully there will be many more.

Nevertheless, by now you know I'm skeptical about a workless future. For the foreseeable future work will still be the main source of income for the typical person, as well as a community. Work ties people to the wider society. The value of work extends far beyond income.

You may like some of these ideas and reject others. The devil is always in the design details and the political system can absorb only so much change. Nevertheless, policy proposals like these would go a long way toward not only helping an aging workforce stay engaged and productive in the new economy, but all workers.

Harvard professor David Riesman wrote several decades ago: "What I am asking for now are explorations in reorganizing work itself so that man can live humanely on as well as off the job."[33] Sociologist Lane Kenworthy more recently elaborated on Riesman's desire. "If most people are expected to be in employment, policy also ought to improve the quality of work life. Low-end service jobs may offer limited mental stimulation or opportunity to participate in decision making, and some are stressful. There is a limit to the amount of stimulation that some of these jobs will ever be able to provide, but most could do better, and we should try to figure out how and to push firms in that direction. Indeed, we should aim to improve working conditions in all jobs, rather than assuming that higher-skilled, better-paying positions automatically have decent work quality."[34]

The stated goals of Riesman and Kenworthy are worth pursuing. All workers would benefit, including those in the second half of life or in their unretirement years.

EPILOGUE

To Have a Go

Let's work. Be proud: Stand tall. Touch the clouds.

—MICK JAGGER[1]

Kieran Folliard is a 60-something Irish immigrant and serial entrepreneur. He grew up in Ballyhaunis, a small farming town in County Mayo, Ireland. After graduating from the Galway-Mayo Institute of Technology, he "flogged" milk in the Middle East for an Irish-Saudi dairy company. He moved to New York in the 1980s for work and adventure. In 1997, he moved to Minnesota to consult with some local companies. He soon launched his own entrepreneurial ventures.

Folliard is well known in Minnesota for his former pubs in the Twin Cities—Kieran's, the Local, the Liffey, and the Cooper. He sold the pubs in 2011 to start 2-GINGERS, an Irish whiskey named after his red-headed mother and aunt. A year later, 2-GINGERS was sold to liquor giant Beam Suntory. Kieran heads up the 2-GINGERS operation even as he set up another venture: The 26,000-square-foot "Food Building" in Minneapolis. Food Building is an urban home for craft food producers.

When asked about his zeal for entrepreneurship, Folliard is fond of quoting something his father used to say to him: "You'll be a long time dead, so don't waste any time."

Second-life entrepreneurs and experienced workers are heeding that insight in swelling numbers. No point in waiting.

Entrepreneurs and the self-employed in the second half of life are in the vanguard of the working longer revolution. Encore career entrepreneurs are taking their experience, skills, and creativity to start new enterprises, often with a social conscience. Older entrepreneurs are a driving force behind the rise of artisan capitalism, among the most dynamic movements in the U.S. economy. Entrepreneurs in their unretirement years are deeply engaged in their communities, talking to customers, community leaders, and fellow risk-takers. They're enthusiastically joining forces with the younger generation— including family members—to innovate and develop new products and services. They're embracing the latest information technologies to retain current customers and attract new ones. They're seizing new opportunities and creatively solving problems. From the solopreneur operation to a venture capital backed high-tech company, we're all better off for their second-life spirit.

What do second-life entrepreneurs need? Communities could do much more to encourage an even more vibrant startup culture in the second half of life. Cities and towns could take deliberate steps to welcome older entrepreneurs into their innovation districts, incubators, accelerators, and coworking spaces. Small business leaders and startup mentors could deliberately reach out to older entrepreneurs. Local startup ecosystems could create connections that smooth the startup path for second-life entrepreneurs eager to transform their skills, their ideas, and their human capital into a new enterprise. "Entrepreneurship drives economic growth regardless of the age of those involved," writes Jessica Lee in a report for the Brookings Institution. "As such, districts should explore how to increase the participation of older adults in their entrepreneurial ecosystems."[2]

Thanks to the tight labor market and the aging of the workforce, management is waking up to the economic potential of experienced workers. Yes, there is still a long way to go. But the turn has been made. There's no going back. The narrative about experienced workers is far more positive and nuanced compared to even three years ago, let alone ten years or four decades in the past. Experienced workers are creative and productive. Older workers have the knowledge and the skill to push their organizations to innovate more and to connect the dots in new ways, especially working in multigenerational teams. Management seems willing to experiment with flexible work schedules, part-time employment options, and phased retirement programs to keep experienced workers on payroll (or on call during times of need). Many Americans will make their greatest contributions to the workplace in their 60s, 70s, and 80s. Bank on it.

For individuals, transitions are always stressful. Key to success—defined as purpose and a paycheck—is a willingness to experiment, to see what jobs might intrigue you and steering clear of pursuits that leave you cold. Everyone needs an entrepreneurial mind-set when it comes to exploring what comes next, even if starting your own enterprise isn't in the cards.

The most valuable asset experienced workers have is their network of colleagues and acquaintances built up over the years, some existing at fourth, fifth, and sixth degrees of separation. Experienced workers usually find new jobs and opportunities through their network. To the people in your network, you're a person with skill and character and experience, not a number defined by chronological age. Working longer can mean leaving old careers and occupations behind and trying something different. "These transitions may involve pursuing employment that is more personally fulfilling but less financially rewarding than previous jobs," writes Richard Johnson of the Urban Institute. "They may involve moves from wage and salary jobs to self-employment. Or they may represent a gradual shift into retirement, with workers moving from demanding, full-time work into less stressful part-time work."[3]

Transitions like these are easier to manage with planning and savings to tap. But that sensible combination isn't always possible or practical to create in the first half of life. Don't despair. Saving is important. But broaden the typical personal finance approach toward the economics of the unretirement years beyond retirement savings, Social Security, and Medicare/Medicaid. Focus on creating a portfolio of engaging pursuits that keep you involved in the community, including some activities that generate an income.

For the broader society, impatience is a virtue when it comes to fighting age discrimination and creating more opportunities for experienced workers. Ignore calls to see an aging population as cause for alarm and an ominous burden. Instead, support efforts to speed the embrace of the incredible economic and social dividends opened by the longevity economy. The challenge is to advocate for employer benefits and government policies that encourage working longer at something meaningful.

Put it this way: How can society's major institutions work together to build a more equitable and inclusive economy, a life course that encourages experienced workers to pursue their purpose while earning an income? I've given a number of suggestions in the previous chapter. You may vehemently disagree with some or most of them. That's fine. The grassroots movement reimagining the second half of life to include entrepreneurship and work opportunities is gaining momentum. The rethinking is pragmatically and morally right with increased longevity. Designing the right path toward a more inclusive second-life society is much less clear. That's where the politics of democracy comes in.

Nevertheless, societal expectations of what a normal second half of life looks are changing rapidly. It's exciting to see the traditional silos segregating the life course into three distinct stages—school, work, and retirement—crumble. Age segregation is poisonous to the spirit, while variety nourishes it. With work and the search for purpose intertwined in the modern economy, people should find it increasingly easy to seek out multiple careers in different parts of the economy. Shifts from full-time work to part-time work, self-employment, volunteer, school, and leisure activities will blend more throughout a lifetime. Variety is good for our physical and mental health. "Aging and old age has been different in the past and it will be different for our children and grandchildren," says Columbia University's Staudinger.

This book has focused on aging and work in America. But aging is a global phenomenon, a megatrend. Much of the world—especially Asia and Europe—is aging faster than the United States. The number of people 65 years and older is projected to reach 1.3 billion in 2040. That's double the current estimate today. Two-thirds of the world's 65 and over population will live in emerging markets. The same demographics forces are at work: People are having fewer children and living longer.

The global aging megatrend signifies that the business and investment opportunities are much larger than typically discussed. The rise of older populations will profoundly shape the financial markets and consumer markets. "Everything from travel and lifestyle products to financial services, health, home, media, transportation, and food offerings will increasingly feel this group's massive footprint," as the Milken Institute Center on the Future of Aging put it in a report. "Smart companies will focus product development, service delivery, and marketing in ways that respect and acknowledge this economic force."[4]

Governments, businesses, and other major institutions in much of the world are responding to an aging society. A major thrust of reform is encouraging longer work lives. American business leaders and policymakers should study these policies and emulate what works by adapting them to U.S. circumstances. Third-age entrepreneurship is a hot public policy topic in Britain and Australia. Many intriguing experiments training older employees are being tried in Singapore and Sweden. German management groups are developing a toolkit of attractive options for retaining experienced employees, including flexible working conditions. Perhaps the United States should emulate New Zealand and open apprenticeship programs to experienced workers looking for their next chapter.

Another area for American leaders to learn from involves retirement security. A glaring failure in the United States is the more than one-third of private-sector workers without access to an employer-sponsored retirement savings plan. Tax breaks and years of personal finance stories on how to save for retirement hasn't "nudged" everyone to set aside money for their elder years, say, with an IRA.

Heard of the term superannuation? Maybe everyone should become familiar with this Australian word; it's a mandatory defined contribution retirement savings system. (Think 401(k) and 403(b).) The widely admired plan was introduced in 1992 and more than 90 percent of workers participate. Other countries have introduced mandatory private pension contributions, such as Israel and Britain. There is much information about innovation and reforms to share about aging.

The grassroots social movement redefining aging in America holds the promise of better days ahead. The major economic imbalance of our time is a lack of inclusion in the world of work generally, and into employment and jobs, specifically. What does inclusion mean? In Deidre McCloskey's phrase, *To Have A Go*. Inclusion focuses on bringing more people into the workplace, boosting the prospects of generating innovative ideas, and launching more new businesses and social enterprise.

Here's where workers and entrepreneurs in the second half of life come in. The outcomes of their fight against workplace discrimination, the struggle for choice when it comes to staying employed (or not), and the lobbying for policies that support longer work lives will make a huge difference to everyone. Older workers and aging entrepreneurs are in the vanguard of inclusion.

America's creativity flourishes at society's borders, the "fertile verges" of historian Daniel Boorstin. "A verge is a place of encounter between something and something else. America was a land of verges—all sorts of verges, between kinds of landscape and seascape, between stages of civilization, between ways of thought and ways of life," Boorstin writes. "The creativity of our nation will depend on finding and exploring the verges between our new world and the next."[5]

Hip-hop artist Lin-Manuel Miranda turned Ron Chernow's massive biography *Alexander Hamilton* into a groundbreaking multiethnic musical. Vietnamese refugees who started arriving in New Orleans in the mid-1970s married their French-influenced cuisine with French-inspired Creole food to create something slightly new and definitely delicious. Singer Nina Simone transfixed audiences with her powerful songs that drew on jazz, folk, and blues traditions.

The most intriguing fertile verge of our time involves the demographics of aging. A new vision of the second half of life is being created. Older Americans are reimagining the workplace and the startup enterprise. The prospects for a much brighter economy and more engaged society are enticing.

There has never been a better time to be in the second half of life in America.

ACKNOWLEDGMENTS

M any of the people you met in this book were initially interviewed for PBS's Next Avenue, the online magazine targeted at
the 50-plus demographic. I write a biweekly column for Next
Avenue edited by Rich Eisenberg, managing editor and senior editor
of the Money and Work & Purpose channels. Rich is a brilliant editor
and wonderful colleague. I can't thank Rich enough for his deft edits,
wise counsel, and good humor. Next Avenue is giving voice to people
in the second half of life wanting to make a difference. Next Avenue
is in the forefront of battling ageism and pernicious stereotypes that
diminish the modern elder. Thanks also to Shayla Stern, director of
editorial and context for Next Avenue. Many of my Next Avenue interviews were updated in the course of writing the book.

Most important are the people I've interviewed over the years in
all kinds of fields and occupations in the second half of life. They're
trying out various ventures and contributing to their wider communities. Their stories and struggles are inspiring and their willingness
to share generous. Thank you.

Several years ago, I was lucky enough to join an informal community of scholars, researchers, journalists, social entrepreneurs,
think-tank leaders, and positive aging advocates pushing hard to
bury the Still Syndrome. The ecosystem is expanding every year with
growing numbers of media stories and research studies challenging
dire jeremiads about aging. Everyone involved in the aging ecosystem

feeds off and learns from one another. Of course, we don't always agree. I know that some will strongly object to parts or all of *Purpose and a Paycheck*. That's for the good. I look forward to their criticisms and continuing spirited conversations about the new narrative being written about the second half of life.

In the aging ecosystem I've met so many wonderful journalists. Savvy writers and thinkers like Kerry Hannon, Mark Miller, Carol Hymowitz, Sally Abrahms, Nancy Collamer, Peter Gosselin, and Paul Kleyman. I've learned much from scholars doing exciting research, especially Ruth Finkelstein of Hunter College, Linda Fried of Columbia University, Laura Carstensen of Stanford University, Alicia Munnell of Boston College, Ursula Staudinger of Columbia University, Joseph Coughlin of the MIT Age Lab, and Nicole Maestas, associate professor of health care policy at Harvard Medical School. Several scholars I've never met or interviewed have influenced me with their writing, particularly historian W. Andrew Achenbaum, anthropologist Mary Catherine Bateson, and sociologist Richard Sennett.

Like so many people involved in rethinking aging, I've benefitted from the insights of social entrepreneurs Marc Freedman, Marci Alboher, and Betsy Werley of Encore.org. Irving Picard, executive director of the Milken Institute Center for the Future of Aging, is always willing to engage in thoughtful discussions. Fellows Howard Gleckman and Richard Johnson of the Urban Institute are doing incredible work that I consistently rely on. Author Richard Leider has been an inspiration in his books and in several conversations. Ross Levin, co-founder of Accredited Investors Wealth Management, is always thinking through finance and values in the second half of life. A special thank you to Bevan Gray-Rogel, Catherine "Kitty" Preziosi, and Rosemary Nixon for welcoming me into their south Florida communities and their encore career initiatives.

Minnesota, my adopted state, has a vibrant aging ecosystem. Several people stand out. Phyllis Moen is a professor at the University of Minnesota and Kate Schaefers is a consultant, executive coach, and volunteer state president of AARP Minnesota. They're cofounders of the University of Minnesota Advanced Careers Initiative. Will Phillips is State Director of AARP Minnesota. Patsy Bartley is executive director of Shift. The consultant George Dow is always encouraging about encore careers and activist Mary Jo Schifsky is breaking down ageist barriers.

I love public radio, it's mission and its voice, which is why I'm glad I work at American Public Media/Minnesota Public Radio. Thanks to chief executive officer Jon McTaggart for his support and interest in the reimagining of the aging movement. Mike Reszler, senior vice president for strategy and experimentation, chief digital officer, and my boss cheerfully and thoughtfully backs my various initiatives. Marketplace Morning Report host David Brancaccio and producer Michael Lipkin (and before him producer Justin Ho) are wonderful to work with.

Numerous people helped with this book. Dylan Hicks provided much-needed editing early on. A big shout out to Catherine Sullivan, associate professor, Department of Occupational Therapy at the Henrietta Schmoll School of Health, St. Catherine University. Sullivan read several chapters and gave me informed feedback on the discussions about creativity, cognitive well-being, and aging. Louis Johnson, economic historian at the College of Saint Benedict and Saint John's University is always willing to offer an insightful historical example. Meir Statman, finance professor at Santa Clara University, has offered wise counsel over the years, and his insights show up periodically in the book. Producer Lauren Dee was my partner in crime for our APM Unretirement podcast series. Stephen Smith, Sasha Aslanian, Richard Yankwich, Jim Robinson, Benjamin Ruxin, and Sarah Lutman provided critical feedback at various stages. Deepest thanks to Carolyn Wall for all her support.

Thanks to my long-time agent Joelle Delbourgo. I'm glad editor Tim Burgard of HarperCollins Leadership took a chance with this book.

ENDNOTES

CHAPTER 1
The Frontier of Experienced Workers
and 50-Plus Entrepreneurs

1. "My Shot," *Hamilton*, Act 1, lyrics by Lin-Manuel Miranda.
2. John Kenneth Galbraith, "Notes on Aging," Encyclopedia Britannica. https://www.britannica.com/topic/Notes-on-Aging-1756520.
3. Sandra L. Colby and Jennifer M. Ortman, *Projections of the Size and Composition of the U.S. Population: 2014 to 2060*, Current Populations Reports (Washington, DC: U.S. Census Bureau, March 2015), 25–1143. https://www.census.gov/content/dam/Census/library/publications/2015/demo/p25-1143.pdf.
4. U.S. Census Bureau, "Older People Projected to Outnumber Children for First Time in U.S. History," Release Number CB18-41, March 13, 2018. https://www.census.gov/newsroom/press-releases/2018/cb18-41-population-projections.html.
5. Samuel Ullman, "Youth," Samuel Ullman Museum. https://www.uab.edu/ullmanmuseum/.
6. U.S. Federal Reserve Board Chairman Ben Bernanke, "The Coming Demographic Transition: Will We Treat Future Generations Fairly?" (Speech before the Washington Economic Club, October 4, 2006). https://www.federalreserve.gov/newsevents/speech/bernanke20061004a.htm.
7. Ewing Marion Kauffman Foundation, 2017 Kauffman Index of Startup Activity: National Trends, p. 5. https://www.kauffman.org/kauffman-index/reporting/~/media/c9831094536646528ab012dcbd1f83be.ashx.

8. David Leonhardt, "A Time for Big Economic Ideas," *The New York Times*, April 22, 2018, p. 15. https://www.nytimes.com/2018/04/22/opinion/big-economic-ideas.html.

9. Linda Fried, "Getting More from a Longer Life," *Trend*, January 26, 2018. https://trend.pewtrusts.org/en/archive/winter-2018/getting-more-from-a-longer-life.

10. Oxford Economics, "The Longevity Economy: Generating Economic Growth and New Opportunities for Business," p. 9. https://www.aarp.org/content/dam/aarp/home-and-family/personal-technology/2013-10/Longevity-Economy-Generating-New-Growth-AARP.pdf.

11. Julika Erfurt, Athena Peppes, Mark Purdy, "The Seven Myths of Population Aging: How Companies and Governments Can Turn the 'Silver Economy' into an Advantage" (Washington, DC: Accenture Institute for High Performance, February 2012), p. 4. https://ec.europa.eu/research/innovation-union/pdf/active-healthy-ageing/accenture.pdf.

12. Fried, "Getting More From a Longer Life."

13. John Rowe, "Aging in the U.S.: Where Do We Stand Globally" (Speech given at the Robert N. Butler and Jack Rosenthal Age Boom Academy, Columbia University, "The Future of Work: New Technology and an Aging Workforce," May 31–June 2, 2018).

14. Gila Bronshtein, Jason Scott, John B. Shoven, Sita N. Slavov, "The Power of Working Longer," Working Paper 24226, NBER, January 2018.

15. Fidelity, "A Couple Retiring in 2018 Would Need an Estimated $280,000 to Cover Health Care Costs in Retirement," April 19, 2018.

16. Johannes Koettl and Wolfgang Fengler, "Should We Work Forever?" Brookings Institute, April 9, 2015. https://www.brookings.edu/blog/future-development/2015/04/09/should-we-work-forever/.

17. Bureau of Labor Statistics, "Older workers: Labor force trends and career options," May 2017.

18. Joint Center for Housing Studies, Harvard University, "The State of the Nation's Housing, 2018."

19. David Brooks, "The Man Who Changed the World, Twice," *The New York Times*, May 7, 2018.

20. Robert Shiller, "Narrative Economics," Cowles Foundation Discussion Paper No. 2069, January 2017.

21. Howard Harriott, "Old Age, Successful Ageing and the Problem of Significance," *Ethical Perspectives: Journal of the European Ethics,* Network 13, no. 1 (2003): 119–143, March 2016. http://www.ethical-perspectives.be/viewpic.php?TABLE=EP&ID=966.

22. Age Smart Employer, Robert N. Butler Columbia Aging Center. https://www.mailman.columbia.edu/research/age-smart-employer/about.

23. Chris Farrell, "Splitting Work and Fun in Retirement," PBS Next Avenue, October 27, 2014.

24. Robert William Fogel, *The Fourth Great Awakening and the Future of Egalitarianism* (Chicago: University of Chicago Press, May 2000), p. 205.

25. Chris Farrell, "Should Entrepreneurship Be A Company Benefit?" *Forbes*, June 10, 2016.

26. Ursula Staudinger, "Living Longer: Working Longer? Living Longer: Retiring Longer? Is That the Question?" (at the 2016 Age Boom Academy, "The Future of Work and Retirement," June 9–11, 2016).

27. Bertrand Russell, *Principles of Social Reconstruction* (New York: Routledge, 1997).

28. Milton Friedman, "The Social Responsibility of Business Is to Increase Its Profits," *The New York Times Magazine*, September 13, 1970.

29. James Montier, "The World's Dumbest Idea," GMO white paper, 2014.

30. Studs Terkel, *Working: People Talk About What They Do All Day and How They Feel About What They Do* (New York: The New Press, 1997).

31. Michael Mandel, "Connections as a Tool for Growth: Evidence from the LinkedIn Economic Graph," November 2014. Research supported by LinkedIn.

32. W. Andrew Achenbaum, *Old Age in the New Land: The American Experience Since 1790* (Baltimore, MD: Johns Hopkins University Press, 1978).

33. Achenbaum, *Old Age in the New Land.*

34. Barry Schwartz, *Why We Work* (New York: Simon & Schuster Ltd., 2015).

35. Laura Carstensen, "In search of a word that won't offend 'old' people," *The Washington Post*, December 29, 2017.

CHAPTER 2
The Myth of Creative Decline

1. *Design Matters* with Debbie Millman: Milton Glaser, 2009 podcast.

2. Simon Schama, "How Matisse and Picasso turned old age into art," *Financial Times*, April 4, 2014.

3. Alastair Sooke, *Matisse: A Second Life* (New York: Penguin, 2014).

4. Judith Thurman, "Wilder Women: The Mother and Daughter Behind the Little House Stories," *The New Yorker*, August 10, 2009. https://www.newyorker.com/magazine/2009/08/10/wilder-women.

5. Jon Pareles, "Madonna Talks About 'Rebel Heart,' Her Fall and More," *The New York Times*, March 5, 2015.

6. Andrew Russeth, "The Storyteller: At 85, Her Star Still Rising, Faith Ringgold Looks Back on Her Life in Art, Activism, and Education," *ArtNews*, March 1, 2016. http://www.artnews.com/2016/03/01/the-storyteller-faith-ringgold/.

7. Alexis Petridis, "Keith Richards: 'You Don't Stop Growing until They Shovel the Dirt In.'" *The Guardian*, September 17, 2015.

8. Chris Farrell, "The Age Discrimination Law at 50: A Mixed Bag," PBS Next Avenue, February 14, 2017. https://www.nextavenue.org/age-discrimination-law-50-mixed-bag/.

9. Chris Farrell, "The Problem With Job Boards for Older Job Seekers," PBS Next Avenue, April 10, 2017.

10. Chris Farrell and Jeffrey Bissoy-Mattis, "Minority-owned businesses are growing, but they're still struggling," Minnesota Public Radio, December 28, 2017. https://www.mprnews.org/story/2017/12/28/minority-businesses.

11. Bureau of Labor Statistics, "Older Workers: Labor Force Trends and Career Options," May 2017.

12. Michael D. Giandrea, Kevin E. Cahill, Joseph F. Quinn, "Self-Employment Transitions among Older American Workers with Career Jobs," BLS Working Paper 418, April 2008.

13. Chris Farrell, "Episode #3: Should You Quit Your Day Job? Starting a Business in Retirement," Unretirement, APM Podcast Dec. 1, 2015.

14. Matthew B. Crawford, "The Case for Working With Your Hands" *The New York Times,* May 21, 2009. https://www.nytimes.com/2009/05/24/magazine/24labor-t.html.

15. Chris Farrell, "How Older Performers Are Helping Us Rethink Aging," PBS Next Avenue, October 30, 2015. https://www.nextavenue.org/how-older-performers-are-helping-us-rethink-aging/.

16. Author interview.

17. Nussbaum, Bruce, *Creative Intelligence: Harnessing the Power to Create, Connect, and Inspire* (New York: HarperBusiness, 2013).

18. Margaret Kane, "Say What? 'Young People Are Just Smarter'" CNET, March 28, 2007.

19. James Kaufman and Ronald Beghetto, "Beyond Big and Little: The Four C Model of Creativity," *Review of General Psychology* 2009, vol. 13, no. 1, 1–12.

20. Weisberg, Robert, *Creativity: Understanding Innovation in Problem Solving, Science, Invention, and the Arts* (Hoboken, NJ: Wiley; April 28, 2006).

21. Herbert Simon, "How Understanding Creativity Builds Creative Management," Digital Collections Library, Carnegie Mellon University.

22. Michael Mandel, "Connections as a Tool for Growth: Evidence from the LinkedIn Economic Graph."

23. John Seely Brown, "The Social Life of Learning: How Can Continuing Education be Reconfigured in the Future?" *Continuing Higher Education Review,* vol. 66, 2002.

24. Arthur Cropley, "Creative Performance in Older Adults," in *Reflections on Educational Achievement*. Edited by Wilford Bos and Rainer Lehmann, Waxman Publishing, 1995.

25. Cropley, "Creative Performance in Older Adults."

26. Barry Matthew Kudrowitz, "HaHa and Aha!: Creativity, Idea Generation, Improvisational Humor, and Product Design (Dissertation, Massachusetts Institute of Technology, September 1, 2010).

27. Author interview with Jim Robinson.

28. Chris Farrell, "Act 2: Learning and Teaching the Arts After 60," PBS Next Avenue, August 6, 2016.

29. Author interview with Tim Carpenter.

30. "Batman," This American Life, January 9, 2015.

31. Oliver Sachs, "The Joy of Old Age. (No Kidding)," *The New York Times*, July 6, 2013.

32. Christopher Farrell, "Disproving Beliefs About the Economy and Aging," *The New York Times*, May 13, 2016.

33. Joshua Hartshorne and Laura Germine, "When does cognitive functioning peak? The asynchronous rise and fall of different cognitive abilities across the lifespan," *Psychological Science*, March 13, 2015.

34. Paul Irving with Rita Beamish and Arielle Burstein "Silver to Gold: The Business of Aging" Milken Institute Center for the Future of Aging, 2018.

35. Florian Schmiedek, Martin Lövdén, Ulman Lindenberger, "Hundred Days of Cognitive Training Enhance Broad Cognitive Abilities in Adulthood: Findings from the COGITO Study," *Frontiers in Aging Neuroscience,* 2010.

36. Gary Charness and Marie-Claire Villeval "Cooperation and Competition in Intergenerational Experiments in the Field and the Laboratory," *American Economic Review*, Vol. 99, NO. 3, June 2009.

CHAPTER 3
The Economics of Optimism

1. Betty Friedan "How to Live Longer, Better, Wiser" *Parade*, March 20, 1994.
2. W. Andrew Achenbaum, "What Is Retirement For?" *Wilson Quarterly*, Spring 2006.
3. Peter Coy, "Old. Smart. Productive," *Bloomberg Businessweek*, June 26, 2005.
4. David Harris, "Demographics," Global Foresight, Rockefeller & Co., Third Quarter, 2015.
5. "Soaring Numbers of Elderly Reshaping U.S. Economy," Federal Reserve Bank of Atlanta Annual Report, March 21, 2016.
6. Christopher Farrell, "Disproving Beliefs About the Economy and Aging," *The New York Times*, May 13, 2016.
7. Johannes Koettl "Did We Get the 'Old-Age Dependency' of Aging Countries Wrong?", Brookings Institution Future Development Economics to End Poverty, May 20, 2015.
8. Author interview.
9. Census Bureau, *Older Americans with a Disability, 2008–2012*, December, 2008.
10. Peter Cappelli, "Engaging Your Older Workers," *Harvard Business Review*, November 5, 2014.
11. Axel Börsch-Supan, Matthias Weiss, "Productivity and Age: Evidence from Work Teams at the Assembly Line." Munich Center for the Economics of Aging (MEA) at the Max Planck Institute for Social Law and Social Policy, 2011.
12. PwC, Golden Age Index, "Unlocking a Potential $3.5 Trillion Prize from Longer Work Lives," June 2018.
13. Accenture, "The Seven Myths of Population Aging: How Companies and Governments Can Turn the "Silver Economy" into an Advantage," February 2012.
14. Tyler Cowen, "Forget New Robots. Keep Your Eye on the Old People," *Bloomberg*, May 17, 2018.
15. Sarah McFarlane, "The Battery Pioneer Who, at Age 96, Keeps Going and Going," *Wall Street Journal*, August 9, 2018.
16. Pagan Kennedy, "To Be a Genius, Think Like a 94-Year-Old," *New York Times,* April 7, 2017.
17. Chris Farrell, "Employers Are Rethinking Older Stereotypes," July 8, 2016.
18. Christopher Farrell, "Boomerang Boom: More Firms Tapping the Skills of the Recently Retired," *The New York Times*, December 6, 2016.

19. Farrell, "Boomerang Boom."

20. Government Accountability Office, "Unemployed Older Workers: Many Experience Challenges Regaining Employment and Face Reduced Retirement Security," April 25, 2012.

21. AARP Research, "The Value of Experience Study," July 2018.

22. U.S. Equal Employment Opportunity Commission (EEOC), Charge Statistics (Charges filed with EEOC) Fiscal year 1997 through Fiscal year 2017.

23. EEOC, "The State of Age Discrimination and Older Workers in the U.S. 50 Years After the Age Discrimination in Employment Act (ADEA), June 2018.

24. Victoria A. Lipnic "The State of Age Discrimination and Older Workers in the U.S. 50 Years After the Age Discrimination in Employment Act (ADEA)," U.S. Equal Employment Opportunity Commission, footnote No. 32, June 2018.

25. Peter Gosselin, "Supreme Court Won't Take Up R. J. Reynolds Age Discrimination Case," ProPublica, June 26, 2016.

26. Written Testimony of Laurie McCann, Senior Attorney, AARP Foundation Litigation, EEOC Meeting of June 14, 2017. The ADEA @ 50—More Relevant Than Ever.

27. Lisa Madigan, Illinois Attorney General, "Madigan Probes National Job Search Sites over Potential Age Discrimination," March 2, 2017.

28. Peter Gosselin, "Restaurant Chain Settles Age Bias Case for $12 Million," ProPublica, April 4, 2017.

29. David Neumark "The Age Discrimination in Employment Act and the Challenge of Population Aging," NBER Working Paper No. 14317, September 2008.

CHAPTER 4
What about the Robots? Not.

1. As quoted in "Art Buchwald Celebrates His Life," a profile on *CNN Newsroom* (2 November 2006). http://transcripts.cnn.com/TRANSCRIPTS/0611/02/cnr.06.html.

2. Henry Adams, *The Education of Henry Adams*, Modern Library; 1st THUS edition (May 1999).

3. Paul David, "The Computer and Dynamo: An Historical Perspective on the Modern Productivity Paradox," *American Economic Review*, vol. 80, No. 2, May 1999.

4. PwC, "Will Robots Really Steal Our Jobs? An International Analysis of the Potential Long-Term Impact of Automation," 2018.

5. Carl Benedikt Frey and Michael Osborne, "The Future of Employment," Published by the Oxford Martin Programme on Technology and Employment, September 17, 2013.

6. Rob Lever, "Tech World Debate on Robots and Jobs Heats Up," *Science X*, March 26, 2017. https://phys.org/news/2017-03-tech-world-debate-robots-jobs.html.

7. Jeremy Rifkin, *The End of Work: The Decline of the Global Labor Force and the Dawn of the Post-Market Era,* (New York: Tarcher; 1996).

8. Rodney Brooks, "2015: What Do You Think About Machines That Think?" *Edge,* August 30, 2018. https://www.edge.org/annual-question/what-do-you-think-about-machines-that-think.

9. Robert Atkinson and John Wu, "False Alarmism: Technological Disruption and the U.S. Labor Market, 1850–2015," Information Technology & Innovation Foundation, May 8, 2017.

10. James Manyika and Charles Roxburgh, "The Great Transformer: The Impact of the Internet on Economic Growth and Prosperity," McKinsey Global Institute, October 2011. https://www.mckinsey .com/~/media/McKinsey/Industries/High%20Tech/Our%20 Insights/The%20great%20transformer/MGI_Impact_of_Internet_ on_economic_growth.ashx.

11. James Feyrer, Erin T. Mansur, Bruce Sacerdote, "Geographic Dispersion of Economic Shocks: Evidence from the Fracking Revolution," National Bureau of Economic Research, Working Paper No. 21624, October 2015. http://www.nber.org/papers/w21624.

12. Michael Mandel, *U.S. App Economy Update* (Washington, DC: Progressive Policy Institute, May 2017). https://www.progressivepolicy.org/ wp-content/uploads/2017/05/PPI_USAppEconomy.pdf.

13. James Bessen, "Artificial Intelligence: The Impact on Jobs," Economist, June 25, 2016.

14. James Bessen, "How Computer Automation Affects Occupations: Technology, Jobs, and Skills," Boston University. School of Law, Law and Economics Research Paper No. 15-49 (Last revised: 4 Oct 2016).

15. Benjamin Shestakofsky, "More Machinery, Less Labor?" *Berkeley Journal of Sociology*, December 10, 2015.

16. Barry Eichengreen, "Two Myths About Automation, Debunked," World Economic Forum/Project Syndicate, December 13, 2017. https://www.weforum.org/agenda/2017/12/two-myths-about-automation-debunked.

17. Jeffrey Short, "Analysis of Truck Driver Age Demographics Across Two Decades," American Transportation Research Institute, December 2014.

18. Bureau of Labor Statistics, "Fastest Growing Occupations" *Occupational Outlook Handbook* (Last Modified Date: Friday, April 13, 2018).

19. Howard Gleckman, "Where Will Our Home Care Aides Come From?" *Forbes*, February 28, 2018.

20. Paraprofessional Healthcare Institute (PHI), "U.S. Home Care Workers: Key Facts," August 31, 2018.

21. Lisa Gurgone and Hayley Gleason, "2016–2017 Home Care Industry Assessment," Home Care Aide Industry Council, February 2018.

22. Chris Farrell, "Could This Idea Help Fix America's Shortage of Home Care Workers?" PBS Next Avenue, August 15, 2017.

23. Edmund Phelps, "The Aristotelian Ethic and the "Good Economy," in *Arguments for a Better World: Essays in Honor of Amartya Sen*, Kaushik Basu, Ravi Kanbur, S. M. Ravi Kanbur, eds. (Oxford, UK: Oxford University Press, 2009), p. 48.

24. Lawrence Katz, in interview with Paul Solman, "Get a Liberal Arts B.A., Not a Business B.A., for the Coming Artisan Economy," *PBS NewsHour*. https://www.pbs.org/newshour/nation/get-a-liberal-arts-b-a-not-a-business-b-a-for-the-coming-artisan-economy.

CHAPTER 5
The Returns to Work

1. Ralph Waldo Emerson, "Works and Days," *The Complete Works of Ralph Waldo Emerson* (Boston and New York: Houghton, Mifflin and Company, 1904), p. 18.

2. William Handwerker and Jayne Pearl, *Nathan's Famous: The First 100 Years of America's Favorite Frankfurter Company* (New York: Morgan James Publishing, May 2016).

3. Joseph Biden, "Remarks by the Vice President at Yale University Class Day," White House Office of the Vice President, May 17, 2015.

4. "American Bank Note Building, Hunt's Point," Forgotten New York, November 23, 2015.

5. Federal Reserve, "Survey of Consumer Finances," 2016. https://www.federalreserve.gov/econres/scfindex.htm.

6. Government Accountability Office, "Retirement Security: Most Households Approaching Retirement Have Low Savings," GAO-15-419, May 2015.

7. Sar A. Levitan and Clifford M. Johnson, *Second Thoughts on Work* (Kalamazoo, MI: Upjohn Press, 1982).

8. Jonathan Gershuny and Kimberly Fisher, "Post-Industrious Society: Why Work Time Will Not Disappear for Our Grandchildren," Sociology Working Papers, Number 2014–03, University of Oxford. Also, Arthur Brooks, "It Took A Village," *Politico*, August 8, 2015.

9. Peter Drucker, *The New Society: The Anatomy of Industrial Order*, 2nd ed. (Piscataway, NJ: Transaction Publishers, 1993).

10. Nicole Maestas, Kathleen J. Mullen, David Powell, Till von Wachter, Jeffrey B. Wenger, "The American Working Conditions Survey Finds That More Than Half of Retirees Would Return to Work," (Santa Monica, CA: RAND Corporation, 2017). https://www.rand.org/pubs/research_briefs/RB9973.html.

11. Axel Börsch-Supan and Morten Schuth, "Early Retirement, Mental Health, and Social Networks," in *Discoveries in the Economics of Aging*, David A. Wise, ed. (Chicago: University of Chicago Press, June 2014), pp. 225–250. https://www.nber.org/chapters/c12982.

12. Susann Rohwedder and Robert J. Willis, "Mental Retirement," *Journal of Economic Perspectives*, 24(1), 2010.

13. Author interview with Catherine Sullivan, professor of occupational science and occupational therapy at St. Catherine University.

14. Richard Johnson and Claire Xiaozhi Wang, "Educational Differences in Employment at Older Ages" (New York: Urban Institute, July 2017).

15. Johnson and Wang, "Educational Differences in Employment at Older Ages."

16. Robert Gordon, *The Rise and Fall of American Growth: The U.S. Standard of Living since the Civil War* (The Princeton Economic History of the Western World) (Princeton, NJ: Princeton University Press, January 12, 2016).

17. Gordon, *The Rise and Fall of American Growth*.

18. Jan Oltmanns, Ben Godde, Axel H. Winneke, Götz Richter, Claudia Niemann, Claudia Voelcker-Rehage, Klaus Schömann, Ursula M. Staudinger, "Don't Lose Your Brain at Work – The Role of Recurrent Novelty at Work in Cognitive and Brain Aging," *Frontiers in Psychology*, August 2017.

19. Christopher Farrell, "Migrant Workers in Recreational Vehicles," *The New York Times*, October 21, 2016.

CHAPTER 6

The Rise of 50-Plus Entrepreneurship

1. This quote is from Seamus Heaney's acceptance speech when he received the 1995 Nobel Prize for literature, and it was inscribed as an epitaph on his gravestone when he died in 2013. https://www.independent.ie/irish-news/news/walk-on-air-against-your-better-judgement-inscribed-on-seamus-heaney-headstone-31451644.html.

2. Herbert Gutman, *Work, Culture and Society in Industrializing America: Essays in American Working-Class and Social History* (Oxford, England: Basil Blackwell, 1977).

3. Chris Farrell, "From Professor to Pizza Shop Owner," PBS Next Avenue, February 2, 2018.

4. T. S. Eliot, "The Hollow Men." https://www.d.umn.edu/~tbacig/cst1010/chs/eliot.html.

5. Author interview.

6. Center for an Urban Future, "Starting Later: Realizing the Promise of Older Entrepreneurs in New York City," September 2018.

7. Chris Farrell, "The Senior Planet Course that Launches Entrepreneurs Over 60," PBS Next Avenue, July 17, 2018. (Also, notes from presentation by Alex Glazebrook, Senior Planet's director of training and technology at the 2018 Age Boom Academy at Columbia University.)

8. Chris Farrell, "Episode #7: Grandma Drives an Uber: Why the Gig Economy Is Better for Boomers than Millennials," Unretirement, APM Podcast, January 5, 2016.

9. Email correspondence with Richard Sutch. (I also recommend reading Roger L. Ransom and Richard Sutch, "The Labor of Older Americans: Retirement of Men On and Off the Job, 1870–1937," *Journal of Economic History*, vol. 46, no.1 [March 1996], pp. 1–30).

10. Louis Cain, "Entrepreneurship in Antebellum United States," in *The Invention of Enterprise: Entrepreneurship from Ancient Mesopotamia to Modern Times*, eds. David Landes, Joel Mokyr, William Baumol (Princeton, NJ: Princeton University Press, 2010).

11. Scott Shane, *Is Entrepreneurship Dead?* (New Haven, CT: Yale University Press, May 2018).

12. Robert Sobel, David Sicilia, *The Entrepreneurs: An American Adventure* (New York: Houghton Mifflin Harcourt, October 1986).

13. David Riesman, "Leisure and Work in Postindustrial Society," *Abundance For What? & Other Essays* (New York: Anchor Books, 1965).

14. Daniel Bell, *Work and Its Discontents: The Cult of Efficiency in America* (Boston, MA: Beacon Press, 1956).

15. Chris Farrell, "Work-From-Home in Retirement: One Win-Win Solution," *Forbes,* May 29, 2015.

16. Richard Eisenberg, "2 Nifty Disruptors Helping Older People Get Jobs," PBS Next Avenue, May 8, 2018.

17. Chris Farrell, "Running a Second-Act Business with Your Kid," PBS Next Avenue, December 22, 2014.

18. Christopher Farrell, "With Adult Children as Partners, Taking an Entrepreneurial Leap," *The New York Times*, November 3, 2017.

19. Encore.org https://encore.org/purpose-prize/dr-samuel-lupin/.

20. Richard Sennett, *The Craftsman* (New Haven, CT: Yale University Press, 2008).

21. Chris Farrell, "Second Career: Join the Craft Foods Movement," *Forbes,* January 8, 2015.

22. Richard Sennett, "Labours of Love," *The Guardian,* February 2, 2008.

23. I interviewed Eddie Ermoian while in Boulder, Colorado, during a shoot for my public television series *Right on the Money* in the late 1990s. He died in 2017. An admiring obituary is by Charlie Brennan, "'Fast Eddie' Ermoian, Beloved Boulder Hot Dog Slinger, Dies at 80," *Boulder News,* June 20, 2017.

24. Chris Farrell, "Episode #2: From the Bronx to the Barn: Planning for a Sustainable Unretirement," Unretirement, APM Podcast, November 24, 2015.

CHAPTER 7
Doing Well by Doing Good

1. Tony Bennett, in Jordan Hoffman, "At Cannes, a Remarkable Documentary about Amy Winehouse's Tragically Short Life," *Vanity Fair,* May 18, 2015. At the end of the documentary, Tony Bennett shares the words he wished he could have told Amy Winehouse. The full quote is: "Slow down. You're too important. Life teaches you how to live it, if you live long enough." https://www.vanityfair.com/hollywood/2015/05/amy-winehouse-documentary.

2. Chris Farrell, "The Senior Planet Course that Launches Entrepreneurs Over 60," PBS Next Avenue, July 17, 2018.

3. Richard Leider and David Shapiro, *Work Reimagined: Uncover Your Calling* (Oakland, CA: Berrett-Koehler Publishers, November 2015).

4. Corporation for National and Community Service, "Older Americans Provide Services Valued at $78 Billion to U.S. Economy," May 16, 2017.

5. Daniel Boorstin, *Hidden History: Exploring Our Secret Past* (New York: Vintage Books, April 1989).
6. Chris Farrell, "Add Volunteering to Your Unretirement Plan," PBS Next Avenue, December 11, 2015.
7. Marc Freedman, "Why John Gardner Is My Retirement Role Model," *Wall Street Journal*, April 4, 2014.

CHAPTER 8
Management (Increasingly) Embraces Experienced Workers

1. Oprah interviews Maya Angelou in *O, The Oprah Magazine*, Dec. 2000.
2. "The Right People in the Right Seats on the Right Bus," Enterprise Minnesota, Fall, 2017 (Issue on "How to Retain Skilled Employees.").
3. Christoph Loch, Fabian J. Sting, Nikolaus Bauer, Helmut Mauermann, "The Globe: How BMW Is Defusing the Demographic Time Bomb," *Harvard Business Review*, March 2010.
4. Center on Aging & Work at Boston College, "Workplace Flexibility." www.bc.edu/research/agingandwork/about/workFlexibility.html.
5. Center on Aging & Work at Boston College, "Workplace Flexibility" (lightly edited). www.bc.edu/research/agingandwork/about/work Flexibility.html.
6. Chris Farrell, "Why Phased Retirement May Arrive Where You Work," PBS Next Avenue, November 13, 2014.
7. Farrell, "Why Phased Retirement May Arrive Where You Work."
8. Chris Farrell, "Hiring Older Workers Is Suddenly in Season," November 17, 2017.
9. Christopher Farrell, "Boomerang Boom: More Firms Tapping the Skills of the Recently Retired," *The New York Times*, December 16, 2016.

CHAPTER 9
Taking Lifelong Learning Seriously

1. Edith Wharton, "A First Word," *A Backward Glance* (New York: D. Appleton & Company, 1934).
2. White House Council of Economic Advisers, "Addressing America's Reskilling Challenge," July 2018.
3. Senior Citizen Education Program, University of Minnesota.
4. Joshua Wright, "The Rise of Postsecondary Certificates in the US," EMSI, May 31, 2016.

5. Chris Farrell, "Episode #6: Back to School: Are Professional Certification Programs Worth It?" Unretirement, APM Podcast, December 22, 2015.

6. University of Minnesota Advanced Career Initiative (https://cla.umn.edu/umac).

7. Encore!Hartford (https://dpp.uconn.edu/nonprofit-leadership/encore-connecticut/encore-hartford/).

8. Christopher Farrell, "Nonprofit Work After Retirement? Maybe You Can Make It Pay," *The New York Times,* June 24, 2016.

9. Philip A. Pizzo, "Navigating Transitions and Charting New Paths," *JAMA: Journal of the American Medical Association,* April 25, 2017.

10. "Lifelong Learning Is Becoming an Economic Imperative," *Economist,* January 12, 2017.

11. Carl E. Van Horn, Kathy Krepcio, Maria Heidkamp, "Improving Education and Training for Older Workers," AARP Public Policy Institute, March 2015.

12. Matteo Picchio and Jan C. van Ours, "Retaining through Training: Even for Older Workers," Institute for the Study of Labor, Discussion Series, March 2011.

13. Peter B. Berg, Mary K. Hamman, Matthew M. Piszczek, Christopher J. Ruhm, "The Relationship between Establishment Training and the Retention of Older Workers: Evidence from Germany," NBER Working Paper No. 21746, November 2015.

14. Robert D. Atkinson, "How to Reform Worker-Training and Adjustment Policies for an Era of Technological Change," Information Technology & Innovation Foundation, February 20, 2018.

15. Stephen A. Wandner, David E. Balducchi, Christopher J. O'Leary, "Selected Public Workforce Development Programs in the United States: Lessons Learned for Older Workers," March 2015.

16. Senior Community Service Employment Program, United States Department of Labor, Employment and Training Administration. From the Department of Labor's website, www.doleta.gov/seniors/.

17. Chris Farrell, "Trump Should Fix, Not Scrap, Job-Training Program for Older Adults," *Forbes,* June 12, 2017.

18. Robert D. Atkinson, "How to Reform Worker-Training and Adjustment Policies for an Era of Technological Change," Information Technology & Innovation Foundation, February 20, 2018.

19. John F. Kennedy, "Special Message to the Congress on the Needs of the Nation's Senior Citizens," February 21, 1963.

CHAPTER 10
The Personal Finances of Aging—Don't Despair

1. Mary Catherine Bateson, *Composing a Further Life: The Age of Active Wisdom* (New York: Vintage Books, October 4, 2011), p. 19.

2. Vickie Bajtelsmit and Anna Rappaport, "Retirement Adequacy in the United States: Should We Be Concerned?" Society of Actuaries, March 2018, p. 5.

3. C. Adam Bee and Joshua W. Mitchell, "Do Older Americans Have More Income than We Think?" U.S. Census Bureau, Working Paper Number SEHSD-WP2017-39, July 25, 2017. https://www.census.gov/library/working-papers/2017/demo/SEHSD-WP2017-39.html.

4. Matt Fellowes and Lincoln Plews, "The State of Retirees: How Longer Lives Have Changed Retirement," United Income, n.d. https://unitedincome.com/documents/papers/UnitedIncomeStateOfRetirees.pdf.

5. Derek Thompson, "Why Do Millennials Hate Groceries?" *The Atlantic*, November 2, 2016.

6. Pew Research Center, "Stepfamilies," February 3, 2011. http://www.pewresearch.org/fact-tank/2011/02/03/stepfamilies/.

7. Karen L. Fingerman, Karl A. Pillemer, Merril Silverstein, J. Jill Suitor, "The Baby Boomers' Intergenerational Relationships," *Gerontologist*, April 2012.

8. Katherine Anne Otis, "Everything Old Is New Again: A Social and Cultural History of Life on the Retirement Frontier, 1950–2000," Carolina Digital Repository, May 2008.

9. Amalavoyal V. Chari, John Engberg, Kristin Ray, Ateev Mehrotra, "The Opportunity Costs of Informal Elder-Care in the United States," *Health Services Research*, vol. 50, no. 3, June 2015.

10. Susan C. Reinhard, Lynn Friss Feinberg, Rita Choula, Ari Houser, "Valuing the Invaluable: 2015 Update Undeniable Progress, but Big Gaps Remain," AARP Public Policy Institute, July 2015.

11. Chris Farrell, "The Painful Struggles of America's Older Immigrants," PBS Next Avenue, December 9, 2016.

12. Kao Kalia Yang, "My Father the Song Poet," Literary Hub, April 25, 2016.

13. John Shoven, Gopi Shah Goda, Sita N. Slavov, "Implicit Taxes on Work at Older Ages," NBER Reporter, Number 2, 2018.

14. Gila Bronshtein, Jason Scott, John B. Shoven, Sita N. Slavov, "The Power of Working Longer," NBER Working Paper No. 24226 (Revised in January 2018).

15. Alicia H. Munnell, Francesca Golub-Sass, Anthony Webb, "How Much to Save for a Secure Retirement," Center for Retirement Research at Boston College, November 2011.

16. Alicia Munnell, "Millennials and Retirement: How Bad Is It?" *Politico*, June 7, 2018.

17. Mark Lino, Kevin Kuczynski, Nestor Rodriguez, TusaRebecca Schap, "Expenditures on Children by Families, 2015," United States Department of Agriculture, Center for Nutrition Policy and Promotion, January 2017.

18. Michael Kitces, "Why the Empty Nest Transition Is Crucial for Retirement Success," Nerd's Eye View at Kitces.com, May 25, 2016.

19. Bruce Wolfe and Robert Brazier, "Spending Retirement Assets . . . or Not," Blackrock Retirement Institute, February 18, 2018.

20. Anna Mamdamba and Stephen Utkus, "Spending and Saving in Retirement," Vanguard Center for Retirement Research, July 2015.

21. Chris Browning, Tao Guo, Yuanshan Cheng, Michael S. Finke, "Spending in Retirement: Determining the Consumption Gap," *Journal of Financial Planning*, 29 (2).

22. John Bailey Jones, Mariacristina De Nardi, Eric French, Rory McGee, Justin Kirschner, "The Lifetime Medical Spending of Retirees," NBER Working Paper No. 24599 (revised in July 2018).

23. Matt Fellowes and Lincoln Plews, "The State of Retirees: How Longer Lives Have Changed Retirement," United Income, n.d. https://unitedincome.com/documents/papers/UnitedIncomeStateOfRetirees.pdf.

24. Joanne Binette and Kerri Vasold, "2018 Home and Community Preferences: A National Survey of Adults Age 18-Plus," AARP Research, August 2018.

CHAPTER 11
Gains from a Multigenerational Society

1. Muhammad Ali, "Muhammad Ali: In His Own Words." CBSNews.com, June 5, 2016. https://www.cbsnews.com/news/muhammad-ali-in-his-own-words/.

2. Marion White, "Rethinking Generation Gaps in the Workplace" UNC Executive Development, July 2, 2015.

3. Brenda Kowske, "The 'Generations' Debate Degenerates: Finding Facts Among the Myths," Kenexa Research Institute, 2010.

4. IBM Institute for Business Value, "Myths, Exaggerations and Uncomfortable Truths," 2015.

5. Richard Tyler, "Workers Over 60 Are Surprise Key to McDonald's Sales," *The Telegraph*, August 13, 2009.

6. Great Places to Work, "The Best Workplaces for Millennials, Gen Xers and Baby Boomers," June 28, 2016.

7. Laura Sydell, "At 90, She's Designing Tech for Aging Boomers," National Public Radio, January 19, 2015.

8. Brendan Flinn, "Millennials: The Emerging Generation of Family Caregivers," AARP Public Policy Institute, May 22, 2018.

9. Robert Samuelson, "Generational Warfare, Anyone?" *Washington Post*, November 29, 2015.

10. Marc Freedman, *How to Live Forever: The Enduring Power of Connecting the Generations* (New York: PublicAffairs, November 2018).

11. Pew Research Center, "Little Appetite for Considering Reductions in Social Security," in *Campaign Exposes Fissures Over Issues, Values and How Life Has Changed in the U.S.* (Washington, DC: Pew Research Center, March 31, 2016).

12. Paul Taylor, "Generational Equity and the 'Next America,'" Pew Research Center, April 18, 2014.

13. D'Vera Cohn and Jeffrey Passel, "A Record 64 Million Americans Live in Multigenerational Households," Pew Research Center, April 2018.

14. "2017 Parents and the High Cost of Child Care," Child Care Aware of America, 2017.

15. Una Osili, Chelsea Clark, and Jonathan Bergdoll, "A Tradition of Giving: New Research on Giving and Volunteering Within Families," Lilly Family School of Philanthropy and Vanguard Charitable Trust, May 2016.

16. John Tarnoff, "The Coming Design Revolution: It's All About Boomers," Huffington Post, March 17, 2015.

17. Chris Farrell, "Family Businesses Hand the Reins to the Next Generation," PBS Next Avenue, November 22, 2016.

18. Gen2Gen website: https://generationtogeneration.org/.

19. Marc Freedman, *How to Live Forever: The Enduring Power of Connecting the Generations* (New York: PublicAffairs, November 2018).

20. Mentor: The National Mentoring Partnership, "Mentoring Impact." https://www.mentoring.org/why-mentoring/mentoring-impact/.

CHAPTER 12

Reimagining the Common Good

1. John Maynard Keynes, *The Essential Keynes*, Robert Skidelsky, ed. (New York: Penguin, 2016), p. 124.

2. Richard Leider and Alan Webber, *Life Reimagined: Discovering Your New Life Possibilities* (Oakland, CA: Berrett-Koehler Publishers; 2013).

3. Rick Wartzman, *The End of Loyalty: The Rise and Fall of Good Jobs in America* (New York: Public Affairs, May 2017).

4. Wartzman, *The End of Loyalty*.

5. Robert D. Atkinson, "How to Reform Worker-Training and Adjustment Policies for an Era of Technological Change," Information Technology & Innovation Foundation, February 20, 2018.

6. Government Accountability Office, "Retirement Security: Challenges and Prospects for Employees of Small Businesses," Statement of Charles A. Jeszeck, director, Education, Workforce and Income Security, July 16, 2013.

7. Henry J. Kaiser Family Foundation, 2018 Employer Health Benefits Survey, October 3, 2018.

8. Lane Kenworthy, *The Good Society*, March, 2018. From the chapter "Employment." https://lanekenworthy.net/employment/.

9. Shayna Strom and Mark Schmitt, "Protecting Workers in a Patchwork Economy," The Century Foundation, April 7, 2016.

10. Soumitra Dutta, Bruno Lanvin, Sacha Wunsch-Vincent, eds., "Global Innovation Index 2018," Cornell SC Johnson School of Business, INSEAD, WIPO, 11th edition.

11. Gareth Olds, "Food Stamp Entrepreneurs," HBS Working Paper series, 2016.

12. Gareth Olds, "Entrepreneurship and Public Health Insurance," Working Paper 16–144, 2016.

13. Robert W. Fairlie, Kanika Kapur, Susan Gates, "Is Employer-Based Health Insurance a Barrier to Entrepreneurship?" *Journal of Health Economics*, vol. 30, issue 1, January 2011.

14. Christian N. Brinch, Ola L. Vestad, Josef Zweimüller, "How Does Retirement Behavior Respond to Drastic Changes in Social Security Rules? Evidence from the Norwegian 2011 Pension Reform," NBER Retirement Research Center Paper No. NB 16-10, September 2016.

15. Andrew Haldane and Vasileios Madouros, "The Dog and the Frisbee," Speech given at the Federal Reserve Bank of Kansas City's economic policy symposium, Jackson Hole, Wyoming, August 31, 2012.

16. Dean Baker, Sarah Rawlins, David Stein, "The Full Employment Mandate of the Federal Reserve: Its Origins and Importance," The Center for Economic and Policy Research, Fed Up, The Center for Popular Democracy, July 2017.

17. Robert Eisner, *The Misunderstood Economy: What Counts and How to Count It,* (Boston: Harvard Business Review Press, August 1995).

18. Lawrence Ball, "Monetary Policy for a High-Pressure Economy," Center for Economic and Policy Research, March 30, 2015.

19. Catherine Stephen, "Ins-and-Outs of the Danish Flexicurity Model," BNP Paribas economic research department, July 11, 2017.

20. Carmen Hall, "Number of Apprentices Over 50 Climbing Year on Year," *Bay of Plenty Times,* May 1, 2016.

21. Robert D. Atkinson, "How to Reform Worker-Training and Adjustment Policies for an Era of Technological Change," Information Technology & Innovation Foundation, February 20, 2018.

22. White House Council of Economic Advisers, "The Economics of Family-Friendly Workplace Policies," chapter four in the 2015 Economic Report of the President.

23. Sandra E. Black, Diane Whitmore Schanzenbach, Audrey Breitwiese, "The Recent Decline in Women's Labor Force Participation," The Hamilton Project, Brookings Institution, October 2017.

24. "The 2018 Annual Report of the Board of Trustees of the Federal Old-Age and Survivors Insurance and Federal Disability Insurance Trust Funds," Social Security Administration.

25. Frank Levy, "The Impact of Increased Inequality on the Social Security Trust Fund, and What to Do Now," An Economic Sense: It's the Economy Stupid (blog), March 22, 2016.

26. Stanford Center on Longevity. Interview with Dr. Axel Börsch-Supan by SCL Postdoctoral Research Scholar Marti DeLiema, February 2016.

27. Gene Sperling, "A 401(k) for All," *The New York Times,* July 22, 2014.

28. Tony James and Teresa Ghilarducci, "The Retirement Savings Plan" Teresa Ghilarducci blog, October 21, 2015.

29. J. Mark Iwry and David C. John, "Pursuing Universal Retirement Security Through Automatic IRAs," Brookings Institution, July 1, 2009.

30. Lane Kenworthy, "Low-Wage Jobs and No Wage Growth: Is There A Way Out?" New America Foundation, June 2011.

31. Lori G. Kletzer, "Why the U.S. Needs Wage Insurance," *Harvard Business Review,* January 25, 2016.

32. Charles Murray, "A Guaranteed Income for Every American," *Wall Street Journal,* June 3, 2016.

33. David Riesman, "Leisure and Work in Postindustrial Society," *Abundance For What? & Other Essays* (New York: Anchor Books, 1965).

34. Lane Kenworthy, in chapter "Employment," from *The Good Society,* March 2018.

EPILOGUE
To Have a Go

1. Excerpt from the lyrics to Mick Jagger's 1987 song, "Let's Work." https://en.wikipedia.org/wiki/Let%27s_Work_(Mick_Jagger_song).
2. Jessica Lee, "Beyond Millennials: Valuing Older Adults' Participation in Innovation Districts," Brookings Institution, March 22, 2017.
3. Richard Johnson, Janette Kawachi, Eric K. Lewis, "Older Workers on the Move: Recareering in Later Life," Urban Institute April 2009.
4. "Summit on Business and the Future of Aging, 2017" Milken Institute Center on the Future of Aging, 2017.
5. Daniel Boorstin, "Prologue: The Fertile Verge," in *Hidden History: Exploring Our Secret Past* (New York: Vintage Books, April 1989).

INDEX